THE **PRECIS**
INDEX SYSTEM
PRINCIPLES, APPLICATIONS, AND PROSPECTS

THE **PRECIS**
INDEX SYSTEM

PRINCIPLES, APPLICATIONS, AND PROSPECTS

PROCEEDINGS OF THE INTERNATIONAL **PRECIS** WORKSHOP
Sponsored by the College of Library and Information Services of the
University of Maryland October 15–17, 1976

EDITED BY HANS H. WELLISCH

NEW YORK • The H. W. WILSON COMPANY • 1977

Library of Congress Cataloging in Publication Data

International Precis Workshop, University of Maryland,
    1976.
    The PRECIS index system.

    Includes index.
    1. PRECIS (Indexing system)—Congresses.
I. Wellisch, Hanan. II. Maryland. University.
College of Library and Information Services. III. Ti-
tle.
Z695.92.I56 1976   029.5   77-1932
ISBN 0-8242-0611-8

PREFACE

PRECIS (*PRE*served *C*ontext *I*ndex *S*ystem) is probably the most significant development in the field of subject indexing since Charles Ammi Cutter first tried to formulate rules for the construction of subject headings in 1876. PRECIS approaches the task of subject indexing and the construction of subject headings for books and other documents from a completely new direction. PRECIS is based on the fundamentals of natural language and an ingenious conjunction of human indexing skills and computer capabilities. It is also a practical system that has been applied by the *British National Bibliography (BNB)* to more than 30,000 titles annually since 1971.

The International PRECIS Workshop was sponsored by the University of Maryland's College of Library and Information Services and held from October 15–17, 1976. Its primary aim was to present the system to librarians, indexers, and subject specialists in the United States—at present the only major English-speaking country in which the system has not yet found any practical application.

The Workshop was an international one in several respects. Firstly, the principal lecturers came from the United States, England, Denmark, and Canada. Secondly, the participants—though mostly from the United States—also included persons from Canada and Australia. And finally, although PRECIS was originally designed for English subject indexing only, it became apparent from Jutta Sørensen's paper that the system has the potential to be applicable to any language, thus becoming the first translingual indexing language.

The papers included in this volume fall into three distinct groups: those in Part I explain the principles of the system; Part II contains reports on research projects and comparative studies with traditional indexing systems; and Part III contains papers dealing with the practical applications of the system.

The papers in Part I include many examples with their worked-out answers, though they cannot, of course, substitute for the more comprehensive *Manual* (Derek Austin, *PRECIS: A Manual of Concept Analysis and Subject Indexing*, London: Council of the British National Bibliography, 1974). The *Manual* is indispensable for anyone who wishes to apply the system to the most variegated possible range of subjects. In a sense, however, these papers go beyond the *Manual*, for they incorporate recent insights and approaches that have been developed by the designers of the system during the period between the publication of the *Manual* (in 1974) and the Workshop. They thus constitute a complement to the *Manual*, and may be especially useful for students in library schools and for beginners in PRECIS indexing who wish to become acquainted with the system.

In Part II researchers report on quantitative and qualitative comparisons of PRECIS with traditional indexing systems. These systems include the Library of Congress subject headings and purely computer-derived systems, such as Key Word In Context (KWIC) indexing. These papers adduce evidence that lend credence to the assertion that PRECIS—in regard to the number of user access points and the clarity of subject relationships—is more efficient than any of the older indexing systems currently in use.

The practical applications of PRECIS (other than its current primary one in *BNB*) are discussed by the papers in Part III. Librarians of smaller libraries, for instance, may be interested in the fact that PRECIS, though essentially a computer-dependent system, can also be applied manually, though on a more limited scale. The final paper, by C. Donald Cook of the University of Toronto, examines the possible application of PRECIS throughout the North American continent and raises questions that will have to be addressed in the near future—primarily by librarians in the United States.

The task of making PRECIS word strings available on a nationwide basis (perhaps in collaboration with the Library of Congress and networks such as the Ohio College Library Center) will not be an easy one. The difficulties are not only organizational and financial, but, as several discussions during the Workshop have demonstrated, are linguistic as well. This is particularly true on the socio-linguistic plane, due to the fact that the British and Americans are "two peoples divided by one language." These problems will almost certainly become the focus of future research and development aimed at forging PRECIS into a more efficient and universally applicable system.

Most of the participants in the Workshop expressed their desire to gain more practical knowledge about PRECIS indexing, and many considered possible future applications of the system in various indexing enterprises. It is my hope that the International PRECIS Workshop of 1976 will in the future be regarded as the starting point for the introduction of PRECIS indexing to the United States, supplementing—or in time even replacing—the subject retrieval methods conceived exactly one hundred years earlier.

February 1977   Hans H. Wellisch

CONTENTS

I. The PRECIS System

The Development of PRECIS, and Introduction to Its Syntax

Derek Austin
Subject Systems Office, Bibliographic Services
Division, British Library

1   INTRODUCTION

1.1   Before trying to describe what PRECIS is, it might be as well to dispel any possible misconceptions, and explain what the system is *not*:

    (1)   it is not a fully automated index system. Computer programs are available, and can generate and interfile large quantities of index entries and references extracted from machine-held files, but the preparation of input to these files calls for human intellectual effort. A PRECIS index can be produced manually (see Audrey Taylor's paper, p. 157).

    (2)   PRECIS does not consist of a fixed set of indexing terms or phrases such as a list of subject headings. Instead, it consists of a set of generalized indexing procedures which can be applied to any subject field, to any medium, and to an increasing range of natural languages.

    (3)   it is not a classification system in the library sense, despite the fact that one of its components—the thesaurus—is clearly based on classificatory principles. The origins of the system as a whole can be traced back to research into the fundamentals of library classification which was carried out in the 1960's, but the system is now based explicitly, and increasingly, upon linguistic principles.

1.2   Having established these negative attributes, we should now consider what PRECIS *is*. The easiest way to start any explanation of the system is to set it into some kind of historical context. This serves two purposes: firstly, it shows the kind of problems we faced when we first set out to design this system; this, in turn, may help to explain why certain things are now done in certain ways. I shall therefore start by glancing back some years to the time when the *British National Bibliography (BNB)* (which was then produced by a private organization, not the British Library) became involved in the MARC Project. At that time, the concept of a machine-readable catalog was still new, and the full

potential of these records had not been realized. The national bibliography was still being produced by traditional means: that is, catalog entries were written on cards, complete with their class numbers; index entries were extracted from a separate card file, and these various cards were then sent away as copy to a printer. The same entries were then re-created by a second team of catalogers, who recorded the data on worksheets inscribed with mysterious symbols which most of us would now recognise as indicating MARC fields, subfields, and so on. Finally, these new records were sent for keyboarding and processing, to become the magnetic tapes which were mailed from *BNB* to the Library of Congress. At that time, these two organizations comprised the whole of the international MARC network.

1.3   It was soon realized, of course, that these machine-readable data could also be utilized in various ways, including the production of the national bibliography itself. After all, MARC is founded upon the concept of a set of uniquely identified data elements (such as author, title, publisher, and so on) which can be organized and output, through a simple instruction to the computer, in any order stipulated by the user, including that used for entries in the national bibliography. The decision was therefore taken to produce *BNB* directly from MARC tapes, and to close down the manual system, from about the end of 1969.

1.4   From its earliest issues, *BNB* has contained three kinds of sequence:
(1)   a classified "front end," in which full catalog entries are arranged under DC class numbers.
(2)   an alphabetical index of authors, titles, editors, series, etc.
(3)   an alphabetical subject index.
As one might expect, it was a relatively simple matter to reproduce the first and second of these sequences (that is, the classified file and the name index) directly from MARC tapes, since all the necessary data are held in clearly labelled fields. However, no satisfactory source of subject index data existed at that time. With some hesitation, *BNB* therefore launched a research project, seeking a means to generate an alphabetical subject index directly from machine-readable records.

1.5   At first, and quite naturally, we tried to automate the production of the chain index which had been a familiar feature of *BNB* for almost twenty years, but the attempt proved to be abortive. This may seem surprising to anyone familiar with this technique, since to all intents and purposes the chain index is based on a step-by-step application of logical principles which would appear to be well-suited to mechanization. Our study showed, however, that *BNB*'s chain index to the Decimal Classification called for a number of human intellectual decisions which are quite beyond the capacity of the computer. Once we had accepted this fact, we took what was probably a fairly courageous decision; we set up a project with the aim of re-thinking entirely the concept of a machine-produced subject index.

1.6   Some basic desiderata for this index were set down as guidelines at the start of this enquiry, while others were, inevitably, added as the work proceeded. This additon of extra demands appears to be typical of many computerization projects. They frequently begin, simply enough, as a search for the means to mechanize an existing manual system, but extra requirements tend to be added once it is realized that these machines are, in fact, capable of handling large quantities of complex data in ways which, however desirable, had previously been beyond the scope of human operators. Furthermore, these machines can do these things faster and more efficiently than human indexers, without tiring, and without losing their tempers.

1.7   Various desiderata for the new subject index were established in this way. These can be summarized broadly under five main headings:

(1)   It was decided that the computer, *not* the indexer, should produce all the index entries. The indexer's task would be limited to writing one or more input strings containing terms which are the components of index entries, plus machine-readable instruction codes indicating how that string should be transformed into a set of multiple entries, but the indexer would not write the entries himself.

(2)   Each of these entries should express, in summary form (a kind of précis), the complete theme or topic of a document. This should be seen in contrast to: (a) the chain index previously used by *BNB*, where only the final entry is fully co-extensive with the subject; (b) a subject heading system, where each heading assigned to a multi-concept document frequently expresses only one aspect of the overall subject.

(3)   Each of these entries should be meaningful and intelligible according to what we might call "normal frames of reference". This meant that we wanted to avoid unnatural entries, including inverted headings (such as "Bridges, concrete"), and other entries which take no account of the conventions of natural language (e.g. "Women: Mass production", which appeared in an issue of *BNB*'s chain index). Furthermore, the meaning of the various entries should not be distorted by the computer during its manipulation of the input string.

(4)   The system should be based upon a single set of logical principles which could be applied consistently throughout the entire subject spectrum. This was partly required to ensure that computer programs could be based upon a single set of logical procedures, but mainly to ensure consistent output from a team of varied and normal human indexers.

(5)   Finally, it was decided that the entries produced in this mechanical way should be supported by an adequate system of references between semantically related terms. No such provision had been made in *BNB*'s chain index, except when the index happened to refer to a part of the Dewey Classification (DC) schedules which is organized hierarchically in this way.

1.8   If these various desiderata are considered overall, it can be seen that we were, in effect, committed to the study of two fundamentally different kinds of relationships between concepts. These can be distinguished broadly as:

(1) *syntactical:* i.e. the relationships between the terms in input strings which together express the subject of a document, and in the entries generated by algorithms out of those strings.

(2) *semantic:* i.e. those *a priori* relationships between terms in index entries and other (unstated) terms which might also occur to the user who would regard a particular entry term as falling within the scope of his enquiry, including the names of its broader classes and other associated terms. These extra terms are usually excluded from index entries, but are nevertheless present by implication. They are handled in PRECIS by *See* and *See also* references extracted from a machine-held thesaurus.

This exclusion of semantically related terms from subject statements is also, of course, a feature of natural language. Whenever we speak of "Computer systems" we do not need to state explicitly that we mean tools for "Data processing", nor do we need to refer to "Cereals" whenever we speak of "Wheat." In each case, one of the terms (i.e. "Data processing" and "Cereals") is present by implication as part of our normal frames of reference.

1.9   We shall consider these two kinds of relationship in separate sessions, concentrating here on the syntax of PRECIS, and examining later the mechanism for producing references between semantically related terms. Syntax itself will be considered from two viewpoints:

(1) the format and structure of index entries

(2) the grammar, based on a schema of codes which represent grammatical roles, used to regulate the writing of input strings.

2   FORMAT OF INDEX ENTRIES

2.1   From the beginning of the research project, we encountered a particular problem in connection with the format of index entries. This can best be demonstrated by considering an example of a string of four terms summarizing a subject:

UNITED STATES — AIRCRAFT INDUSTRIES —
SKILLED PERSONNEL — TRAINING

We shall take this and similar subjects as the basis for many of the explanations which follow.

2.2   Before going on to further explanations, however, I should like to point out two special characteristics of this string, since these bear directly on the techniques of PRECIS. In the first place, it should be noted that these terms have been written in what we call a context-dependent order. This simply means that each term sets the next term into its obvious context. The concept, "United States", for example, establishes the environment in which the "Aircraft industries" (and therefore the rest of the concepts) were considered; the "Aircraft industries" identifies the contextual whole of which the "Skilled personnel" form a part, while the act of "Training" was applied to the entity "Skilled personnel". If a string of terms has been organized in accordance with this principle of context-dependency, it frequently also forms what we call a "one-to-one related sequence"; that is, each term is directly related to the next term in the string. These two notions—context dependency and one-to-one relations—are closely related, and both are important factors in rendering an index entry intelligible and unambiguous, regardless of the index system in use. In many cases, the presence of ambiguous or unclear entries in a subject index can be explained in terms of the failure to recognize the strength of these basic relationships. In expressing "meaning" in an index entry, it is possible that one-to-one relationships play the more important role. Indeed, this factor carries so much weight that a string of terms organized in this way is capable of expressing exactly the same message whether it is organized as a context-dependent sequence —as seen above—or is read from back to front:

TRAINING — SKILLED PERSONNEL —
AIRCRAFT INDUSTRIES — UNITED STATES

Consequently, either the first or the last term could be made to function, without further problems, as an entry point in an alphabetical index which satisfies many of the criteria considered earlier. Each is fully co-extensive with the subject; each is a meaningful statement; in neither case was the meaning distorted.

2.3   We shall start to encounter problems, however, when we try to construct an entry under one of the middle terms in the sequence, such as "Skilled personnel". It would be quite a simple matter to transpose this term to the start of the sequence so that it would function as an entry point to the index:

SKILLED PERSONNEL/UNITED STATES —
AIRCRAFT INDUSTRIES — TRAINING

But we then find that the subject has become blurred or ambiguous to some extent: it is no longer clear from this sequence whether the "Skilled personnel" is being trained, or is engaged in the training of other kinds of person. It is not difficult to hypothesize how this ambiguity occurred. The human mind seems to like these one-to-one relationships, and when the middle term was transposed to the start of the string, the mind automatically closed the resulting gap, and recognized a new and unintended one-to-one relationship between, say, "Aircraft industries" and "Training". The problem we face in this situation can therefore be expressed as follows: How can we generate an entry under one of the middle terms in an input string, without disturbing the original one-to-one relationships, and without losing any of the terms in the process?

2.4   We could have resolved this problem quite simply by adopting some
standard technique, such as KWIC, KWOC or KWAC, in which the
basic one-to-one relationships remain undisturbed as the various
entries are generated by the computer. For various reasons, however,
we decided that these systems are not well suited to the production of
an index to a large pan-disciplinary catalog or bibliography where a
high level of collocation is desirable. We therefore set out to explore
some new approach to the format of a machine-produced index entry,
and found almost immediately that we had to abandon the single line
entry which is a feature of traditional subject indexes.

2.5   In order to preserve these important one-to-one relationships, we devised a two-line format, following a line of reasoning which is best
illustrated by an example. We need to consider a sequence of four
terms representing a compound subject, as shown by the letters:

As we have seen, we face a problem when we try to make an entry under one of the middle terms in such a sequence: for example, C. This
is due to the fact that C is related simultaneously to each of the terms
on either side:

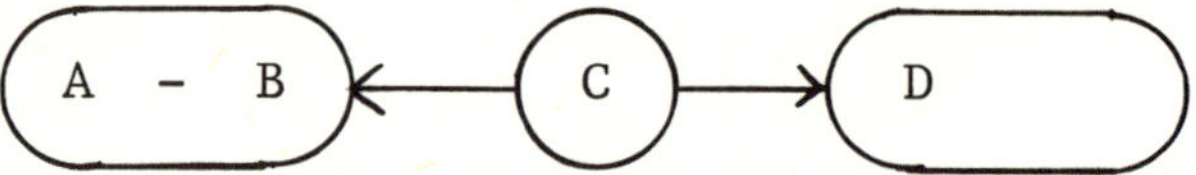

In order to preserve and express these simultaneous relationships, we
devised a two-line and three position format:

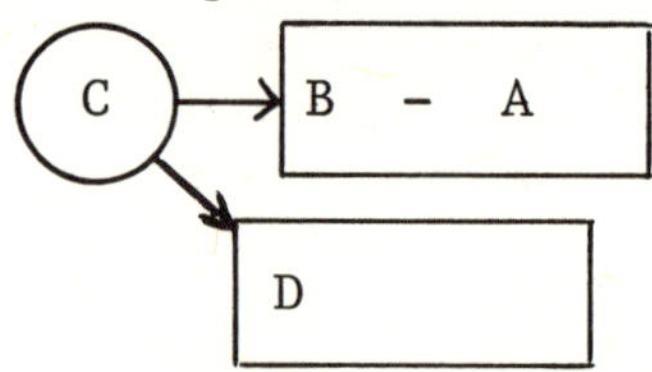

This demonstrates the fact that the term C is related not only to the
terms B and A which are printed on the same line, but also to D which
is indented below on a second line.

2.6   The diagram above clearly shows a three-part structure which has become the basis of a typical PRECIS entry. Names have been given to
each of the positions in this structure, as follows:

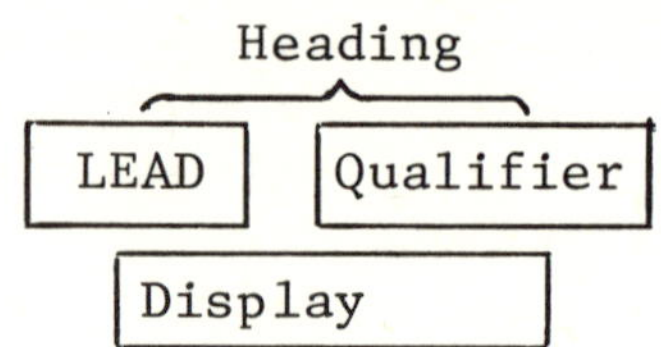

3   THE STANDARD ENTRY FORMAT

3.1   The adoption of this structure, with its three named positions, not only allowed us to express the one-to-one relationships between terms in index entries; it also gave us the basis for a fairly simple mechanism for generating a set of entries from a single input string. This procedure leads to entries in what is known as the *standard format,* which is by far the most commonly used of three formats used in PRECIS.

3.2   Entries in the standard format are produced by an operation known as "shunting." To understand this choice of name, we shall run step-by-step through the procedure, starting from the point shown in the following diagram:

```
United States. Aircraft industries. Skilled personnel. Training
```

In this diagram, we can see that a string of terms, organized as a context-dependent sequence, has been marshalled in the display position, but the lead has not yet been occupied: that is, no entry has yet been generated. As the procedure starts, the first term is shunted out of the display and into the lead, and the rest of the terms in the display are shifted to a standard indentation position. This gives us the first entry:

United States
    Aircraft industries. Skilled personnel. Training

As any term moves into the lead, it is automatically printed in roman bold, while the rest of the terms are printed in roman or italic, depending on factors we shall consider later.

3.3   At the next step, the term in the lead is shunted across into the qualifier, and the lead is then occupied by the next term in the display. Again, the remaining terms in the display move to the standard indentation point. This gives us the following entry:

Aircraft industries. United States
    Skilled personnel. Training

The lead and qualifier together form what is called the "heading". When more than one string gives rise to the same heading (which frequently happens), the second and subsequent common heading is automatically cancelled by the computer, while the terms which are context-dependent on the heading are alphabetically displayed as a column.

3.4   This same procedure is then repeated twice more, giving us the following entries:

> **Skilled personnel.** Aircraft industries. United States
> Training
> **Training.** Skilled personnel. Aircraft industries. United States

In these examples, all the terms appeared in the lead position. However, the generation of leads is not quite that mechanical. It is always under the control of the indexer, who indicates his choice of leads, and various other factors, through a code which is written as a prefix to each of the terms in the input string.

3.5   In addition to this standard format, PRECIS possesses two further procedures which are known as the "Predicate transformation" and the "Inverted format". Each of these will be considered later.

4   COMPOUND TERMS — THE TECHNIQUE OF DIFFERENCING

4.1   The procedures used to generate entries in the standard format were devised originally to deal with a certain category of compound subjects— that is, subjects which are expressed as more than one term. We realised, however, that a similar technique could also be applied to the treatment of separate words in a compound term, such as "Expanded polystyrene containers." To understand the treatment of compound terms, we first need to draw a distinction between their various parts according to their logical functions. We distinguish between two kinds of component:

(1)   the *focus:* that is, the noun or substantive element, which generally (but not invariably) specifies the class of ideas to which the term as a whole belongs. In a term such as "Expanded polystyrene containers", it is the word "Containers" which functions as the focus.

(2)   the *difference* or differences. "Difference" is used here in its logical sense, and expresses that part of the term which defines a subclass of the focal concept. In the term "Expanded polystyrene containers," the adjectives "Expanded" and "Polystyrene" function as differences which indicate a particular class of containers.

4.2   Differences are themselves divided into two types, known as "direct" and "indirect" differences. This distinction can be illustrated as follows:

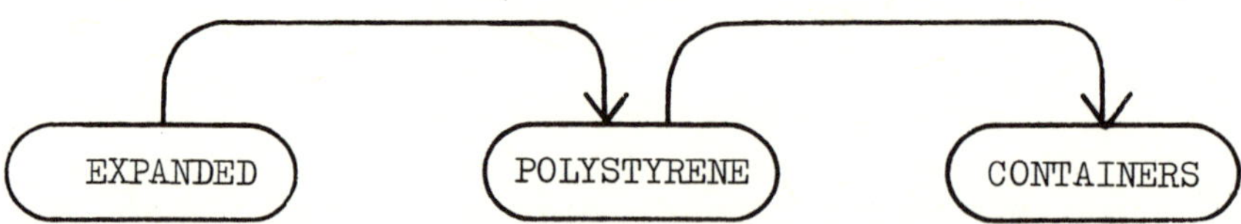

It can be seen that the adjective "Polystyrene" directly qualifies the noun: that is, it specifies a kind of container in terms of its material. The adjective "Expanded", however, has a different function. It does not refer directly to the focus (these are not "Expanded containers"), but it differences instead the material "Polystyrene".

4.3   An entry can be produced under any part of such a compound term. When the term is written as part of an input string, its elements are set down in the reverse of their natural language order, so that the noun precedes the adjective or adjectives. Each part is then prefixed by a code which indicates, firstly, whether or not that part should be printed in the lead, and, secondly, whether it functions as the focus, a direct difference, or an indirect difference. An example of a coded input is as follows:

(1) containers $i polystyrene $m expanded

—where the code $i indicates a lead direct difference, and the code $m identifies a lead indirect difference. This input is then handled by the computer using a variation of the shunting procedure considered earlier, and leading to the following entries:

> **Containers**
>   Expanded polystyrene containers
> **Polystyrene containers**
>   Expanded polystyrene containers
> **Expanded polystyrene containers**

Two points should be noted about these entries:

(1)   unless the whole of the compound term appears in the lead, the term as a whole is always printed in the display, which ensures that each entry is still co-extensive with the subject as perceived by the indexer.

(2)   in generating the output, a compound term is always printed in natural language order. An inverted heading, such as "Containers, polystyrene", cannot be produced by PRECIS procedures.

4.4   Various combinations of direct and indirect differences can occur at one and the same time. An example of a more complex term and its coding is shown below:

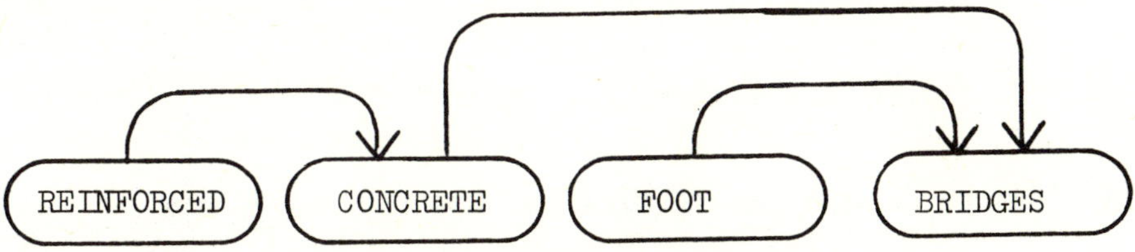

> *Term:* Reinforced concrete foot bridges
> *Input:* (1) bridges $i foot $i concrete $m reinforced
> *Entries:* **Bridges**
>   Reinforced concrete foot bridges
>   **Foot bridges**
>   Reinforced concrete foot bridges
>   **Concrete bridges**
>   Reinforced concrete foot bridges
>   **Reinforced concrete bridges**
>   Reinforced concrete foot bridges

It is worth pointing out that this system, which was devised for dealing with typical combinations of nouns and adjectives in English, is not sufficiently flexible or powerful to handle all compounds in other languages, such as German. A new set of codes to deal with these languages has therefore been specified, and these will be described in Jutta Sørensen's paper (p. 81).

5   DEFINITION OF A CONCEPT; CONTEXT DEPENDENCY; THE ROLE OPERATORS

5.1   These differencing procedures are not applied indiscriminately to any compound term, but only to those terms which represent valid concepts according to the underlying grammar of PRECIS. Some of these grammatical criteria are expressed in what are called the "Rules of differencing". These general guidelines were established empirically to ensure that a practicing indexer can distinguish between those compound terms which express single concepts according to the grammar of PRECIS (on the grounds, as we shall see later, that each can be introduced by its own role operator), and, on the other hand, those multi-word terms which should be broken down into separate substantive components, each introduced by its operator. Some of these rules represent strong recommendations rather than mandatory instructions, but one is regarded as binding in any circumstance. This is the rule which states that a compound term consisting of an adjective and a noun is *not* acceptable as an indexing unit (to be handled by differencing) if the adjective indicates the whole of which the focus is the part. Given a clear rule such as this, the various members of an indexing team will be equipped with a predictable logic such that they all know how to deal with compound terms such as "Aircraft engines" and "Secondary school teachers". Compounds of this type are common in natural language, but they should not be handled in PRECIS by using the differencing operators. Instead, they should be fragmented into their components (e.g. "Aircraft" and "Engines"), each of which should be written in its noun form in an input string, and introduced by its own specific role operator.

5.2   This means that the "Rules of differencing" are one of the means used in PRECIS to establish exactly what is meant by an indexing "term". A term is a word, or combination of words, whose function in a subject statement can be indicated by one of the role operators which are used to organize terms into strings. In a PRECIS string, as seen earlier, terms are organized into a sequence according to the principle of context-dependency, and the terms which represent the "core" of a subject generally form one-to-one related sequences. As a general rule, it is a simple matter to recognize when a string of terms has been organized in this way. It is quite a different matter to write such a string in practice. For the practicing indexer, something more definite is needed—we need to provide constraints, in the form of an indexing "grammar", which guide the indexer during the act of writing strings. In other words, we need to impose a syntax, which functions as a normalizing device, upon the index system.

5.3   The basis for the syntax of PRECIS has changed with the development of the system. It was originally based upon classificatory principles, influenced by the work of the Classification Research Group in England in its search for a "standard" citation order. PRECIS, however, has moved steadily towards an explicit linguistic basis for organizing terms in input strings; we shall hear more about this later when we consider the application of PRECIS in different natural languages. We generally say that the order of terms in a PRECIS string tends to favour the passive mood as seen in a declarative sentence, on the grounds that the object on which an action has been performed is stated before the name of the action, and the action precedes the name of the agent. The syntax which is intended to ensure that different indexers consistently achieve this order of terms (and by different indexers I would also include the same indexer on different occasions), is embodied in the schema of *Role operators* which is shown in Figure 1. One of these operators has to be written as a prefix to each of the terms in an input string.

5.4   These codes serve two principal functions:
(1)   The numbered operators, in the range from 0 to 6, have built-in filing values (low numbers before high). These are the operators which identify the main components of an index string, and the built-in filing value ensures that a team of indexers will consistently achieve the same results.
(2)   The operators also serve as computer instructions. They determine not only the format of index entries, but also the typography of each term and its associated punctuation. Punctuation is generated in a right-to-left direction: that is to say, each operator regulates the punctuation mark which is printed in front of the term introduced by the operator.

5.5   During a full course on PRECIS, we spend almost a week studying these operators, by which time most indexers have completely mastered the syntax of the system, and are using the codes correctly and almost intuitively. Here we shall consider only those operators which are most used in practice, paying particular attention to the "Main line" operators and the "Dependent element" codes which are printed in the upper half of the list. These two groups of operators are clearly distinguished by their characters: the "main line" operators consist of numbers in the range from 0 to 6, while the "dependent element" codes consist of lower case letters. Certain logical conditions are associated with the use of these operators, and these will be checked by the computer when a new string is first submitted as input:
(1)   every string must begin with a main line operator in the range from 0 to 2.

Main line operators

Environment of observed system	0	Location
Observed system (Core operators)	1	**Key system:** *object of transitive action; agent of intransitive action*
	2	**Action/Effect**
	3	**Agent of transitive action; Aspects; Factors**

A ─────────────────────────────

Data relating to observer	4	**Viewpoint-as-form**
Selected instance	5	**Sample population/Study region**
Presentation of data	6	**Target/Form**

Interposed operators

Dependent elements	p	**Part/Property**
	q	**Member of quasi-generic group**
	r	**Aggregate**
Concept interlinks	s	**Role definer**
	t	**Author attributed association**
Coordinate concepts	g	**Coordinate concept**

B ─────────────────────────────

Differencing operators

(prefixed by $)	h	**Non-lead direct difference**
	i	**Lead direct difference**
	j	**Salient difference**
	k	**Non-lead indirect difference**
	m	**Lead indirect difference**
	n	**Non-lead parenthetical difference**
	o	**Lead parenthetical difference**
	d	**Date as a difference**

Connectives

(Components of linking phrases; prefixed by $)	v	**Downward reading component**
	w	**Upward reading component**

C ─────────────────────────────

Theme interlinks

	x	**First element in coordinate theme**
	y	**Subsequent element in coordinate theme**
	z	**Element of common theme**

Figure 1. Role operators used in PRECIS

(2)   every string must also contain a term which is prefixed by the
operator 1 and/or 2.

The interposed operators, such as the dependent elements, can be
introduced into a string at any point, and as often as necessary, so
raising the exhaustivity of the index entries, but these operators cannot be used to start a string. This means, briefly, that we cannot start
a string by declaring (through the operator) that the first term represents a "part"; we must begin the string by using a main line operator
which indicates the "whole."

5.6   If we consider the first four main line operators, i.e. 0, 1, 2 and 3, it is
a fairly simple matter to recognize a direct connection between the
terms introduced by these codes and certain everyday parts of speech.
For example, the operator 0 is related to the locative case in grammar,
while the operators 1, 2 and 3 introduce terms which usually (but not
invariably) correspond to the object, verb and subject of a sentence. The
interposed operators, such as p and q, do not strictly indicate grammatical roles as such. The role of a term which is prefixed by a dependent
element code is determined instead by whichever main line (or numbered)
operator was assigned to an earlier term in the string, and so sets the
dependent element into its logical context. We shall consider examples
of this mechanism at work later.

6   **STAGES OF CONCEPT ANALYSIS, AND THE USE OF THE OPERATORS**

6.1   Complete mastery of the schema of operators is entirely a matter of
practice, but we can nevertheless consider, by studying examples, the
stages of analyzing a compound subject, and the general procedures for
assigning appropriate operators when preparing an input string. We can
start with a fairly typical compound subject, then go on to add further
complexities in successive stages. Let us consider the subject, "Training
skilled personnel in the Canadian footwear industries", which is simply
a variant of the topic considered earlier.

6.2   When considering the stages of subject analysis, we have to assume that
the indexer has already examined the document and determined its subject content. This preliminary stage is common to all types of indexing,
abstracting and classifying. To a large extent this skill depends on what
we might call indexer flair or know-how, but certain teachable stages of
document analysis can be identified, and these are now being set down
as a code of practice being prepared by the International Standards
Organization. One point, which is stressed in the proposed standard,
also needs to be stressed here; indexing has to be based on an analysis
of the text as a whole; it is never based only on titles. The indexer needs
to examine the document (or a synopsis, in the case of non-print media)
to the point where he can state "This is about . . .", and then express
a subject or subjects in the form of one or more "title-like phrases".
PRECIS helps at the stage of document analysis by suggesting, through

the operators, that the indexer needs to be on the look-out for certain
important factors, answering questions such as the following:
—what happened?
—to what or to whom did it happen?
—who or what did it?
—where?
Each of these factors takes a specific operator. The result is a title-like
phrase on which we can then carry out a syntactical analysis.

6.3 In the first place, the indexer needs to consider this phrase, asking whether or not a term which denotes an action is present. If such a term
occurs, it usually determines how the rest of the subject should be
handled, much as the verb tends to dominate the sentence in traditional
grammar. In the present example, "Training skilled personnel in the
Canadian footwear industries", we can detect an action term in "Training". This should therefore be prefixed by the operator "2", which indicates an action or the effect of an action, i.e.

  (2) training

6.4 We next have to consider the kind of action which this term represents, and make a distinction between transitive and intransitive actions. "Training" represents a transitive action, insofar as it is capable
of taking an object (that is, somebody can be trained). We should therefore next examine the topic to see whether such an object is present; the
object is frequently coded as the "key system" (operator 1). In the
present example, it is the "Skilled personnel" who is being trained, so
the string should now appear as follows:

  (1) skilled personnel
  (2) training

6.5 In this particular instance, however, the "Skilled personnel" is actually
part of some other system which is also named in the subject: that is,
the "Footwear industries". Consequently, we need to revise our coding
to indicate this whole-part relationship, and we do this by using the
operator *p*, which introduces a part or property, to prefix the concept
"Skilled personnel". The operator "1" is then assigned to the name of
the greater whole, i.e. "Footwear industries". This gives us the string:

  (1) footwear industries
  (p) skilled personnel
  (2) training

6.6 This still leaves one term which has to be coded: that is, "Canada",
which clearly functions as the environment or widest context in which
the author considered all the other phenomena. We shall then finish up
with the string:

  (0) Canada
  (1) footwear industries

(p) skilled personnel
(2) training

In this case, check marks have been written above certain terms to indicate that they are needed as leads. In practice, this decision is indicated to the computer by a special coding system which is considered in a later session.

6.7 It is worth pointing out that the practicing indexer does *not* proceed in this fashion, going step-by-step through the separate stages of document analysis, then the formulation of a subject statement or title-like phrase, followed by its analysis in grammatical terms. Instead, the act of analysis and indexing form an integrated whole, and I doubt whether a skilled indexer would be able to describe his mental processes in this systematic way, even though this way is well-suited for teaching purposes. One point should be noted about this process of syntactical analysis, followed by the use of the operators to indicate the role of each term in the subject, and the filing of the terms according to the value of each operator: it has led to exactly the same order of concepts as that achieved in a subject considered earlier, "Training of skilled personnel in the American aircraft industries", although that subject was considered only in terms of context-dependency and one-to-one relationships. It can also be seen that the main line or numbered operators, owing to their built-in filing values, carry most of the load in indexing. It is these which determine the order of terms, and also regulate the format of the index entries. The computer will recognize that this string forms a "0-1-2" pattern of main line operators. This pattern calls for a set of entries in the standard format, produced by the shunting procedure considered earlier. Since each term has been marked as a lead, this will generate the entries below:

Canada
  Footwear industries. Skilled personnel. Training
Footwear industries. Canada
  Skilled personnel. Training
Skilled personnel. Footwear industries. Canada
  Training
Training. Skilled personnel. Footwear indsutries. Canada

7 **INCREASING THE COMPLEXITY OF A STRING: ADDING FURTHER DEPENDENT ELEMENTS**

7.1 We can now go on to increase the complexity of this string by adding further dependent elements at various points. For the sake of demonstration, we could specify that this subject has been considered in relation to Quebec, not the whole of Canada. We would therefore code "Canada" as the environment (as before), but identify "Quebec" as one of its parts:

        (0) Canada (NU)
        (p) Quebec
        (1) footwear industries
        (p) skilled personnel
        (2) training

In this case, a conventional sign (NU)—i.e. "Not upwards"—has been added to the term "Canada". This sign causes the term to which it has been attached to be suppressed from the qualifier when an entry in the standard format is generated under any term later in the string.

7.2 Similarly, we could indicate that the document referred to the training of a special class of "Skilled personnel", i.e. "Women". This relationship between the class ("Skilled personnel") and its member ("Women") is indicated by the operator q:

        (0) Canada
        (p) Quebec
        (1) footwear industries
        (p) skilled personnel
        (q) women
        (2) training

7.3 We could also go on to indicate that the author was concerned with a special kind of training, but this time we could use a differencing operator to increase the specificity:

        (0) Canada (NU)
        (p) Quebec
        (1) footwear industries
        (p) skilled personnel
        (q) women
        (2) training $i in-service

7.4 In these ways we have introduced new concepts into the string which clearly raise both its exhaustivity and specificity. Nevertheless, as far as the computer is concerned, this is still basically a "0-1-2" string, as indicated by the main line operators. The terms will therefore be shunted in a standard fashion to produce the following entries:

Canada
    Quebec. Footwear industries. Skilled personnel: Women.
        In-service training
Quebec
    Footwear industries. Skilled personnel: Women. In-service
        training
Footwear industries. Quebec
    Skilled personnel: Women. In-service training
Skilled personnel. Footwear industries. Quebec
    Women. In-service training
Women. Skilled personnel. Footwear industries. Quebec
    In-service training

        Training. Women. Skilled personnel. Footwear industries. Quebec
         In-service training
        In-service training. Women. Skilled personnel. Footwear industries.
         Quebec

8   THE INVERTED FORMAT: OPERATORS 4, 5 AND 6

8.1   We shall now move on to consider the second of the three formats used in PRECIS: in this case, an entry structure known as the *inverted format.* This format is produced by the computer whenever a lead is generated under a term prefixed by one of the operators in the range 4, 5 and 6, or a dependent element of any of these concepts.

8.2   The most frequently used of these codes is the operator 6, which introduces two different kinds of concept:

(1)   the name of a bibliographical form, when this differs from those usually handled by an indexing agency.

(2)   the name of a special category of user for whom a given document is intended (known as the "target user").

Both kinds of concept justify their places in a subject index, even though they fall outside the central theme of a document, so that they deal, in effect, with "extra-subject" factors. A subject index is more than a tool for selection; it is also a means for rejecting documents according to any factor which may be relevant for the user, including their forms and their users. For example, a nuclear physicist might be interested in an index entry such as:

        Elementary particles
        Collisions

But his interest is likely to evaporate if this were followed by the name of a target user, as in:

        Elementary particles
        Collisions—*Secondary school texts*

8.3   The viewpoint of the author is another extra-subject factor which could influence the user's judgement concerning the relevance of a given document. This factor is introduced by the operator "4", which also produces the inverted format. Examples of strings containing these operators are shown below:

(1)   (0) United States
        (1) aircraft industries
        (6) bibliographies

(2)   (0) United States
        (1) aircraft industries
        (p) skilled personnel
        (2) training
        (4) labor union viewpoints

8.4   A special set of computer instructions have been built into these operators which introduce extra-subject elements. These instructions can be summarized as follows:

(1)   A term prefixed by one of these operators is printed in italics when it appears in the display or qualifier. In the display position, it is preceded by a long dash.

(2)   When one of these terms serves as a lead, it is printed in roman bold, and the inverted format is generated: (a) the display consists of the terms in the string printed in their input order; (b) the term in the lead is repeated in the display *except when* the whole of the term is in the lead *and* it is the final term in the string.

These instructions account for the form of the final entries in the examples of output from the strings considered above:

Entries from String (1)

> **Aircraft industries.** United States
>   *—Bibliographies*
> **Bibliographies**
> United States. Aircraft industries

Entries from String (2)

> **Aircraft industries.** United States
>   Skilled personnel. Training—*Labor union viewpoints*
> **Skilled personnel.** Aircraft industries. United States
>   Training—*Labor union viewpoints*
> **Training.** Skilled personnel. Aircraft industries. United States
>   *—Labor union viewpoints*
> **Labor union viewpoints**
> United States. Aircraft industries. Skilled personnel. Training

8.5   The same instructions are built into the operator "5", which is used by the indexer when he wishes to indicate that the author was engaged in a general study, and has clearly indicated that he chose a specific example as his data source. This would occur, for example, if an author was concerned with the general problems of training in the American aircraft industries, and had stated, quite explicitly, that this general survey was based on facts and figures gathered from a study made at the Boeing International Corporation. Documents of this kind are not uncommon, and frequently cause problems for classifiers, who have to decide whether they should be classed at the author's intended subject (i.e. the whole aircraft industry), or at the specific instance (i.e. Boeing). In PRECIS, we can express both factors in the same string using the operator "5" to make the necessary distinction. The use of this operator is shown below:

(0) United States
(1) aircraft industries
(p) personnel
(2) training
(5) study example
(q) Boeing International Corporation

This string would lead to the entries below:

> **Aircraft industries.** United States
>> Personnel. Training—*Study example: Boeing International Corporation*
>
> **Personnel.** Aircraft industries. United States
>> Training—*Study example: Boeing International Corporation*
>
> **Training.** Personnel. Aircraft industries. United States
>> —*Study example: Boeing International Corporation*
>
> **Boeing International Corporation.** *Study example*
>> United States. Aircraft industries. Personnel. Training

8.6 In the final entry, we can see two format instructions functioning at the same time:

(1) the term which was coded "5" (i.e. "Study example") appears in the qualifier, and has been printed in italic. Logically, the qualifier is the correct place for this term, since its link with the lead (Boeing Aircraft Corporation) is one of direct dependency, as shown by the operator *q* assigned to the specific example.

(2) at the same time, the rest of the string was printed in the display in input order. This is due to the fact that it is the numbered operators (in this case, the operator "5") which govern the overall structure of an entry, and in this case generates the inverted format. The operator *q*, which precedes the name of the corporation, identifies a standard condition of context-dependency, so that "Study example" is shunted into the qualifier.

9 **ENTRIES GENERATED BY THE PREDICATE TRANSFORMATION**

9.1 We shall now consider the third and last of the formats used in PRECIS. This is an entry structure produced by a routine known as the "predicate transformation", for reasons which may become clear when we see the conditions which generate this format. The subjects which trigger this mechanism differ from those considered so far; they include not only the name of an action, prefixed by the operator "2", but also the name of the agent of the action, identified by the operator "3". This can be seen in the following string:

(0) United States
(1) aircraft industries
(p) personnel $h unskilled
(2) training $i in-service $v by $w of
(3) foremen

This coding indicates that "Foremen" are here regarded as the agents responsible for the in-service training of unskilled personnel.

9.2   This string also includes two other codes which have not been used in previous examples. These are the connective codes, $v and $w, attached to the term 'Training". These are not strictly indicators of grammatical roles, but they introduce instead certain components of phrases which the computer will generate out of terms which are adjacent in a string. The first code, $v, is called the "Downward-reading connective"; when an entry is being produced under a term which is earlier in the string, such as "Personnel", the term to which the connective is attached (in this case, the compound term "In-service training") will be linked to the next lower term (i.e. "Foremen") by the datum which follows $v (i.e. the preposition "by"). These elements will be organized as a phrase with no intervening punctuation, and with an upper case initial only on the first term in the phrase unless some other term was written in the string itself with an upper case initial (e.g. a proper name). The product is then a phrase, such as "In-service training by foremen," which can be seen in the first four entries generated from that input string:

> **Aircraft industries.** United States
>   Unskilled personnel. In-service training by foremen
> **Personnel.** Aircraft industries. United States
>   Unskilled personnel. In-service training by foremen
> **Training.** Unskilled personnel. Aircraft industries. United States
>   In-service training by foremen
> **In-service training.** Unskilled personnel. Aircraft industries
>   United States
>   By foremen

The other connective code, $w, has a similar function, but is used to construct appropriate phrases when the string is read in a reverse direction: that is, an entry is being constructed under a term which occurs *later* in the string than the connective. This can be seen in the entry produced under the term "Foremen":

> **Foremen.** Aircraft industries. United States
>   In-service training of unskilled personnel

9.3   If we examine the string from which these entries were produced, it can be seen that the first four terms were coded as a "0-1-2" pattern similar to some of the subjects we have already considered. This pattern of operators always generates entries in the standard format. However, a special set of computer instructions came into operation when the name of the agent, coded "3," was due to appear in the lead:

(1)   The computer can recognize, from the role operator, that it is dealing with the name of an agent.

(2)   It then automatically checks the operator assigned to the next preceding term, and establishes whether or not that term was coded as an action. This, too, is indicated by the role operator, three of which (i.e. "2", *s* and *t*) all indicate action terms of various types.

(3) If this condition is encountered (as it is in the present example,
     where "Training" is prefixed by "2"), the name of the action
     is then printed at the start of the *display* position; it is not
     shunted across into the qualifier.

(4) If, as in this example, the name of the action ("Training") is also
     accompanied by an upward-reading connective ($w), the connec-
     tive is printed as the next component of the display.

(5) The machine then completes the phrase by running-on to pick up
     the next preceding term, i.e. "Unskilled personnel". Since there
     is no upward-reading connective attached to this term, the phrase
     is then complete. Any earlier terms still left in the string (e.g.
     "United States") are then assigned automatically to the qualifier.

9.4   The predicate transformation was introduced into PRECIS for two
      special purposes:

(1) To ensure that the actions in which an entity are engaged are
     treated in exactly the same way as all its other attributes. When
     the name of an agent appears in the lead, its actions (and possibly
     the objects of these actions, as in the example above) are assigned
     to the display, and they then constitute a kind of "predicate"
     which collocates with other attributes of the agent, such as its
     parts and properties.

(2) It also ensures that we can retain certain one-to-one relationships
     between concepts which may have become separated in the input
     strings, due to their different grammatical roles. For example,
     there is an obvious whole-part relationship between "Aircraft
     industries" and their "Foremen", just as there is between "Aircraft
     industries" and their "Unskilled personnel". If we were dealing with
     a document which referred to a simpler subject, such as "Foremen
     in the American aircraft industries", we would index this by writ-
     ing the following string:

     (0) United States
     (1) aircraft industries
     (p) foremen

This string would lead to the following entries:

Aircraft industries. United States
    Foremen
Foremen. Aircraft industries. United States

Due to the predicate transformation, the final entry above at Position
5 under the term "Foremen" collocates exactly with that produced
from the earlier string, even though the term "Foremen" was treated
quite differently in the earlier subject: it was coded as an agent, not a
part, and was separated by two intervening terms from the whole of
which it logically forms a part.

10.1   We shall now consider the functions of one more operator before we draw various threads together and see how these different parts of the system interact when they occur together in a complex subject. This is the operator *s*, which is used to introduce two slightly different kinds of concept: firstly, what we call "role defining" terms; secondly, "directional properties". We shall deal with these separately, beginning with the use of *s* to introduce a role defining term.

10.2   When analysing a compound subject, it is usually a straightforward matter to deduce that a given term indicates an agent, but nevertheless it is not always easy to state the exact action in which the agent is engaged. This applies especially when an agent is responsible for a diffuse range of actions which cannot be specified exactly by a single term or phrase. It is sometimes enough to juxtapose the name of the object and the agent, leaving the action unstated, and relying on our normal frames of reference to make the distinction—i.e. commonsense will tell who did what to whom. This is not always sufficient, however, and we then need to introduce an explanatory word or phrase into the string to make a role more explicit, using the operator *s* to introduce the "role defining" term. An example of this is shown in the string below, which represents the coding of the subject "The role of consultants in the training of skilled personnel in the American aircraft industries":

> (0) United States
> (1) aircraft industries
> (p) skilled personnel
> (2) training $w of
> (s) role $v of $w in
> (3) consultants

—where the term "role", prefixed by "s", has been introduced to explicate the relationship between "Training" and "Consultants".

10.3   The entries which would be generated from this string are shown below:

> **Aircraft industries.** United States
>   Skilled personnel. Training. Role of consultants
> **Skilled personnel.** Aircraft industries. United States
>   Training. Role of consultants
> **Training.** Skilled personnel. Aircraft industries. United States
>   Role of consultants
> **Consultants.** Aircraft industries. United States
>   Role in training of skilled personnel

These entries demonstrate two mechanisms at work which were encountered in previous examples: firstly, the use of the connective codes $v and $w to introduce prepositions, and which lead to the production of phrases such as "Role of consultants"; secondly, the predicate transformation, which caused the term "Role" to be assigned to the display position, not shunted across into the qualifier, when the name of the agent, "Consultants", appeared in the lead. In this case, the transformation is triggered by the fact that an agent, coded "3", immediately follows a term ("Role") which is introduced by one of the three operators ("2", *s* and *t*) which identify actions.

10.4   By applying this routine, we have not only caused the computer to assign the phrase "Role in training of skilled personnel" to the display position, which is where it logically belongs; we have also ensured that the entry under the term "Consultants" will collocate with those entries produced from a quite different string such as the following:

> (0) United States
> (1) aircraft industries
> (p) consultants

This string will give rise to the following entries:

> **Aircraft industries.** United States
>   Consultants
> **Consultants.** Aircraft industries. United States

10.5   The operator *s* is usually used in this way to introduce terms and connectives, such as "Role-of-in" or "Applications-of-in", which have simply an explanatory function, and do not justify marking as leads. It can be seen, however, that they have an almost "transitive" quality—that is, they are actively related to some term *earlier* in the string—but it was not at first realized that these terms are also invariably *properties* of the next term later in the string: that is, of the agent. This special characteristic can be seen if we consider a simple two-term subject such as "The role of consultants". This would be coded as follows:

> (1) consultants
> (p) role

The use of the operator *p* indicates that the consultants *have* a role, just as they have various other attributes. It can also be seen, however, that the terms "Consultants" and "Role" have been set down in the string in an order which differs from that seen in the earlier example, in which "Role" preceded "Consultants". This simple two-element string would give rise to the following entries:

> **Consultants**
>   Role
> **Role.** Consultants

10.6   Terms such as "Role" in the examples above have been given the special name "Directional properties"—which indicates that they function, when they are introduced by the operator *s*, as the attribute of the term which is written *later* in the string, and at the same time they refer, in an almost transitive sense, to some earlier term in the string. A number of terms possess this characteristic, a typical example being "Attitudes." We can say that the attitudes of a person constitute part of their mental make-up or personality, and as such should be coded in certain cases by the use of the operator p. This coding is shown in the following subject:

> (1) students
> (p) attitudes

This represents the coding of the subject "Students' attitudes", where the attitudes have been studied in a general sense, not related to any specific object. This string would generate entries in the standard format:

> **Students**
>   Attitudes
> **Attitudes.** Students

10.7   It is these entries, produced from a simple string, which we have to keep in mind when we are assigning operators to a more complex subject in which the author considered the students' attitudes to some particular object, such as the revision of the curriculum. This is expressed in the following string:

> (0) United States
> (1) universities
> (p) curriculum
> (2) revision $w of
> (s) attitudes $v of $w to
> (3) students

This string will generate the following entries:

> **Universities.** United States
>   Curriculum. Revision. Attitudes of students
> **Curriculum.** Universities. United States
>   Revision. Attitudes of students
> **Attitudes.** Students. Universities. United States
>   To revision of curriculum
> **Students.** Universities. United States
>   Attitudes to revision of curriculum

10.8   The first three of these entries are quite straightforward: they simply represent further examples of the "standard format". We can also recognize the predicate transformation in operation in the final entry under the term "Students": since this term was introduced by the operator "3" in the input string, and follows a term prefixed by s, the term "Attitudes" was assigned to the display, and it then began the compound phrase, "Attitudes to revision of the curriculum", which was generated by a succession of $w connectives. However, something quite different happened in the entry which begins with the term "Attitudes". This is the entry which begins with a term coded s in the input string (i.e. "Students"), and assigns that term to the qualifier, not the display. At the same time, the preposition "to" (which was introduced by the connective $w) was assigned to the display, and started the construction of the phrase "To revision of curriculum". Any terms earlier in the string which did not form part of this phrase (since they were not linked by connectives) were automatically assigned to the qualifier. By applying these procedures, we have ensured that the entries produced from this string under the terms "Attitudes" and "Students" collocate with the entries under the same terms produced from the simpler string considered earlier.

11   ANALYSIS OF A COMPOUND SUBJECT COMBINING VARIOUS FACTORS

11.1   Finally, we can see a demonstration string and set of index entries which show most of the techniques we have been considering (Figure 2). This string introduces one further factor, known as *substitution:* this is a mechanism which allows the indexer to insert a term or phrase into a string so that it substitutes for, or replaces, some stated number of earlier terms whenever a later term comes into the lead. This is generally necessary when a second or subsequent action is introduced into a subject, and a restructured phrase may then be required to maintain an appearance of naturalness in the output.

11.2   Fortunately, we do not have to deal with subjects of this complexity all the time; nevertheless, the mechanisms are there if we should need them. In conclusion, I should like to emphasize three points which these entries demonstrate:

(1) It is the computer, not the indexer, which produced all the entries.

(2) This appears to be a formidable subject, but I hope it can now be seen as a combination of fairly simple elements linked by straightforward relationships which are amenable to analysis.

(3) Finally, the production of the entries clearly called for a number of complex transformations of the original input string. This complexity, however, resides entirely within the computer, which is where it rightly belongs. Writing the string itself is not a difficult task, and the technique of string writing (given the motivation) can be mastered within a week or so.

(1) *String:*   (0) United States
              (1) aircraft industries
              (p) skilled personnel
              (2) training $w of
              (s) role $v of $w in
              (3) consultants
      (sub 4) (2) role of consultants in training skilled personnel
              (s) attitudes $v of $w to
              (3) foremen
              (6) bibliographies

(2) *Entries:*

Aircraft industries. United States
 Skilled personnel. Training. Role of consultants. Attitudes
  of foremen—*Bibliographies*
Skilled personnel. Aircraft industries. United States
 Training. Role of consultants. Attitudes of foremen—*Bibliographies*
Training. Skilled personnel. Aircraft industries. United States
 Role of consultants. Attitudes of foremen—*Bibliographies*
Consultants. Aircraft industries. United States
 Role in training of skilled personnel. Attitudes of foremen
  —*Bibliographies*
Attitudes. Foremen. Aircraft industries. United States
 To role of consultants in training skilled personnel
  —*Bibliographies*
Foremen. Aircraft industries. United States
 Attitudes to role of consultants in training skilled personnel
  —*Bibliographies*
Bibliographies
 United States. Aircraft industries. Skilled personnel. Training.
 Role of consultants. Attitudes of foremen

Figure 2. Compound subject demonstrating factors in combination

The Semantics of PRECIS: Vocabulary Control and the RIN System

Derek Austin
Subject Systems Office, Bibliographic Services
Division, British Library

1   RELATIONSHIP BETWEEN SYNTAX AND SEMANTICS

1.1   In the previous session we were concerned with the syntax or grammar of string writing, and the mechanics of entry construction. We move on now to the semantic side of the system: that is, establishing terms which, because they are mentally associated with terms in strings, might also function as a user's access points to the alphabetical index. These semantically related terms, such as synonyms and the names of broader classes, are assigned to a machine-held thesaurus which serves as the source of *See* and *See also* references in the printed index. It could be said that these references add a second dimension to the subject index. This new dimension, and the difference between syntax and semantics, are illustrated in the diagram in Figure 1.

Subject: The management of hospitals in West Germany

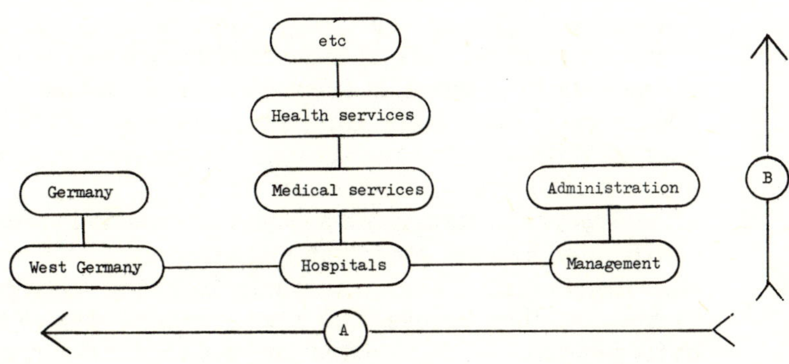

A   Syntactical relationships: a posteriori or document-specific relationships between concepts

B   Semantic relationships: a priori relationships which are independent of the treatment of a concept in any particular document.

Figure 1. Syntactic and semantic relationships

1.2   In PRECIS, as in many other systems, the syntax and semantics are treated as separate components, and are handled by different procedures. In PRECIS, however, we recognize a very strong relationship between syntax and semantics, and we deliberately try to exploit this as far as possible. Our experience has shown that it is a simpler matter to organize terms into logical classes within a thesaurus when we work within certain syntactical constraints which specify exactly what we mean by a term. As we have already seen, the role operators play some part in this process, since they predicate that certain kinds of concept should be treated as separate syntactical units, each prefixed by its own operator, when a string is written by the indexer. The "Rules of differencing" show this procedure at work; remember, in particular, the mandatory rule: "Do not difference the name of a part by the name of its whole". This is the rule which forbids the use of a term such as "Aircraft engines". This kind of compound term is common enough in natural language, but for indexing purposes it has to be treated as two separate nouns, i.e. "Aircraft" (the whole), and "Engines" (the part), each preceded by its own operator. Apart from ensuring consistency in indexing, this also gives us a richer and more logically structured vocabulary. The first element, "Aircraft", will be assigned to a class "Vehicles", while the second, "Engines", belongs to the different class, "Prime movers".

1.3   Several eminent documentalists have warned us that chaos and unpredictability will occur inevitably in any categorial system if the link between semantics and syntax is ignored. Wellisch, in his paper "Subject Retrieval in the Seventies,"[1] has made this point very clearly, using *Library of Congress Subject Headings* (*LCSH*) as the basis for his study, and there is no point in pursuing the matter further here.

1.4   In PRECIS, the act of thesaurus-making differs in two particular respects from many other mechanized systems:

(1)   The necessary *See* and *See also* references are extracted from a computer-held network of interrelated addresses at which terms are held, but the terms, as such, play no special part in this operation. In order to produce a reference to a given term, we have to quote the machine address of that term in a special field which forms part of the indexing data.

(2)   The networks of terms held at these interrelated addresses are constructed in what we call an inductive way. This means that we start from a term which has actually been encountered during indexing, and then proceed "upwards" step-by-step to the names of its genera and other related terms. Other thesauri are usually made deductively: that is, downwards from the names of some pre-established classes or categories.

2.1   Before considering the procedures used in creating the thesaurus, it is
necessary to introduce three concepts which form the basic components
of the semantic side of PRECIS:

(1) *Indexing terms*
These have been considered already, and for the present it is
sufficient to note that, when building the thesaurus, we are concerned only with those terms which are marked as leads in index
entries. There is obviously no point in making a reference to a
non-lead term. Apart from this one constraint, the vocabulary is
entirely open-ended: that is to say, new terms can be admitted at
any time, as soon as they have been encountered in documents.
In the British Library, all lead terms are assigned to the thesaurus
whether they call for references or not, so that the file functions
as the main authority for all the lead terms recorded by previous
indexers.

(2) *Reference Indicator Number (RIN)*
A RIN is a seven-figure number, the final digit serving as a
modulus eleven check. This number identifies the address at
which a term is held in the computer, and is quoted as part of the
indexing data (in field 692 in the present MARC record). Quoting
a valid RIN in this field directs the computer to the appropriate
part of the file, from which it begins the construction of references.
Through constant contact with our data processing team, we have
tended to pick up some rather loose terminology when discussing
the semantics of PRECIS: we now talk of "RINning", "RINfile",
and even "RINput".

(3) *Relational codes*
Various kinds of semantic relationship are recognized in PRECIS,
and each is associated with its own special code. These codes are
used to interrelate the addresses (RINs) in the machine-held file,
which means that the file consists of an interlocked semantic network. We shall consider this procedure in some detail later on. In
practice, the three relationships encountered most often are those
which are now incorporated into a new International Standard
(IS 2788, "Guidelines for monolingual thesauri"). These relationships
are shown in Figure 2.

2.2   The *equivalence relationship* indicates the link between two kinds of
terms:

(1) *Synonyms*, e.g. "Educational attainment" and "Academic
achievement".

(2) *Quasi-synonyms*, that is, terms which are regarded as synonyms
for indexing purposes, even though their meanings are quite
distinct in ordinary usage. These frequently represent different
points on a continuum, e.g. "Hardness" and "Softness".

The equivalence relationship is identified to the computer by a special
code, $m. We shall later consider how we use this code in practice to

EQUIVALENCE RELATIONSHIP

Synonyms, e.g. Hovercraft/air cushion vehicles
Quasi-synonyms, Hardness/Softness

HIERARCHICAL RELATIONSHIP

Generic relations, e.g.

Animals
Vertebrates
Birds
Reptiles

Hierarchical whole-part relations

(a) *Geographical regions*

Canada
Ontario
Ottawa
Toronto

(b) *Systems and organs of the body*

Circulatory system
Cardiovascular system
Arteries
Veins

(c) *Areas of discourse*

Science
Biology
Botany
Zoology

ASSOCIATIVE RELATIONSHIP

Should involve a defining or explaining function, e.g.

Teeth/Dentistry
Birds/Ornithology

Figure 2. General thesaural relationships

generate a *See* reference from an unused term to its preferred synonym or quasi-synonym.

2.3 The *hierarchical relationship*, as laid down in IS 2788, also covers two types of relationship: (i) generic; (ii) hierarchical whole-part.

(1) The *generic relationship* is strictly one of class-inclusion, e.g. between a genus and its species. We need to distinguish between the true generic and the quasi-generic relationship. The difference between them is shown in Figure 3 where it can be seen that the

quasi-generic relationship is one of class-overlap rather than class-inclusion. It is important to distinguish these readily in practice, since the true generic relationship is handled by a *See also* reference extracted from the thesaurus, while the quasi-generic relationship is handled syntactically, a special operator, q, being used for this purpose. We have therefore devised a fairly simple "All-and-some" test which helps us to make this distinction, and this, too, is shown in Figure 3. Even when using this test, it is worth noting that the interpretation of "generic" may vary from one index to another, depending on the frames of reference of the users. In particular, an index to a special subject field may call for references which differ from those in a pan-disciplinary index. In an index devoted to "Pest control", for example, the concept "Mice" may be regarded, in an almost definitional sense, as belonging to the category "Pests", in which case the link between these terms should be handled by a reference. In PRECIS, the treatment of the generic relationship is subject to a rule of the system which states that two terms should not be written as adjacent components in a string if the first serves only to define the class to which the second belongs.

1) The pure generic, or class-inclusion, relationship

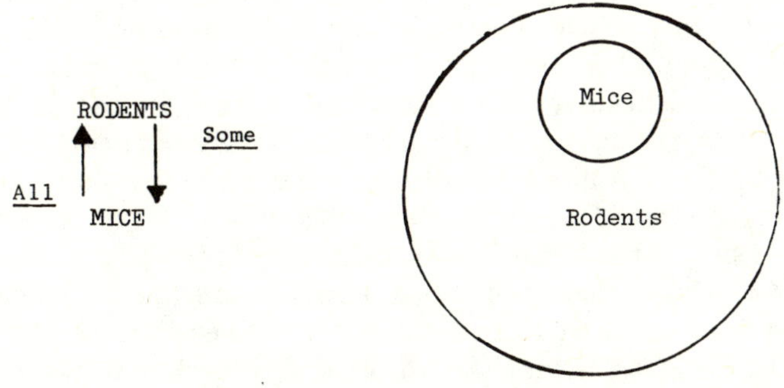

2) The quasi-generic, or class-overlap, relationship

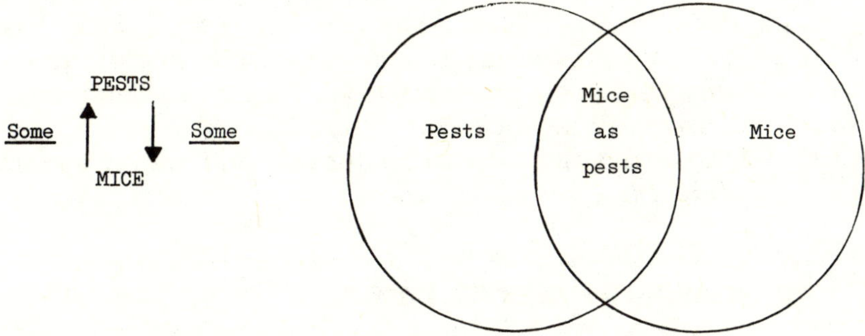

Figure 3. Distinction between "pure generic" and "quasi-generic" relationship

(2)   The *hierarchical whole-part relationship* (shown in Figure 2) may
      appear at first glance to represent a departure from the "standard"
      logic of PRECIS, where the relationship between a whole and its
      part is normally expressed by an operator in the string. In some
      cases, however, a strong and implicit hierarchical link exists be-
      tween a part and its containing whole, so that it can be handled,
      on a once-and-for-all basis, by a *See also* reference. In practice so
      far we have encountered three kinds of concepts which fall into
      this category (all three are listed in the new International Stand-
      ard IS 2788). These are:
      (a)   *geographical regions*
      (b)   *systems and organs of the body*
      (c)   *areas of discourse* (i.e. fields of knowledge)
      In PRECIS, both types of hierarchical relationships are expressed
      by the single code, $o.

2.4   The *associative relationship* covers more or less what is left—that is to
      say, if two terms are mentally associated, without being synonyms or
      hierarchically related, we would say that they are linked by the associa-
      tive relationship. At first glance, this may seem a very loose definition—
      one which would allow too many vaguely connected terms into the
      thesaurus. We have therefore established, as a working guideline, a rule
      which states that two terms can be associated in this way provided that
      one of the terms plays an essential part in defining or explaining the
      other. This applies, for example, to a pair of terms such as "Birds" and
      "Ornithology". These are not synonyms, nor do they form a logical
      hierarchy: "Birds" belong to a class of naturally-occuring things, while
      "Ornithology" is a human activity, so we cannot say that a bird is a
      kind of ornithology. But try to define the word "Ornithology" without
      using the term "Birds"! This associative relationship is represented by
      the code $n, which also produces a *See also* reference. The reference is
      always made *towards* the term which helps to explain the other (i.e.
      from Ornithology *to* Birds). An additional reference in the other direc-
      tion can also be made if required.

2.5   A summary table of the codes which express these various relationships
      is shown in Figure 4. These codes have two specific functions:
      (1)   They indicate the exact nature of the relationship which links the
            terms held at different addresses. We shall see later why we need
            to make this distinction.
      (2)   They also prompt the computer into printing the correct form of
            reference.

3   **ESTABLISHING A SEMANTIC NETWORK**

3.1   In addition to these relational codes, we have also devised a range of
      further codes which are unique to the thesaurus. These are listed in
      Figure 5. Many of these codes play no part in generating references in

Relational codes used to link term addresses (RINs):

$m = EQUIVALENCE RELATIONSHIP

$o = HIERARCHICAL RELATIONSHIPS

$n = ASSOCIATIVE RELATIONSHIP

Machine instructions built into codes:

$m = PRINT *"SEE"* REFERENCE, i.e.   A *See* B

$n
$o   } = PRINT *"SEE ALSO"* REFERENCE, i.e.   A
         (By-pass instruction in $o)
                                                See also
                                                   B

Figure 4. Relational codes and machine instructions in the RIN thesaurus

the printed index, but have been devised to record, in a machine-readable form, information which will be needed when this file is used as the source of a systematically-structured thesaurus. These particular codes will not be considered here. The references in the right hand column on these Figures are to the relevant sections of the *PRECIS Manual.*

3.2   We should now go on to see how these codes work in practice by going through the stages of creating a semantic network. For the sake of this demonstration, we should assume that we are in charge of the RINfile, and we are about to deal with the first string containing the word "Penguins". Let us also assume that none of the higher or other terms related to "Penguins" has yet been admitted into the system. In the first place, we have to ensure that this candidate term is logically acceptable—that is to say, it does not break any of the rules associated with differencing, and so on. Once this has been established, we can then admit the term into the system, proceeding in the way which is shown in Fig. 6.

3.3   The term is first recorded on an input card, and we then strike out the next available RIN from a computer-produced list, and write this number below the term. It needs to be stressed that the RIN does not, in any way, function as a piece of notation in the usual sense: that is, it does not convey any hierarchical or other relational information, but simply indicates the address at which the term will be held in a random-access file.

3.4   We then set out to establish any terms which are directly related to "Penguins", and might therefore function as access points for the user who would be interested in documents on this concept. We make use of any available tools for this task, such as dictionaries, existing thesauri,

Code	Meaning	*PRECIS Manual* Section
Input codes		
#RI#	Record input	32.2
#RA#	Record amend	32.3/16
#RD#	Record delete	32.18/22
#RP#	Report contents of RIN	32.23
Relational codes	The term at the following address:	
See codes		
$m	—*is not used as lead*	30.7/8
See also codes		
$n	—*belongs to a different category*	30.9
$o	—*is a superordinate term in the same category*	30.9; 31.4; 31.16/19
$x	—*is a sibling requiring a crossing reference*	30.9; 32.14/15
$y	—*belongs to a different category, but requires a crossing reference*	30.9; 32.16/17
Redirect codes		
$r	—*belongs to the same category*	33.19/21
$s	—*belongs to a different category*	33.22
Codes used only in construction of thesauri		
$t	—*is the higher generic part of a compound term*	34.6
$u	—*belongs to a different category, but shares a common stem*	34.7

Figure 5. Codes used in construction of references

classification schemes etc. From these we could establish that the term "Penguins" has a synonym, "Sphenisciformes", and that it belongs to a wider class called "Birds". Each of these new terms is also admitted into the system—that is, it is written on a card, and its RIN is assigned. As soon as these terms have been admitted, we can then go back to the card for "Penguins" and add the necessary links to the related terms. The record produced in this way is shown at the start of the second sequence of cards in Fig. 6, where the record for "Penguins" now holds the following additional data:

(1)   The code $m, which indicates the Equivalence relationship, and

Code	Meaning	*PRECIS Manual* Section
Typographic codes		
$e	—*non-filing part in italic preceded by comma*	33.5/7
$f	—*filing part in italic preceded by comma*	33.6/7
$g	—*return to bold*	33.5; 33.7
$h	*filing part in italic preceded by stop*	33.8
$i	—*filing part in italic, no preceding punctuation*	33.9
$j	—*filing part in roman preceded by two spaces and stop*	33.3
$k	—*filing part in roman, no preceding punctuation*	33.10; 35.7
Format codes		
$p	—*term in roman, print in reference display*	33.14/15; 33.18
$q	—*term in italic, print in reference display*	33.16/18
Ancillary data		
$d	—*definition or scope note*	30.4; 31.24

Figure 5. (continued)

    which therefore calls for the construction of a *See* reference from the data held at address 23 (the synonym "Spherisciformes").

(2) The code $o, followed by the RIN 34, which indicates that "Penguins" is hierarchically subordinate to the concept "Birds". This completes what is called the first level of reference.

3.5   The superordinate term, "Birds", is now regarded in its turn as a potential target term, and is treated in exactly the same way as "Penguins". Using the tools at hand, we can establish that this, too, has a superordinate term, "Vertebrates", and that it is associated with a field of study called "Ornithology". This gives us two further terms which have to be admitted into the system. These, too, are recorded on cards, their RINs are assigned, and the appropriate relationships can then be registered on the input card for "Birds".

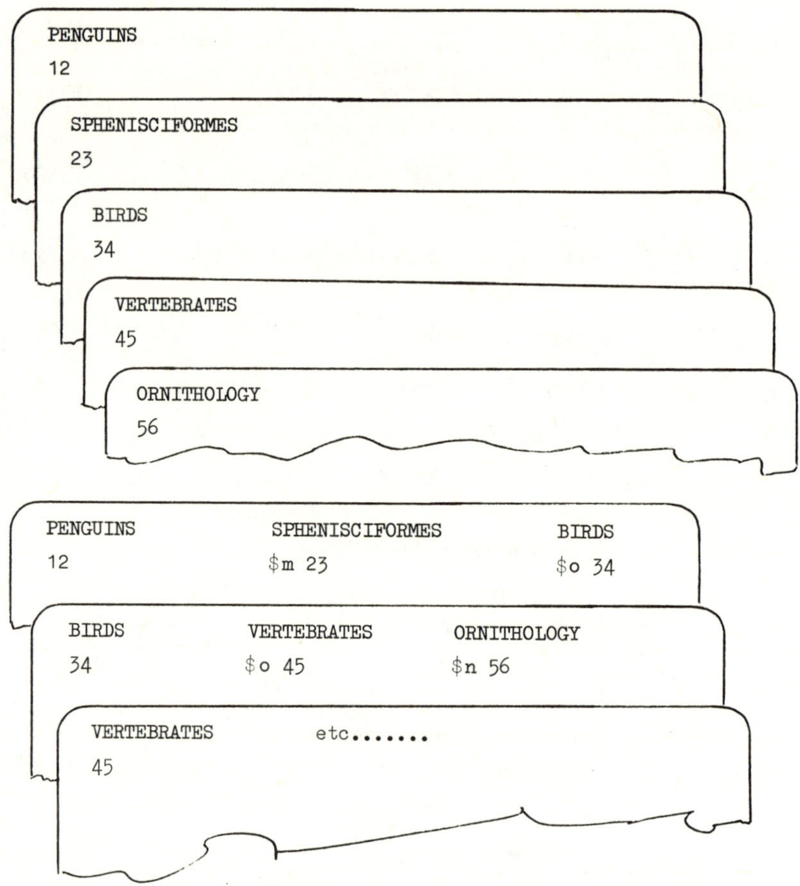

Figure 6. Semantic network for the term "Penguins"

3.6   Exactly the same operation is then repeated at the next higher level of terms, that is, "Ornithology" and "Vertebrates", and this process continues from level to level until the indexer is satisfied that an adequate network of related terms has been recorded, ready to be assigned to the computer. Later experience may show that the network established at this stage is either faulty or inadequate. In designing the system, we allowed for human frailty, and included special mechanisms for changing terms or their relationships, and even for restructuring whole sections of a network. Some of these procedures will be considered later. Any number of higher and other related terms can be associated with any given concept, and what are called polyhierarchical relationships are not uncommon. These occur when a term is designated as belonging, logically and simultaneously, to more than one superordinate class, in the sense in which "Pianos", for example, belongs simultaneously to the three genera, "Keyboard instruments", "String instruments" and "Percussion instruments".

3.7   When this stage of the process is finished, we next have to sort the cards, ready for keyboarding. Some care is necessary at this stage, since

these data must be input in such a way that every address *from*
which a reference will be made is already occupied when the term at
the target end of the reference is admitted into the system. For
example, we cannot submit the data for "Penguins", which includes
a relational code and RIN calling for a reference from "Birds", unless
the address for "Birds" has already been occupied. This condition is
mandatory, and will be checked by the computer at the time of input.

3.8   An example of a set of cards sorted in this way is shown in Fig. 7. This
starts with "Science" at the top of the page, and ends at the bottom
with "Penguins". When these cards are handled by the keyboarders,
they select only some of these data for input to the computer. A string
of input data is shown at position 2, and it can be seen that the following elements were selected:
(1)   The RIN for the newly admitted term.
(2)   The term itself.
(3)   Any associated relational codes, if present, plus the RINs for the
referred-from terms, but *not* the referred-from terms themselves;
these terms will be picked up automatically from their addresses
by the computer.

As each input string is processed, the machine first validates the RIN
(using the modulus 11 digit), then checks that the address for any
referred-from term (i.e. the RIN which follows a relational code) is
already occupied. If this condition is satisfied, the machine records, at
the address of the referred-from term, the reciprocal of the relational
code which called for that reference, plus the RIN (in a condensed version) of the referred-to or target term. This means, in effect, that the
computer can scan either up or down a hierarchy with equal ease, even
though references are printed in only one direction.

3.9   The set of cards in Fig. 7 may appear, at first sight, to hold a jumble of
terms with no obvious structure. Nevertheless, if we organize these
terms strictly in accordance with the logic expressed in the relational
codes, it will be found that, in fact, we created a highly structured and
logical network. This is shown in Fig. 8. It can be seen that the network
consists of two different hierarchies (one of things, and the other of
actions), linked at various points by selected associative relationships
expressed by the code $n, plus a scatter of synonyms, as shown by $m,
down the right-hand side.

3.10   After the input cards have been typed, they are returned to the indexer
responsible for the thesaurus, who sorts them alphabetically into the
main authority file of all the lead terms used. (We also take copies of
these cards, and exchange these data with the National Library of
Australia. A program is now available which allows us to replicate the
main authority file directly from the computer, and copies of this file
are in use in various indexing agencies in London.) At the time when
these data are input to the computer, the machine also responds with a
full set of correctly-formatted references on cards, and these are added

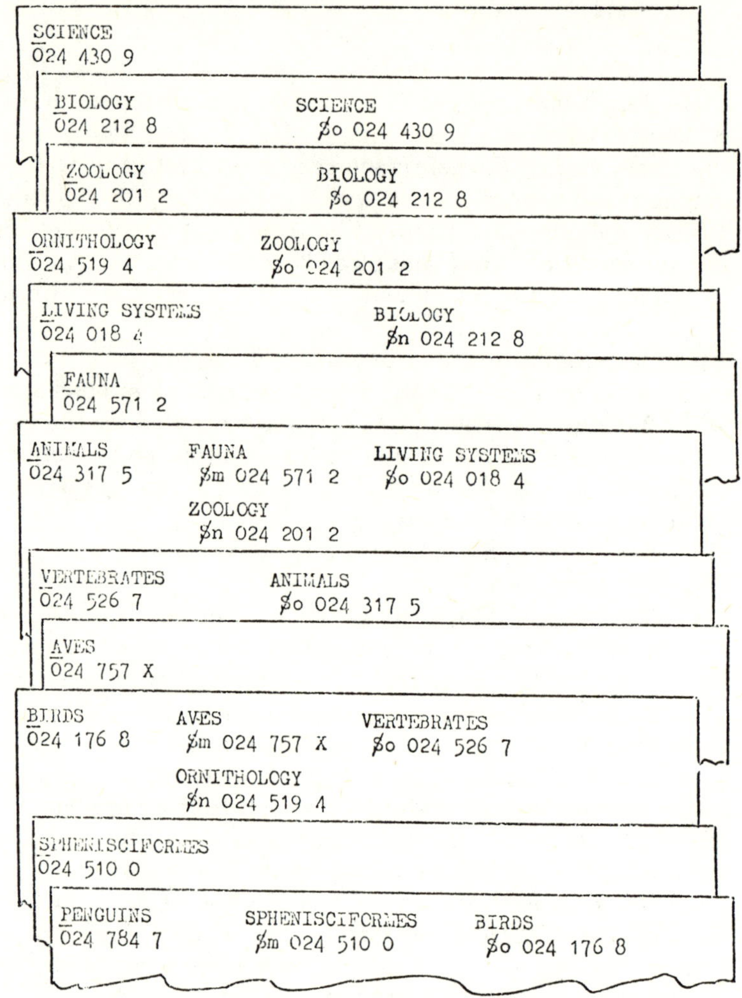

Input record for _Penguins_:

0247847Penguins$m0245100$o0241768#

Figure 7. Thesaurus input records (filed for input)

to the main authority of all index entries and references created in the past. In a later session, we shall consider some of the uses for this full authority file.

4   THE GENERATION OF REFERENCES

4.1   Up to this point, we have been concerned only with the creation of a machine-held semantic network. We can now move on to consider how this network is used in practice, still taking the "Penguin" network as an example. The RIN for "Penguins" would have been written as part of the data associated with the string which first contained this term, and it would also be quoted (in field 692) on any future record which contains this term. The presence of this number (024 784 7) directs the computer to the RINfile, and starts a com-

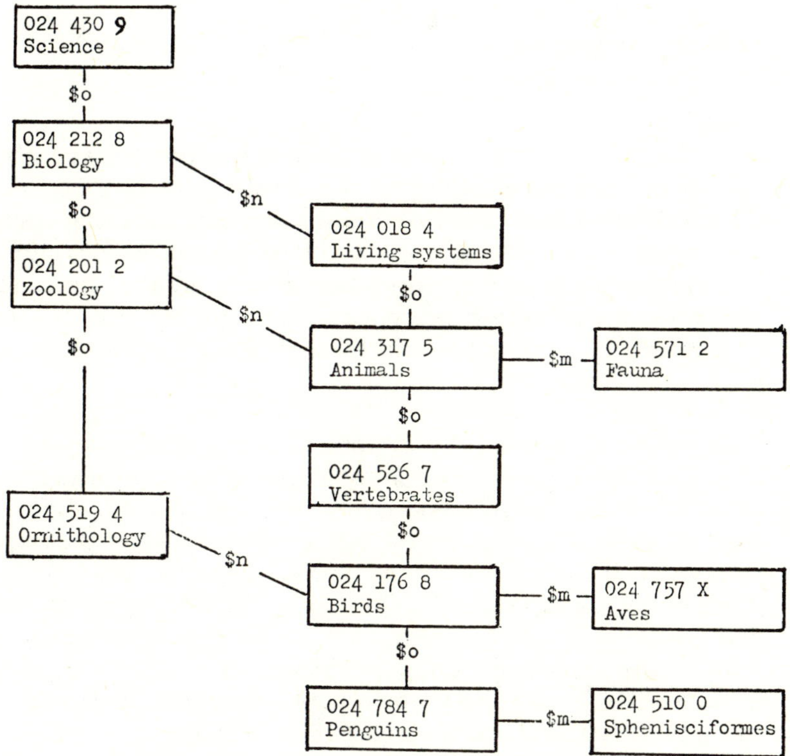

Figure 8. Network of terms linked by thesaural relationships

plex chain reaction which should be followed from the diagram
in Fig. 8:

(1) The machine first extracts the term held at the quoted address
("Penguins").

(2) At this position, it checks for other relational codes. In this
instance, two further codes are present: the symbol $m points
to the address 024 510 0, which contains the term "Sphenisciformes", and the code $o points to 024 176 8, which holds the
term "Birds".

(3) The code $m generates a *See* reference, i.e.

Sphenisciformes *See* **Penguins**

(4) The code $o generates a *See also* reference with a three-line
structure:

Birds
  See also
  Penguins

(5) At the address of the "higher" term ("Birds"), the machine
establishes the presence of three further relational codes, i.e.
$m, $n and $o. Each of these calls for the production of a
further reference, e.g.

(6)   Another set of relational codes is then detected at the next higher level, each code calling for the construction of a new reference, and this operation continues step-by-step until the computer arrives at the top of a hierarchy—that is, it reaches addresses where no further relational codes are present. By that time, a full set of downward-reading references will have been constructed, each reference guiding the user towards the term which appeared in an index entry.

4.2   When we first designed this system of interrelated addresses we had only two codes to express relationships between terms. One led to the production of a *See* reference, and the other to a *See also* reference. Each of these was what we call a one-step reference: that is, it referred the user to the next lower point in the hierarchy, whether or not an index entry also appeared at that point. This did not cause any particular problems in a large index, such as the annual volume of *BNB*, since most of the intervening steps in a hierarchy would by then have acquired index entries. It has to be remembered, however, that *BNB* is a cumulating bibliography, and the PRECIS index first appears in the monthly parts. In any given month, it is possible that only the term "Penguins" in this network had actually appeared in an index entry. From the user's point of view, a step-by-step sequence of re-directions from one term to the next down a hierarchy could then become a very tedious business, especially if the user happened to enter the index at a point near the top of the network, such as "Animals" or "Science". This is the single aspect of PRECIS which provoked critical reactions from *BNB*'s users—and quite understandably.

4:3   In order to overcome this problem, we first examined more closely the relationships which link the terms in a semantic network, then specified these more precisely, using the codes we have been considering here. We then built a special instruction, known as the "By-pass routine", into one of the codes. This is the code $o, which indicates the hierarchical relationship. Whenever the computer is directed, via the code $o, to the RIN for some higher term, the instruction to print a *See also* reference is momentarily blocked, and the RIN for the higher term is assigned to a temporary store. In this way, the computer continues to the top of a $o hierarchy, the RIN at each step being assigned to the store, but not processed. Finally, the RINs held in the temporary store are matched against all the RINs extracted from field 692 in the various subject packets which will go towards the making of that particular index. Whenever a match is found, which means that a particular term will appear as a lead in an index entry, references will be made directly to that point from all the higher positions in the hierarchy. If a match is *not* found, the reference to the empty intervening step will be by-

1. *One-step references produced by $m and $n*

<table>
<tr><td>Biology
   See also
      Organisms</td><td>Zoology
   See also
      Animals</td></tr>
</table>

Ornithology
   See also
      Birds

Fauna *See* Animals

Aves *See* Birds

Sphenisciformes *See* Penguins

2. *By-pass references produced by $o when only entry under "Penguins"*

<table>
<tr><td>Science
   See also
      Ornithology</td><td>Animals
   See also
      Penguins</td></tr>
<tr><td>Zoology
   See also
      Ornithology</td><td>Organisms
   See also
      Penguins</td></tr>
<tr><td>Biology
   See also
      Ornithology</td><td>Vertebrates
   See also
      Penguins</td></tr>
<tr><td></td><td>Birds
   See also
      Penguins</td></tr>
</table>

Figure 9. The by-pass routine

passed, and the reader will be directed instead to the next lower term which actually functioned as a lead. For example, if a given issue of an index contained (of the terms shown in Fig. 8) only a document on "Penguins", the by-pass routine would automatically lead to the construction of the references shown in Fig. 9, e.g.

<table>
<tr><td>**Living system**
   See also
      Penguins</td><td>**Animals**
   See also
      Penguins</td></tr>
</table>

We could, perhaps, have shortened the route even more by building the by-pass instruction into the code $n, but we were not prepared to defend an occasional reference such as:

Science
   See also
      Penguins

5.1   Once we have set up a network such as the "Penguin" hierarchy, we can quote the RIN for any permitted term in the file as soon as an appropriate document occurs. For example, if a work on either "Vertebrates" or "Ornithology" is encountered after the "Penguin" hierarchy has been set up, we can check these terms in the authority file, and quote their RINs without any further effort.

5.2   We can also quote an existing RIN if we wish to graft a new term into the network. If the "Penguin" network has already been established, and we later wish to add a term such as "Snakes" to the system, we can use any relevant part of the hierarchy shown in Fig. 8, and then proceed as follows:

(1)   We would use standard reference tools to establish terms related to "Snakes", such as its synonym "Ophidia", and the higher term "Reptiles".

(2)   All these new terms, and their RINs, would be recorded on input cards, and the relationships between them would be recorded through codes such as $m, etc.

(3)   As far as the term "Reptiles" is concerned, however, we only need to add the code "$o 024 5267" to its card, and this concept will automatically be recorded as a subordinate member of the class "Vertebrates" which already exists in the system. Any number of species can be registered as members of a given category, just as any given concept can be a member of more than one class at the same time.

5.3   It is a straightforward matter to correct faulty data in the file, or to change or extend an existing network if this is shown to be false or inadequate. To see how corrections are applied, we need to consider the input codes which are shown in Fig. 10:

(1)   The first code, #RI#, is a necessary prefix to all normal input messages. The indexer does not need to write this code—this is left to the typist, who understands that any RIN card is an #RI# message unless some other code has been written by the indexer.

(2)   Special instructions are attached to the third and fourth codes, i.e. #RD# and #RP#. We shall consider these codes later, and concentrate for the present on the use of the #RA# message code which is used for data amendment. An analysis of this code is shown in Fig. 11.

5.4   The #RA# message code conveys amendments to the computer. The code is always followed immediately by the RIN which identifies the address where the faulty data occurs, and it is also accompanied by the following two subfield codes:

Type of message	*Code*	*Purpose of message*
Input message	RI	To assign a new thesaurus record to a previously unoccupied address on the disc file.
		NB. Cards for thesaurus records must be sorted, before keyboarding, so that every referred-from term precedes its target term(s).
Amendment message	RA	(a) To correct a record which is already on file.
		(b) To add data to a record which is already on file.
Deletion message	RD	To delete a record
		Invalid unless next message is an RI message which re-uses the RIN of the deleted record.
Report message	RP	To obtain a report on the contents of an address.

Figure 10. Messages for input and correction of thesaurus records

> $a   =   take out the following data
>
> $b   =   insert the following data

Both codes must be quoted on every RA message, though, as we shall see later, either of these subfields can be left empty. This means that we can, if we wish, delete old data without adding anything new, or, alternatively, we can add new data without deleting old ones.

> #RA# (RIN OF RECORD TO BE AMENDED)
>
> $a   =   Data to be deleted
>
> $b   =   Data to be added
>
> NOTE: $a and $b must both be present in message.
> Either can be followed by "No data".

Figure 11. #RA# messages: content of message

5.5   Some typical uses of the RA or amendment messages are shown in Fig. 12:

Example 1:   In this case the RA message is used to correct a misspelled word. It is sufficient to input just enough data to pinpoint exactly where the fault occurred, removing the faulty data with the $a subfield and replacing it with corrected data identified by $b. The faulty spelling "Brids" will thus be corrected to read "Birds". If the same letter or pattern of letters occurs more than once in a word (as in "Canada", which has more than one *a*), the correction will be applied to the earliest occurence. If the fault lies at the second or later

EXAMPLE 1: CORRECTION TO A TERM

Data recorded on file:	023 745 0 Brids
Amendment message:	#RA# 023 745 0
	$a ri
	$b ir #
Amended data on file:	023 745 0 Birds

EXAMPLE 2: CORRECTION TO A RELATIONAL CODE

Data recorded on file:	023 793 0 Traffic
	023 670 5 Road Traffic
	$m 023 793 0 Traffic
Amendment message:	#RA# 023 670 5
	$a $m 023 793 0
	$b $o 023 793 0 #
Amended data on file:	023 670 5 Road traffic
	$o 023 793 0 Traffic

EXAMPLE 3: CHANGING A TERM

Data recorded on file:	023 700 0 Ceylon
Amendment message:	#RA# 023 700 0
	$a Ceylon
	$b Sri Lanka #
Amended data on file:	023 700 0 Sri Lanka

NOTE: The term "Ceylon" should now be assigned to a new address (e.g. 025 593 9), and related to the new name as a non-preferred synonym. This calls for:
a) a new RI message: #RI# 025 593 9 Ceylon #
b) an RA amendment: #RA# 023 700 0
                $a
                $b $m 025 593 9 #
Amended data on file: 025 593 9 Ceylon

Figure 12. #RA# messages: corrections and changes

occurrence, we have to identify the part which is wrong by including
extra letters among the deleted part, then putting them back as part
of the correction. If necessary, we can, of course, always quote the
whole word.

Example 2:   The RA message is used to correct a faulty relational
code. In this case, the term "Traffic" was wrongly input as the unused
synonym of "Road traffic", as shown by the code $m. Since the re-
lationship is, in fact, hierarchical, we have to change $m into $o, using
an amendment message. Whenever we wish to change a relational code
or a RIN, we must quote both as part of the amendment message,
even if one of them is right. We have built this requirement into the

system as a precaution against making a change to the wrong data.
Example 3: In the third example, the amendment message is used
to replace an existing term which has fallen out of use. The whole of
the term has to be deleted, using $a, and the new term substituted,
using $b. All the existing relationships can be left undisturbed. We can,
if we wish, assign the old term to a new address, then treat it as a non-
preferred synonym, using the subfield code $b to add the necessary
reference to the existing address. This use of the RA message is not uncommon, especially when we have to update terminology to keep pace
with official changes, such as "Underdeveloped countries" becoming
"Developing nations", and now "Emergent nations".

5.6   We would also use this amendment message code to correct any fault
in a hierarchy which was revealed through contact with later documents.
Let us go back once more to the "Penguin" network in Figure 8, and
assume that, after we constructed that network, we dealt with a document on "Marine birds". Two facts should then emerge:
(1) The term "Marine birds" has a synonym, "Sea birds", as well as a
     superordinate term "Water birds", which itself has a synonym,
     "Aquatic birds".
(2) "Marine birds" is also the superordinate class to which "Penguins"
     logically belongs.
The procedures for dealing with this are shown in Figure 13. In the
first place, we have to admit all the new terms into the system, and give
each one its own RIN. We can then add the necessary relational codes,
using $o to indicate the generic relationships, and $m to identify synonyms. It can be seen at position 2 that the term "Water birds" has been
linked directly into the existing network, using the code $o 024 1768
to show that it is subordinate to "Birds". Finally, we can use an RA
message to apply a correction to "Penguins", deleting its previous link
with "Birds", and adding a new link to "Marine birds". It is worth
noting, in passing, that this amendment does not impose any extra
steps on the user, thanks to the by-pass routine; we have simply provided some extra access points.

5.7   We have not yet considered the two remaining input message codes
shown in Figure 10, that is, the codes RD and RP. These are not used
a great deal in practice, but merit at least a brief description:
(1) #RD# = *"Record delete"*. A deletion message consists of the
     code RD followed immediately by a RIN; there are no subfield
     codes. This functions as an instruction to the computer to re-
     move all the data from the indicated address: that is, the term, its
     related codes, any reciprocals which point to lower terms, and so
     on. The machine, however, will not execute such a drastic instruc-
     tion unless we confirm our intention by assigning the *same* RIN
     to the *next* term admitted into the system, using the standard RI
     message. If this is not done, the machine will not process the RD
     instruction; our relationship with the computer is one of complete
     and mutual mistrust! When the contents of an address have been

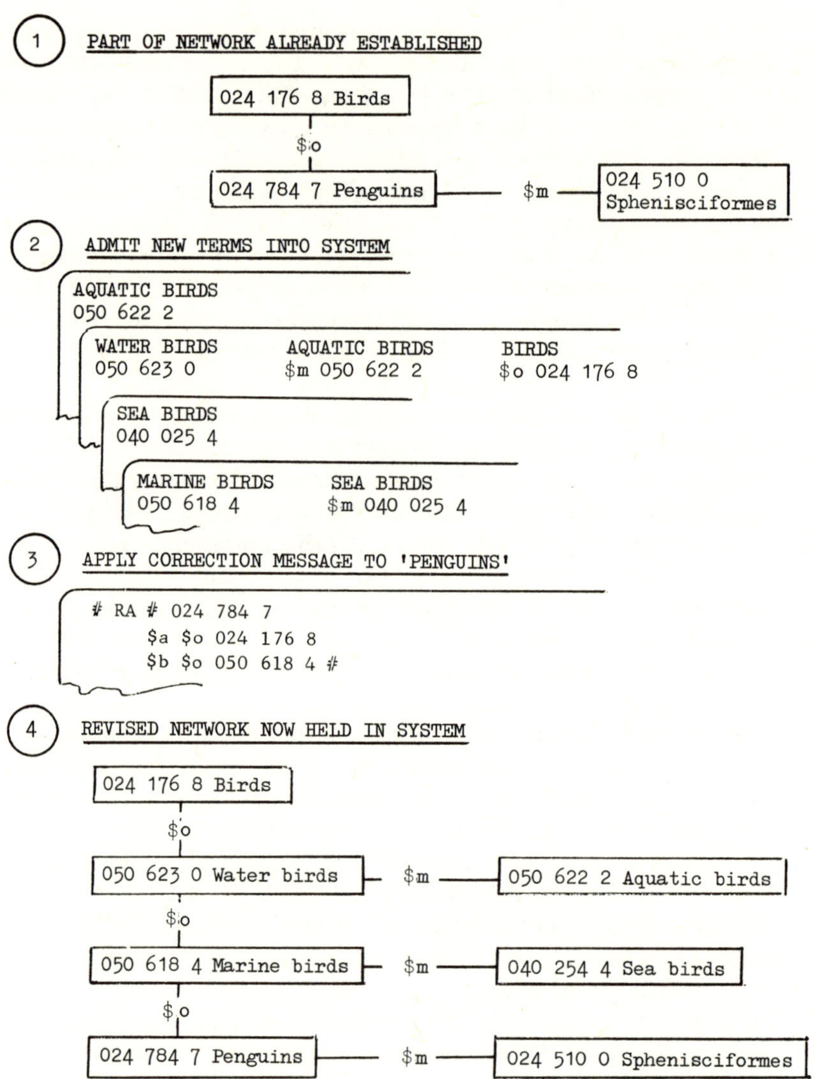

Figure 13. Application of #RA# messages: inserting new terms into an existing network

deleted in this way, the machine will report any terms held at other addresses which *were* related to the now deleted term, and are now, so to speak, left hanging in the air. No references will be produced from that hierarchy until corrections have been applied to all these other terms, using RA messages. In effect, we simply have to mend the hole left by the RD message before the network is usable once more.

(2) #RP# = "*Record report*". The RP message also consists of the code followed by a RIN, with no subfield codes. It has no effect on the contents of the file, but leads only to a report on the contents of the RIN quoted after the code. We would use this only if, for example, the contents of a given address had been modified

48

so often, with RD and RA messages, that we no longer knew for
certain what data it held.

6   CREATING TWO-DIRECTIONAL OR CROSSING REFERENCES

6.1   One further procedure in the RINfile justifies a description, since it
occurs as part of everyday practice. This is the creation of what we
call crossing or two-directional references: that is, each of two terms
calls for a *See also* reference from the other. Various circumstances
call for references of this kind. In *BNB*, for example, we usually make
references in both directions between the name of an object studied,
such as "Birds", and the name of the study itself, that is, "Ornithology".
These references are also made when two terms overlap in meaning, in
the sense in which "Rugs" and "Carpets", for example, share a number of semantic features in common.

6.2   In order to generate these references, we have to use special codes and
procedures. These were devised to cope with a problem which can best
be illustrated by showing what would happen if we tried to set up
crossing references between two terms, such as "Carpets" and "Rugs",
using only the codes which we have considered so far, such as $n and
$o.

6.3   The situation we are facing is shown in a diagram at position 1 in Fig.
14. This shows a small semantic network consisting of a genus, "Floor
coverings", together with two of its species, "Carpets" and "Rugs". The
hierarchical link between the genus and its species is shown, correctly,
by the code $o. For the sake of the demonstration, the two sibling
terms ("Carpets" and "Rugs") have been linked by the code $n, since
their mutual relationship cannot be hierarchical. Let us now run
through the sequence of events which would occur if we quoted one
of these RINs (e.g. the number 023 7906, which identifies the address
of "Rugs") as part of a packet of indexing data:
(1)   The computer would proceed to the indicated address, and
would then be re-directed, via the code $o, to the address
023 7280. It would then print the reference:

> **Floor coverings**
>   *See also*
>   **Rugs**

(2)   It would also be directed, via the code $n, to the address
023 6780, and it would then print:

> **Carpets**
>   *See also*
>   **Rugs**

(3)   Both of the references printed so far are exactly what we need.
Unfortunately, the machine will not stop at this point, but will

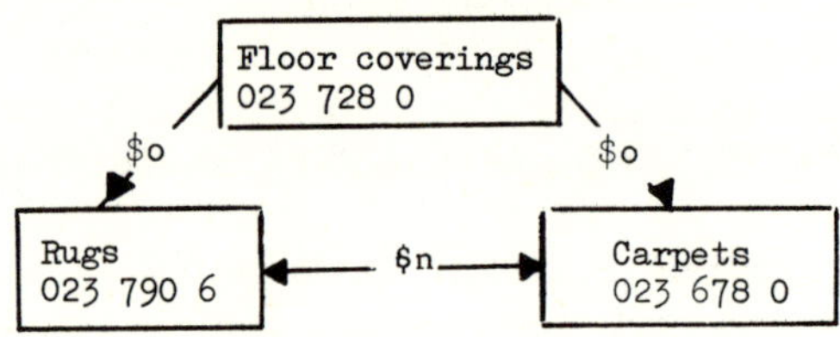

Figure 14. Use of relational codes $x and $y

go on blindly to produce further references. Having arrived at the address for "Carpets", it establishes the presence of two more relational codes. The first code, $o, will generate a reference:

> **Floor coverings**
>> *See also*
>>> **Carpets**

The second code, $n, calls for the reference:

> **Rugs**
>> *See also*
>>> **Carpets**

Both of these are definitely wrong, for the simple reason that we have not had a document on "Carpets".

(4) Unfortunately, worse is to come. The code $n re-directed the computer back to the address for "Rugs"—that is, 023 7906. That address holds two relational codes, $o and $n, which will cause the whole cycle to be repeated: in other words, we have entered a computing nightmare known as the "loop".

6.4   In order to break this vicious circle, we devised two special codes to
deal with crossing references—that is, $x and $y. The relationships expressed by these codes are roughly equivalent to $n, but they incor-
porate extra instructions which are shown at position 2 in Fig. 14.
The third of these instructions is the one which breaks the loop, since
it blocks the construction of any further references, with the single
exception of *See* references produced from synonyms. The revised
network, using the code $x, is shown at position 3. This will give rise
to only two references:

Floor coverings   **Carpets**
See also   *See also*
Rugs   **Rugs**

Beyond that point, the operation is automatically cut off. The exact
meaning of these codes, plus their associated instructions, are shown in
full in Fig. 15.

TWO-DIRECTIONAL CODES:

    $x   =   Relationship between sibling members of the same
category

    $y   =   Relationship between members of different
categories

MACHINE INSTRUCTIONS BUILT INTO CODES:

    $x
    $y   =   Print two-way *See also* references

EXAMPLES OF OUTPUT:

$x references: **Rugs**
    See also
    Carpets

or

Carpets
    See also
    Rugs

$y references: **Ornithology**
    See also
    Birds

or

Birds
    See also
    Ornithology

NOTE: Only *See* references are made to terms at addresses indicated by $x or $y

Figure 15. Relational codes used to link term addresses (RINs):

6.5   We still have one final problem to resolve if we wish to use these codes to produce crossing references, and this involves a further use of the amendment or RA message code. We have to bear in mind the fact that the computer will not accept, as part of its input, any direction to an address which has not yet been occupied. This introduces a problem, since it is clear, in the case of crossing references, that the first term in the pair to go into the system cannot refer to the second, since this second term has not yet been processed. The procedure for dealing with this, using an RA amendment message, is shown in Fig. 16:

(1)   We first input one of the crossing pair (e.g. "Rugs") but without making any attempt to generate a reference from the second term of the pair (e.g. "Carpets").

(2)   The second term, "Carpets", can then be input; this time, we *can* use a code ($x) which calls for a reference from "Rugs", since "Rugs" is already on file.

(3)   Finally, we have to go back to the address of the first term, and use an RA message to add the missing $x link which calls for a reference from "Carpets".

6.6   It is worth adding that this routine is far easier to carry out than to describe. In fact, this probably applies to the whole of the RIN system—many indexers seem to enjoy working with the thesaurus, and would rather construct networks than strings.

NOTES

1.   Hans (Hanan) Wellisch, "Subject Retrieval in the Seventies—Methods, Problems, Prospects," *Subject Retrieval in the Seventies—New Directions*, ed. Hans (Hanan) Wellisch and Thomas D. Wilson (Westport, Connecticut: Greenwood Publishing Company, 1972), pp. 2-27.

(1) In relation to the 'Penguin' network, assume the following
addresses are already occupied:

      024 201 2 ZOOLOGY

      024 526 7 VERTEBRATES

(2) Terms to be added are BIRDS and ORNITHOLOGY, with crossing
references between them.

(3) Proceed in the following steps:

a) Make out a record for one of the terms (e.g. Birds) omitting
$x or $y:

b) Make out a record for the second term (e.g Ornithology). including
the $x or $y link to the cross category term now on file:

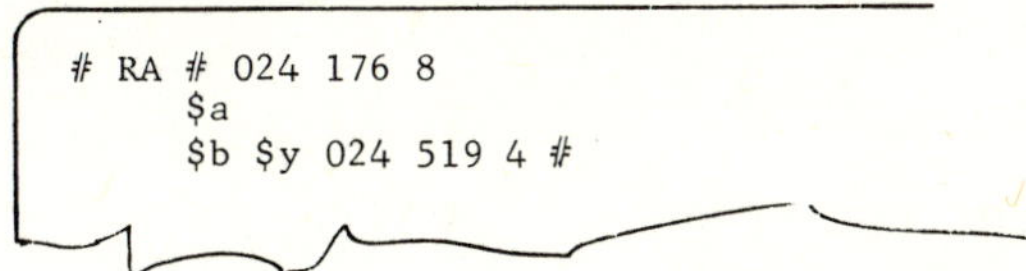

c) Submit an amendment message, adding the $x or $y relationship
to the first term (e.g. Birds):

*Figure 16. Use of #RA# messages to establish "crossing references", creating
references between "cross-category" terms*

Management Aspects of PRECIS, and Current Research and Development

Derek Austin
Subject Systems Office,
Bibliographic Services Division,
British Library

1 INTRODUCTION

1.1 In this final session we shall deal only occasionally with indexing techniques, and consider instead a range of diverse topics, mostly within the field of index production and management. I shall also touch briefly upon some of the current research and development projects going on within the Subject Systems Office of the British Library, where we are exploring new ways of using PRECIS as the subject approach to a large data base. One of the most challenging and exciting of our current projects concerns the use of PRECIS in a range of different natural languages, and our current research into translingual switching (i.e. switching indexing data by computer between different source and target natural languages). However, I shall not deal with this aspect myself—it will be covered instead in Jutta Sørensen's paper. I shall also touch very briefly on the related topics of indexer performance and user evaluation.

2 WORKFLOW IN THE SUBJECT SECTION OF THE BRITISH LIBRARY

2.1 We should now plunge straight into management, and consider the business of indexing and classifying documents in a large organisation—that is, the British Library. Obviously, a collection of this size cannot be taken as a typical situation; nevertheless, we have found, through contact with librarians from various kinds of institutions, that many aspects of the work encountered within the British Library also apply in all kinds of indexing agency. We shall consider later some of the agencies now applying, or experimenting with, PRECIS, and it will be seen that they are not all large institutions.

2.2 In the British Library, documents are cataloged (in the descriptive sense) before they are indexed or classified. Catalog data are recorded on a worksheet which consists of a set of numbered boxes, each

representing a specific MARC field (e.g. 100 = Author). However, only
one field on this worksheet is allotted to any kind of subject data. This
is a small box (labelled 691 on current BL/MARC records) which holds
only a seven figure number: that is, the Subject Indicator Number
(abbreviated to SIN) which identifies the address in a machine-held
file at which all the subject data relevant to that document can be located and retrieved.

2.3   To understand how this system works, let us study the flow of documents through the subject section of the British Library, as shown in
the diagram in Figure 1. Starting at the top of the workflow, we can
see that:

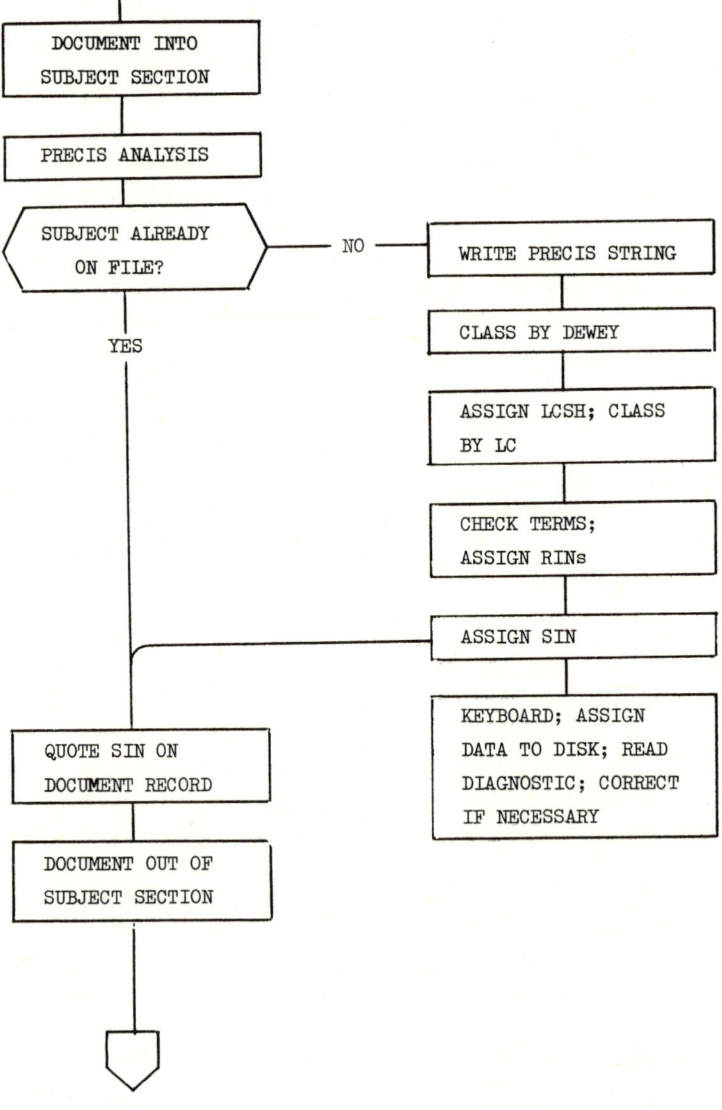

Figure 1. Workflow through subject section of bibliographic services

(1) Documents, accompanied by their cataloging forms, enter the subject section and are handled first by the PRECIS team. This was regarded as something of an innovation when it was first introduced; up to that time, when *BNB* was using a chain index, books had to be classed *before* they could be indexed. In the present system, the concept analysis carried out by the indexer serves as the basis for all the other decisions taken later in the workflow through the subject section.

(2) As we saw earlier, the indexer first examines the document and identifies the concepts which represent its subject content. At this stage, he has already started to formulate a PRECIS string. He then checks the authority file of index entries and references to see whether that subject has been handled in the past. He can, of course, select any significant term as his access point to this authority file. He can check this in various different authorities: for example, the index to a large cumulation, such as an annual volume of *BNB*, or the main authority file on machine-produced cards which is updated daily. Later we plan to introduce regularly updated COM (Computer Output Microfilm) authority files, but these are seen only as an interim measure, lasting until we can introduce on-line access to the data base as a standard working tool.

2.4 Now let us assume that the subject, as established by the indexer, is *not* in the file. In that case, we shall have to proceed down the right hand side of the flow diagram in Fig. 1. Even if the exact subject is not present, the indexer could still have extracted a good deal of useful information from the file: e.g. the correct form of a term, or a parallel subject dealing with either the same terms, or slightly different terms in the same relationships. The indexer then writes the PRECIS string, using the input form which is shown in Fig. 2. We shall consider this form in more detail later. All indexing strings are screened by a senior indexer before they pass on, with the document, through the rest of the subject section.

2.5 The document, together with the indexing form, then goes on to the Dewey Classification (DC) team. Their decisions are based primarily upon the subject as expressed in the string (Why repeat a job which has been done already, especially when subject analysis is the most time-consuming, and therefore most expensive, factor in indexing and classifying?). There is, of course, a feedback from classifiers to indexers, and we shall consider this in more detail later. The DC number is written into Field 082 on the indexing form.

2.6 The document and the form then pass on to the team which is responsible for assigning Library of Congress subject headings and class numbers, again using the string as a basis. We do not, in fact, need these data for the production of *BNB*, and at least as far as the LC class number is concerned, any decisions we record are not, to our knowledge, used by any British libraries, nor are they recognized in Washington. It might even be said that we assign these class marks in an altruistic spirit: that is, for the sake of providing a complete set of subject data to the international MARC network.

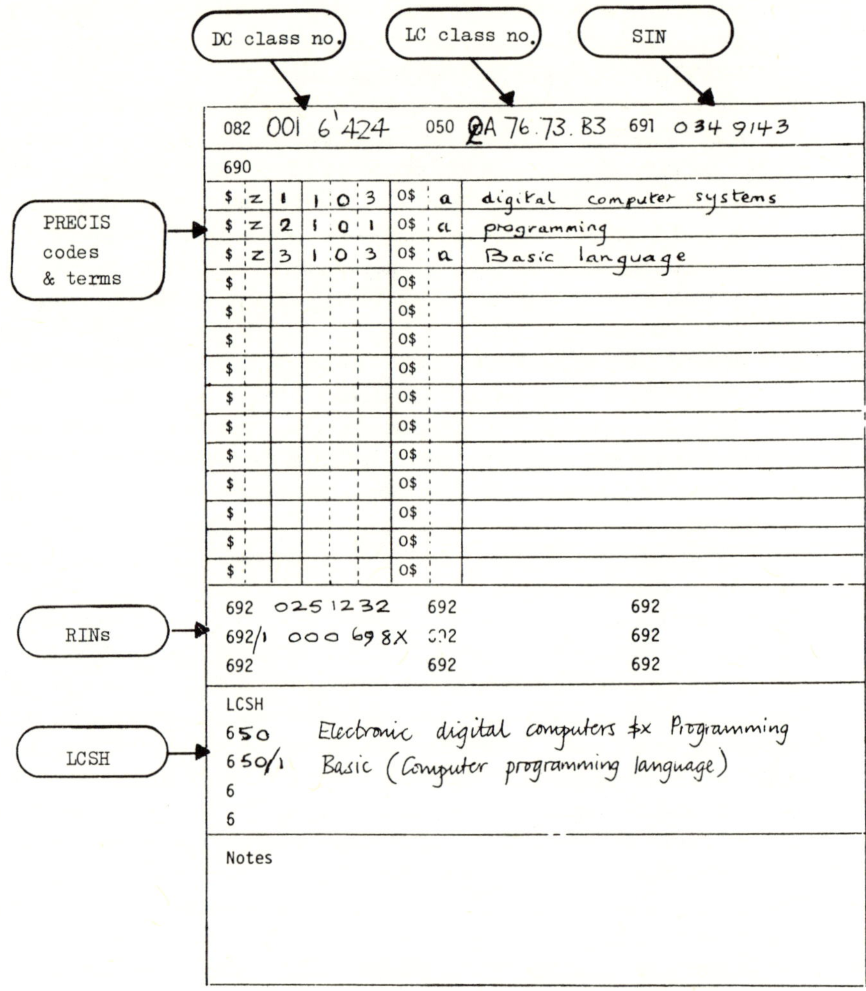

Although this form shows all the subject fields which are required at present for the BNB/MARC record, it is obvious that other data can be added to or substituted for these fields as required.

Figure 2. Input form for classification and indexing of books in BNB

2.7   The book and the form then go to the indexer who is responsible for maintaining the thesaurus; that is, the RINner. She examines the terms in the string from the special viewpoint of the semantic logic, and consequently serves as a final check on all previous decisions. All lead terms are checked in the RINfile, and the RINs for any terms present are written in Field 692. If a term is not present, it is immediately admitted into the system, its RIN is assigned, and this, too, is written into 692; this is a repeater field.

2.8   Finally, the document with its now completed packet of subject data is passed to a clerical assistant, who checks through the form to see that all the necessary fields are present and have been correctly coded. If the data are acceptable, the clerical assistant strikes out the next number from a computer-generated list, and writes this in the one remaining field: that is, Field 691 in the top right-hand corner of the form. This holds the Subject Indicator Number (or SIN), i.e. a seven figure number with a structure like a RIN, where the final digit serves as a modulus eleven check. Henceforth, this number will identify the position at which *all* these subject data will be held in the computer.

2.9   At the same time as the SIN is written on the indexing form, it is also transcribed into the 691 field on the cataloging worksheet. That particular document will then be associated henceforth and automatically with all the relevant subject data. When the catalog record is keyboarded and processed, the various subject data will then be extracted from the machine-held file and assigned to their correct fields in the MARC record. In this way, they become available to any subscriber to the BL/MARC tapes, and they are also used, of course, for producing the national bibliography.

2.10   Let us now consider the point in this operation when the SIN has been assigned, and the form containing the subject package is sent for keyboarding and processing by the computer. In the first place, the computer will carry out a series of validation checks:
(1)   it will ensure that the DC number, the PRECIS string, and so on, are present among the data.
(2)   it will check the validity of the SIN, any RINs which may be present, and the various field indicators.
(3)   it will even carry out the elementary logic checks on the PRECIS string which were mentioned in the first session, to ensure, for example, that the string begins with a numbered operator in the range from 0 to 2.
If any part of the data fails validation, the string will not be processed. Instead, the machine will print out an error warning message identifying where the failure occurred. The fault then has to be corrected, and the subject packet will be re-submitted on a later run. This obviously applies only to batch mode working; things will be much faster and more convenient when we can submit data online.

2.11   If the packet passed validation—which it does most of the time—all these data will be assigned to the computer, and the machine will respond by producing the full set of authority cards which are shown in Fig. 3:
(1)   one card for each index entry produced from the PRECIS string

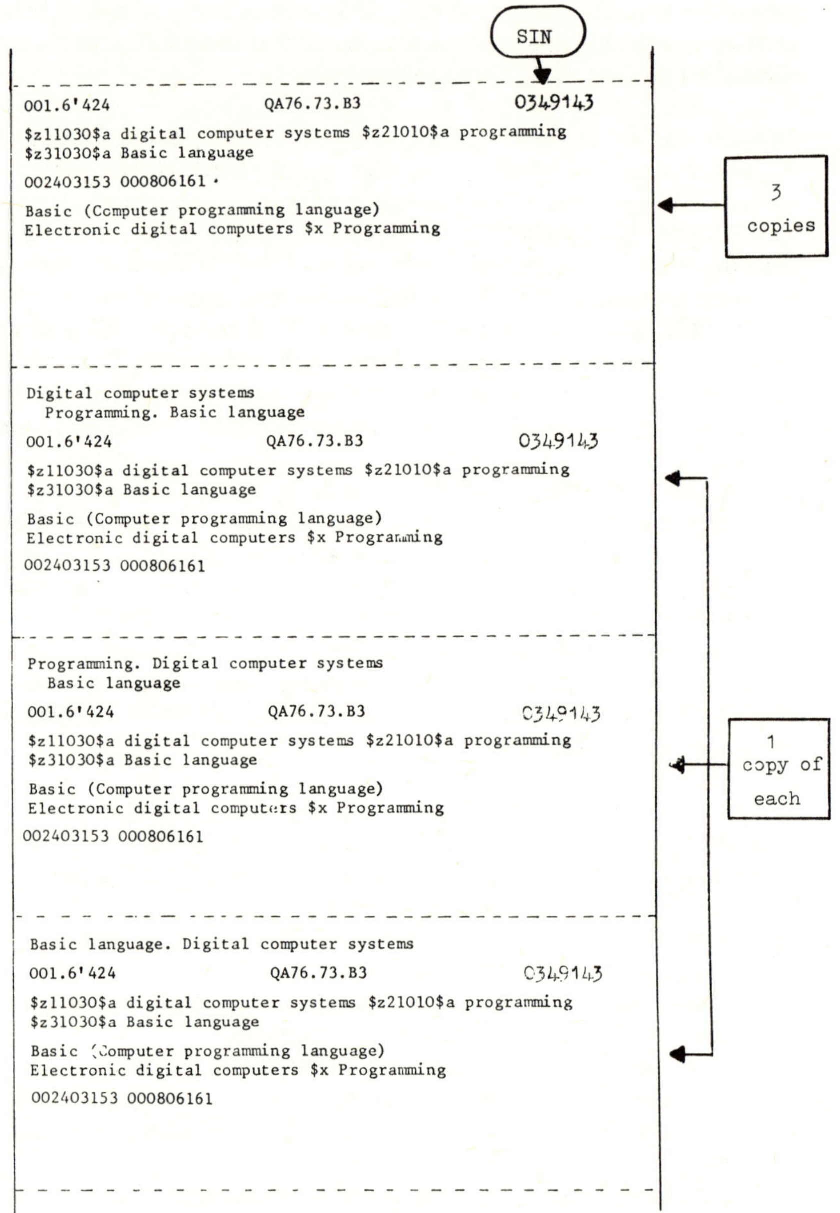

Figure 3. Card set produced from data on an input form

(2)   a set of three cards with class numbers printed along the top line Each of these cards shows the *whole* of the input data, including the SIN itself: this is the number on the right-hand side of each card, i.e. 034 9143.

2.12   These various cards are separated ready for filing. The index entries go into the main PRECIS authority file, which also includes correctly formatted references produced automatically when the RINput is first processed. Two of the three cards with class numbers printed

along the top line go to the DC team, and are added to their classified
authority file. The remaining card is filed under the LC class mark. We
do not make any attempt to produce authorities under Library of
Congress subject headings, though these headings are, of course,
present on all the cards, and on all British MARC tapes.

3   HANDLING "REPEAT" SUBJECTS

3.1   We should now go back to the start of this sequence of operations
(i.e. to the top of the flow diagram in Fig. 1) and consider what happens when an indexer has examined a document, checked his authority
file, and finds that the subject is, in fact, already on file. As we have
seen, each card in the authority file contains a record of the whole of
the subject package, including also the SIN. Unless there are grounds
for questioning some previous decision (e.g. when the document
hand throws a new light on the terminology and/or the relationships),
the indexer can now quote the SIN directly in the 691 field on the
cataloging record. The document will then be linked automatically
to all the relevant subject data in the machine-held file. There is no
need to repeat any work which has already been done, and the document can be routed straight out of the subject section. The benefits of
this facility, in terms of intellectual effort saved, can be seen at a
glance by tracing the route down the left-hand side of the flow diagram. We continually monitored the extent to which this shorter route
is used, and we calculated that approximately 50% of the documents
recorded in *BNB* are handled in this way from an authority file which
is less than three years old.

3.2   In many cases, the indexer will not find an exact match between the
subject of the document in hand and those in the authority file. Every
term and every operator must correspond exactly before an existing
SIN can be quoted. The indexer does, however, frequently find a
parallel subject in the file, i.e. one which differs by one or two terms,
or which has the same terms but slightly different relationships. We
might call these "near misses". The indexer should, for the sake of
consistency, follow precedents as closely as possible, particularly as
far as terminology is concerned, and he should, therefore, take one of
these previous entries as a pattern for a present decision. He should
then go to the DC organized authority file, and extract the second of
the two cards filed under the DC class number (this is why two copies
were printed). This card, together with the new subject form, is then
inserted into the document, and they travel together through the rest
of the subject section—that is, to the DC and LC teams. Obviously,
a good deal of their decision-making should now have been done already, since their own previous decisions are recorded on the card
which expresses the similar subject. We call this "indexing and classifying by analogy". This, too, represents a significant saving in terms

of intellectual effort, though we have not been able to quantify the
extent to which this actually occurs.

4   MANIPULATION CODING

4.1   We shall now consider one of the indexer's tasks which we have mentioned so far only in passing. This is the writing of the manipulation
codes (or machine instruction codes) which precede each of the terms
in the PRECIS string shown in Fig. 2. At first sight, this coding system
may appear to be formidable. In practice, however, we have found
that it does *not* cause any problems for indexers. We have tried to use
stopwatches to time this part of the indexing operation, but found
that, for an average string, it takes as long to operate the stopwatch as
to write the code itself. We can only say, with confidence, that manipulation coding takes less than 10% of the total string writing time,
and we strongly suspect that this is an overestimate.

4.2   A breakdown of the structure of the code is shown in Fig. 4. The code
consists of nine characters, three of which are pre-printed (i.e. two $
signs and a zero), leaving six positions which have to be filled in by the
indexer. Each of these positions carries a character which indicates a
specific property of the term which follows the code—such as, for example, its grammatical role, which is shown by the operator written
into the third position of the code. Only a limited range of characters
can be written in each position, and each character conveys, as an instruction to the computer, the indexer's decision on a specific factor.
For example, the indexer has to decide whether or not a given focus
should appear in the lead position in the index. His choice is expressed
by the character in the fourth position in the code: if the indexer wants
to generate a lead, he writes the figure "1"; if not, he writes a "0". The
indexer clearly has to remember the instruction expressed by the character in each position, as well as the range of options available in each
case, but this is not a difficult task, and we have found that, in practice, the coding system can be mastered within an hour or so.

4.3   There is no point in studying these codes in detail here, but we should
at least consider some of the options made available by this system,
for three main reasons:
(1)   It introduces an opportunity to consider some of the operators
       which were not dealt with in earlier sessions.
(2)   It will help, to some extent, to explain the relationship between
       PRECIS and a classification scheme.
(3)   Finally, it will also serve as the basis for a later review of some of
       the new uses we are finding for PRECIS strings.

4.4   One of the codes which appears in the list of operators, but which was
not considered earlier, is the "theme interlink". This character has to
be written in the second position in every manipulation code. All the

① BREAKDOWN OF MANIPULATION CODE

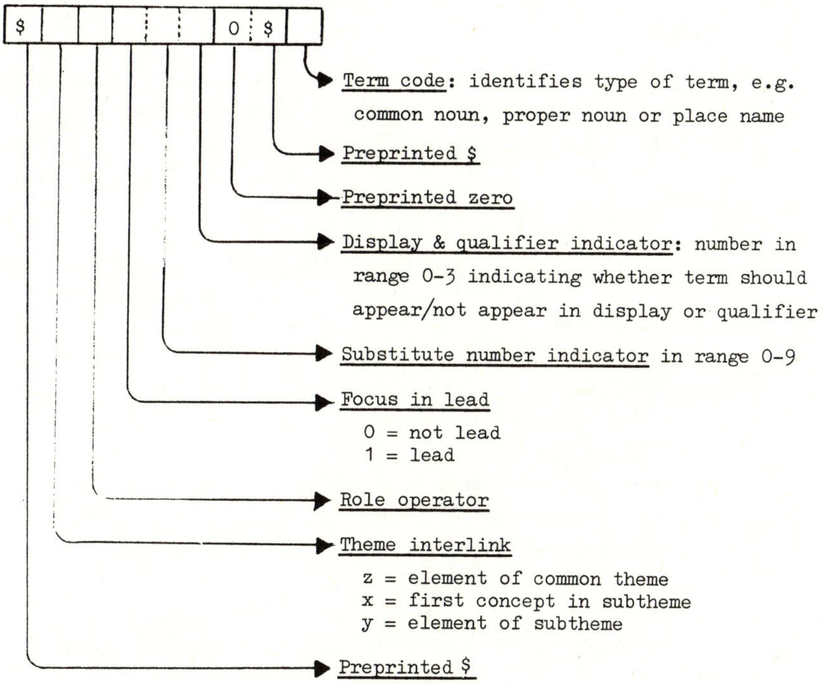

② EXAMPLE OF KEY SYSTEM CODED AS LEAD:

$z 1 103 0$a bridges $i concrete

Figure 4. Manipulation coding

subjects considered as examples in previous sessions consisted of only single themes—that is, each string expressed a single topic. In that case, each concept in the string would be prefixed by a manipulation code which contained the letter "z" in the second position. We can also, however, use this position to indicate that a given string contains two or more separate and identifiable themes. This would occur, for example, if we were dealing with a work on, say, "The anatomy of the legs of amphibia *and* the physiology of the heart of amphibia". The string which expresses this subject is shown in Fig. 5. The computer will immediately recognize, from its reading of the character in the second position of the manipulation code, that this is a string which contains two separate subjects. "Amphibia" is a common element in both topics, and this term is therefore identified by the interlink code *z* at the start of the string. The term "Heart", which begins the first of the two independent themes, is coded *x*, and the term "Physiology", which also belongs to this first sub-theme, is coded *y*. The second independent sub-theme begins with the term "Legs", which is also, therefore, coded

(1) *Subject:* Anatomy of the legs and physiology of the heart of amphibia

(2) *Input strings:*

$z 1 103 0$a	amphibia	←— (Element common to all themes
$x p 103 0$a	heart	←— (Start of first coordinate theme
$y 2 103 0$a	physiology	
$x p 103 0$a	legs	←— (Start of second coordinate theme
$y 2 103 0$a	anatomy	

(3) *Entries produced from multitheme string*

AMPHIBIA
    Heart. Physiology
    Legs. Anatomy
HEART. Amphibia
    Physiology
PHYSIOLOGY. Heart. Amphibia
LEGS. Amphibia
    Anatomy
ANATOMY. Legs. Amphibia

(4) *String unscrambled if each theme refers to a different place in a classified file*

String 1		*Entries*	
$z 1 103 0$a amphibia		AMPHIBIA	
$z p 103 0$a heart		Heart. Physiology	597.604116
$z 2 103 0$a physiology		Legs. Anatomy	597.60449
DC number: 597.604116		HEART. Amphibia	
		Physiology	597.604116
String 2		PHYSIOLOGY. Heart. Amphibia	
			597.604116
$z 1 103 0$a amphibia		LEGS. Amphibia	
$z p 103 0$a legs		Anatomy	597.60449
$z 2 103 0$a anatomy		ANATOMY. Legs. Amphibia	
			597.60449
DC number: 597.60449			

Figure 5. Manipulation coding of a multi-theme subject

x, and its related term, "Anatomy", is then coded y. From its reading of these codes, the computer will produce the set of entries shown at Position 3.

Amphibia
    Heart. Physiology
    Legs. Anatomy
Heart. Amphibia
    Physiology
Physiology. Heart. Amphibia
Legs. Amphibia
    Anatomy
Anatomy. Legs. Amphibia

It can be seen that this string has produced two different display lines under "Amphibia". This occurs automatically whenever a lead, such as "Amphibia" is identified as a component of more than one theme. If a string contains concepts coded z and x, and the term introduced by the theme interlink z was also marked as a lead, the computer will generate as many leads as there are separate x concepts in the same string.

4.5   We can, if necessary, use this technique to pack a considerable amount of information into a single string. Whether or not we use these mechanisms depends, however, on the kind of index we are producing. In some cases, such as *BNB* and the *Australian National Bibliography (ANB)*, the index refers to a list of catalog entries organized under class numbers. We cannot, then, pack several coordinate themes into a single string if *each* of the separate themes is expressed by a *different* class mark in the schedules. In that case, we have to unscramble the themes, and write a separate string for each, as shown at Position 4. The same citation will then appear more than once in the classified section, i.e. once for each class number. It can be seen that index entries are exactly the same.

4.6   We can also use a different technique to pack a good deal of information into a single string. This involves the use of the operator g (one of the codes which was not considered earlier), which indicates a coordinate concept rather than a coordinate theme. This code is written into the third position of the manipulation code—which means that g is one of the role operators. Its use is shown in Fig. 6. In the examples shown, the appearance of the operator g informs the computer that it is dealing with the subject "The anatomy *and* the physiology of the human heart". The entries produced from this string are shown at Position 3, and it can be seen that when each of the coordinate concepts ("Anatomy" and "Physiology") appeared in the lead, the other coordinate concept was automatically suppressed from the entry. Again, this mechanism cannot be used if each of the entries under the coordinate terms refers to a different class number. If the DC classifier received such a string, he would exercise his feedback option, and ask for the string to be unscrambled. For obvious reasons, each PRECIS string should refer to only one class number selected from any given scheme. The result is shown at Position 4, where the string has been unscrambled into two distinct strings, each referring to its own class number.

(1) *Subject:* Anatomy and physiology of the human heart

(2) *Input string:*

```
$z 1 103 0$a   man
$z p 103 0$a   heart
$z 2 103 0$a   anatomy $v &  ← (First coordinate concept
$z g 103 0$a   physiology  ←── (Second coordinate concept
                                (Coordinate concept operator
```

(3) *Entries:*

```
MAN
     Heart. Anatomy & physiology
HEART. Man
     Anatomy & physiology
ANATOMY. Heart. Man
PHYSIOLOGY. Heart. Man
```

(4) *Two strings required if coordinate concepts refer to different places in a classified file:*

String 1:		*Entries:*	
$z 1 103 0$a man		MAN	
$z p 103 0$a heart		Heart. Anatomy	611.12
$z 2 103 0$a anatomy		Heart. Physiology	612.17
DC number: 611.12		HEART. Man	
		Anatomy	611.12
		Physiology	612.17
String 2:		ANATOMY. Heart. Man	611.12
		PHYSIOLOGY. Heart. Man	612.17
$z 1 103 0$a man			
$z p 103 0$a heart			
$z 2 103 0$a physiology			
DC number: 612.17			

Figure 6. Manipulation coding of a subject with coordinate concepts

5   **RELATIONSHIP BETWEEN PRECIS AND A CLASSIFICATION SCHEME**

5.1   The fact that bibliographies, such as *ANB* and *BNB*, use Dewey as the link between the PRECIS index and a classified file of citations has sometimes been criticized. It has been suggested that the logic of PRECIS is necessarily then distorted through its contact with such an alien philosophy. We have already considered the two commonest situations which call for some modification to be made to a PRECIS string—that is, the unscrambling of coordinate themes and coordinate concepts in certain prescribed circumstances. Other situations can also occur which will cause the DC team to bring their special requirements to the indexer's notice. On the whole, however, these are relatively

minor matters. I would emphasize that in *no* circumstances is the logic
which underlies PRECIS distorted for the sake of the classification
scheme. We are not, for example, bound by the terms which appear in
the schedules of the classification (which must, inevitably, be out-of-
date in some areas), nor are we expected to set down strings of terms
in the order in which they appear in the schedules. Apart from the
fact that the syntax of PRECIS is completely "neutral" with respect to
any classification scheme, we should also remember that the string is
written *before* the document is classed. No attempt is made to reduce
either the exhaustivity or the specificity of a string to the level which
is found in the classification. Our DC classifiers know from experience
that approximately 85% of the strings they receive from the indexers
cannot be matched by subject-expressive notation taken from the
schedule. This is not regarded in any way as serious—we feel that the
DC number will have done a reasonable job if it collocates like-with-
like in the classified section of the bibliography or on library shelves,
and serves as the link between the index and the citations file. We do
not expect it to specify subjects exactly—that, we believe, is the job
of the subject index.

6   SUBJECT HEADING CONSTRUCTION

6.1   We realize, of course, that these problems will arise only when class
numbers are used as document addresses in a PRECIS index: that is,
we are producing a classified catalog. We are also aware that catalog
entries can be organized in other ways. In North America generally,
as well as in parts of Europe and the Commonwealth, subject headings are also used for this purpose. The same applies to the subject index to the Department of Printed Books of the British Library (that
is, the old British Museum Library), which has been organized by an
in-house system of subject headings since the catalog was first produced in 1881 (Could anyone seriously consider classifying the entire
stock of the British Museum?). About two years ago, the Board of the
British Library set up a working party on indexing and classification
which considered, among other things, whether the old British Museum
subject headings system should be: (1) continued in its present form;
(2) converted into machine-readable form; (3) abandoned altogether
and replaced by a more up-to-date system. The Working Party com-
missioned an independent enquiry into the feasibility of producing
satisfactory subject headings, by algorithm, directly from the PRECIS
strings which are, in any case, written for the national bibliography.

6.2   The results of the British Library study are summarized in the following Final Report of the Working Party:

". . . PRECIS, as applied in *BNB* and elsewhere, has proved acceptable
to users. It has been shown to be economically viable in comparison
with conventional indexing systems. Investigations have shown that

PRECIS strings can be manipulated to produce mechanically an acceptable subject heading system which could replace the *British Museum Subject Index*,[1] with gains to the user, more efficient indexing information, and without increase in cost. It is seen as the only means of providing a unified subject index to the reference collection."[2]

6.3   I should point out that the Subject Systems Office, which is the office responsible (among other things) for PRECIS research and development, was *not* involved in the preliminary stages of this investigation, which included an exercise in costing, as well as the study of various indexing factors. On the reasonable grounds that we would represent an "interested party", we were excluded from the enquiries. Following these conclusions, however, we were given the task of specifying and testing the computer programs which would achieve the result required by the Working Party. After taking various factors into account, we developed what we now call the "Three-option subject heading package". In order to obtain a range of various output options, we have called into play one of the positions in the manipulation code which had not been used before. This is the character in the seventh position (see Fig. 4). In all the examples we looked at earlier, this position was occupied by a pre-printed zero. The range of options which we acquired in this way is shown in Fig. 7.

(1) *The "0" option:*   Subject heading derived from string
Heading selected by algorithm
Extra heading under proper name(s) if present
Option indicator digit = "0" for all terms

(2) *The "1" option:*   Subject heading derived from string
Heading selected by indexer
Extra heading under proper name(s) if present
Option indicator digit = "1" subject heading
    terms; other terms = "0"

(3) *The "2" option:*   Primary subject heading independent of string
Heading added to string by indexer
Option indicator = "2" for added heading terms

Figure 7. Three-option subject headings

6.4   Let us consider first what we call the "0" option procedure. This is the option which is regarded as most suited to the needs of a general or pan-disciplinary index, such as the subject catalog of the British Library. To produce such a catalog arranged under subject headings, we would leave the seventh position occupied by a zero, exactly as it was in the earlier examples. The procedures for generating the subject headings in this case is shown in Fig. 8. In the first place, the computer will read the role operators (these appear in the third position) in a pre-determined order, looking for the first concept which has been marked as a lead. The order of search is as follows:

(1) *String:*

    $z 1 103 0$a   secondary schools
    $z p 103 0$a   teachers
    $z 2 103 0$a   remuneration
    $z 6 003 0$a   proposals

(2) *Citations file:*

1788   **Secondary schools**
                Teachers. Remuneration—*Proposals*

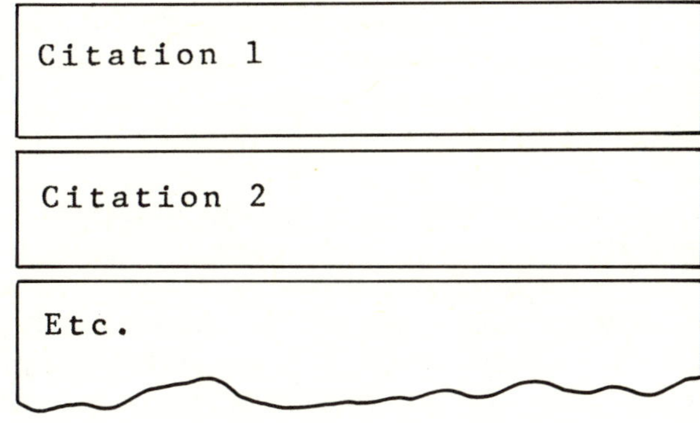

1789   **Secondary schools**
                Teachers. Training . . . . etc

(3) *Subject index:*

Remuneration. Teachers. Secondary schools
    —*Proposals*   1788
Secondary schools
    Teachers. Remuneration—*Proposals*   1788
    Teachers. Secondary schools
    Remuneration—Proposals   1788

Figure 8. Subject index entries created by the "0" option

(1)   the key system or its next dependent element
(2)   an action or its next dependent element
(3)   an agent or its dependent element
(4)   the environment or its dependent element

Somewhere in that sequence, a focus, or perhaps a difference, is bound
to have been marked as a lead. In the example at Position 1 in Fig. 8,
the sought-for condition is encountered at the first term in the string—
that is, the term "Secondary schools" (this is coded as the key system,
and was marked as a lead). The computer will then construct the index
entry which would be generated under that term, and will assign this
entry to a temporary store: this is the entry which will double as a sub-

ject heading. When a complete set of subject headings has been constructed in this way, they are organized into a single alphabetical sequence, and the computer then prints the appropriate citations—that is, the catalog entry or entries—under each heading. The citations themselves can be arranged by any selected factor, such as the author or title. At the next stage, the machine will sequentially number all the subject headings which have been constructed in this way, and which will make up that particular issue of the catalog. Let us assume, in the present case, that the heading under "Secondary schools" happened to acquire the number 1788, as shown at Position 2. This running number is then taken back to the string from which the heading was constructed, and a full set of index entries is generated in the usual way. These entries, however, will *not* now refer to a class number, but to the artificially created running number which indicates where, in the subject headings sequence, the relevant citations can be found. These entries are shown at Position 3.

6.5   It seems reasonable to assume, in the case of a general catalog covering the entire subject spectrum, that the various works on "Secondary schools" should be brought together in this way in a subject headings sequence. However, this might not be a desirable collocation in a special index in the field of education, such as the *British Education Index*. Apart from the fact that a term such as "Secondary schools" would almost certainly be overworked as a subject heading, it is also likely that, from the viewpoint of the educationalist, another term such as "Teachers" would be regarded as more significant. In that case, the indexer can bring another option into play, and can indicate this different choice of the term which starts the heading by changing the character in the seventh position of the manipulation code from zero to one. This change is shown in Fig. 9. Citations will then be organized under a subject heading which begins with the term "Teachers", as shown at Position 2. Again, these headings will be numbered serially (let us assume that, in a given issue, the term "Teachers" acquired the number 2137). This number is then carried back automatically to function as an address indicator, as shown at Position 3.

6.6   The third of the available options is intended to produce an entirely different result. This option was devised especially to introduce a higher level of collocation under pre-selected terms (such as the names of disciplines) which are not regarded as essential components of an index string. It could also be used by library networks which wish to arrange their catalog entries under, say, the names of the faculties or departments which possess particular items. The name of a discipline or faculty can then be written at the beginning of a PRECIS string, as shown in Fig. 10, where the term "Education" has been inserted deliberately as a collocating term. The special status of this term is indicated by the fact that the number in the seventh position of the manipulation code has now been changed to "2". This extra term plays no part at all in producing the subject index. Instead, it functions

(1) *String:*

    $z 1 103 0$a   secondary schools

    $z p 103 1$a   teachers
    $z 2 103 0$a   remuneration
    $z 6 003 0$a   proposals

(2) *Citations file:*

    2137   **Teachers.** Secondary schools
                Remuneration—*Proposals*

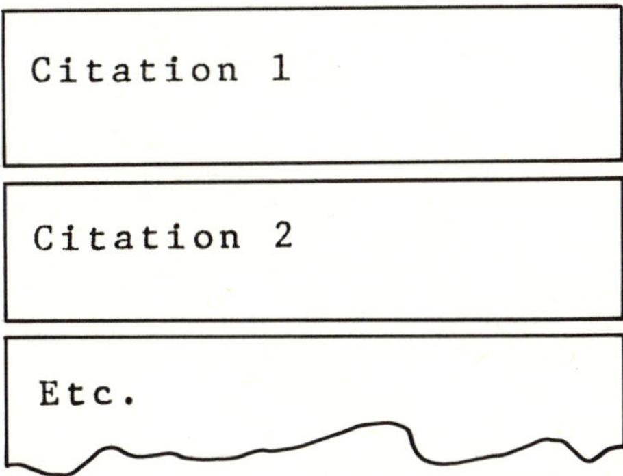

(3) *Subject index:*

Remuneration. Teachers. Secondary schools
   —*Proposals*   2137
Secondary schools
   Teachers. Remuneration—*Proposals*   2137
Teachers. Secondary schools
   Remuneration—*Proposals*   2137

Figure 9. Subject index entries created by the "1" option

as what is called a "Primary subject heading"—that is, it serves to bring
other headings together, as seen at Position 2. The rest of the string is
printed in input order on a second line, where it serves as the "Secondary subject heading". Once again, these headings are numbered serially
(e.g. 566), and this number is then transferred automatically to the
fully shunted subject index.

6.7   It is worth reporting that all three of these options are now fully
operational. They are embodied into a single program, and all or any
of the three options can be extracted on demand from a single data
base; the indexer's choice of option is indicated to the computer
by a special parameter card inserted at the start of the run. The "0"
and "1" options are now already in use. The "0" option was first
used experimentally on an annual volume of *BNB* and gave a complete
bibliography, without a single class number, on three cassettes of

(1) *String:*

        $z 0 000 2$a   education
        $z 1 103 0$a   secondary schools
        $z p 103 0$a   teachers
        $z 2 103 0$a   remuneration
        $z 6 003 0$a   proposals

(2) *Citations file:*

        566   **Education**
                Secondary schools. Teachers. Remuneration—*Proposals*

Citation 1
Citation 2
Etc.

(3) *Subject index:*

Remuneration. Teachers. Secondary schools
   —*Proposals*   566
Secondary schools
   Teachers. Remuneration—*Proposals*   566
Teachers. Secondary schools
   Remuneration—*Proposals*   566

Figure 10. Subject index entries created by the "2" option

16 mm film. A COM version of this kind, with regular cumulations, now serves as the subject index to the entire intake of the Department of Printed Books. This covers both British and foreign intake, a total of more than 60,000 items a year at present. The new subject index is available as a public reference tool in the Reading Room of the British Museum. The "1" option has been used in the *British Education Index* since the first issue of 1976, and a sample from this index, and of the relevant part of the citations file, is shown in Fig. 11.

6.8   In all these subject headings experiments we have still been producing what is known as a "two-stage" index. That is, the subject information is available in one file (the subject index), and the user is then referred to the relevant citations in a second and separate file. We are now conducting experiments, in the British Library, in merging these two files into a single alphabetical sequence. In the experimental version we are now producing, the user might still be referred, through a running number, to citations at a different point in the alphabet, but at least we shall have only one alphabetical sequence. The next step is obvious—print the catalog entries, perhaps in an abbreviated form, under *every* PRECIS entry. So far, we have not had the courage to take this obvious step, possibly because we still had to think in terms of paper costs, and have not fully realized the revolution which COM can offer. We are, however, under some sort of pressure to conduct experiments along these lines—a recent enquiry from South Africa suggested that they might be ready to try out this idea.

(1) <u>Subject index</u>

School leavers
    Attitudes to higher education — *Reports, surveys* 168
    Industrial training. Proposals: Training Services Agency.
       Vocational preparation for young people — *Critical
       studies* 335
    Personnel. Selection. Interviewing — *For school leavers*
       286
    Qualifications, *1973-1974 — Statistics* 336
School magazines 337
School-run factories. China
    Provision of work experience for secondary school
       students — *Study regions: Peking* 361
Schoolchildren *See* **Students.** Schools
Schools
    See also
       Boarding schools
       Comprehensive schools
       Middle schools
       Nursery schools
       Primary schools
       Progressive schools
       Secondary schools
       Sixth forms
       Special schools
Schools
    Confidential records on students. Access. Rights of

Secondary education
    See also
       Comprehensive education
       Comprehensive system
       Sixth form colleges
Secondary education
    Equality of opportunity *related to* sex differences of
       secondary school students 352
Secondary education. North-east England
    Equality of opportunity 353
Secondary schools
    See also
       Names of individual curriculum subjects taught at this
       level
       Comprehensive schools
       Sixth forms
Secondary schools
    Curriculum. G.C.E. (A level) examination subjects.
       Suitability for careers — *Students' guides* 79
    Curriculum subjects. Usefulness of mixed ability group
       teaching. Attitudes of teachers. Case studies 354
    Language laboratories. Teaching materials. Production
       355
    Large secondary schools. Timetables. Construction 409
    Mixed ability groups. Teaching — *Sociological
       perspectives* 356

(2) <u>Citations file of journal articles</u>

341 SCHOOLS COUNCIL
Common system of examining at 16+

A **16** plus disaster? / Mary Warnock. — *New Society.* 35 :
11 Mar 76. — p.547-548.

Pluses and minuses / H.G. Macintosh. — *Times Ednl.
Supp.*. no.3172 : 19 Mar 76. — p.20-21.

**342 SCHOOLS COUNCIL WRITING ACROSS THE
CURRICULUM PROJECT**

Getting it across / Nancy Martin, Bryan Newton and Pat
D'Arcy. — *Times Ednl. Supp.* no.3173 : 26 Mar 76. —
p.19-20.

343 SCHOOLS FOR BLIND CHILDREN. Shrewsbury. Salop
Condover Hall

Condover helps the blind to help themselves / Diane
Spencer. — *Times Ednl. Supp.* no.3167 : 13 Feb 76. —
p.7.

344 SCHOOLS FOR MALADJUSTED CHILDREN

Another kind of handicap / Muriel Colley. — *New Society*
. 35 : 12 Feb 76. — p.327-328.

345 SCHOOLS FOR MALADJUSTED CHILDREN.
Liverpool. Merseyside *(Metropolitan County)*
Kingsway Educational Guidance Unit

The **pupils** who came in from the cold / Margaret
Dennett. — *Teacher.* 28, no.13 : 26 Mar 76. — p.10.

354 SECONDARY SCHOOLS
Curriculum subjects. Usefulness of mixed ability group
teaching. Attitudes of teachers. Case studies

'Which subjects can be taught in mixed ability classes?' -
teachers' views / Ken Hayes. — *Cambridge J. Ed.* 6 :
Lent 76. — p.32-38.

355 SECONDARY SCHOOLS
Language laboratories. Teaching materials. Production

The **preparation** of materials for the language laboratory /
Alistair Campbell. — *Modern Languages in Scotland.*
no.9 : Jan 76. — p.17-41.

356 SECONDARY SCHOOLS
Mixed ability groups. Teaching — *Sociological
perspectives*

The **social** organisation of the classroom and the
philosophy of mixed ability teaching / David Bridges. —
Cambridge J. Ed. 6 : Lent 76. — p.15-23.

357 SECONDARY SCHOOLS
Students, 16 years-. Examinations. Standardisation.
Schools Council. Common system of examining at 16+

A **16** plus disaster? / Mary Warnock. — *New Society.* 35 :
11 Mar 76. — p.547-548.

Pluses and minuses / H.G. Macintosh. — *Times Ednl.
Supp.*. no.3172 : 19 Mar 76. — p.20-21.

ure 11. Example of subject headings from British Education Index, *generated
by the "1" option*

73

7.1   I should now like to consider some of the other research into PRECIS which is now in progress in the Subject Systems Office of the British Library. At present this Office consists of two different teams, the first concerned with new developments in the English language, and the second working under a special government grant to examine the potential of PRECIS as a multilingual, and also a translingual system, which is capable of operating in a range of different natural languages.

7.2   I cannot, as Head of this Office, say that either of these aspects of our research is more important for the system, but I think that our foreign language experiments are certainly more challenging. We have a team of three indexers, with a range of at least six languages, at fluency level, between them. However, it would be quite ridiculous to suggest that research into this aspect of PRECIS is limited to this particular team in the British Library. We have an enormous amount of additional support, and a great range of skills, in indexers all over Europe. That is why I am not going to deal, at present, with the multilingual potentials of PRECIS—I shall gladly leave that instead to "our woman in Copenhagen", Mrs. Jutta Sørensen, who will deal with this matter in her paper.

7.3   Meanwhile, we are also exploring new applications of the system. These experiments can be divided into two types:
(1)   indexing new kinds of media, such as AV materials, and even realia, as well as working at the more exhaustive level of research reports, journal articles, and even on-going research projects.
(2)   applying the system to new specific subject fields, such as musical scores and literature, the performing arts, sociology, and so on.

7.4   We have now produced a prototype *British National Reports Bibliography*, and this being considered by the Board of the British Library. We do not yet know exactly how many research reports, covering all subject fields, are received each year by the various divisions of the national library, but it must run to several thousands. We are aware that no adequate subject approach is provided at present, and that we shall satisfy a genuine need if we can, as I know we shall, produce that bibliography. We are also applying PRECIS to musical scores, as well as documents about music, received in the Music Department of the Reference Division, and we are working very closely with musicologists and music librarians in this task. We have, I think, now reached the stage where all the major problems have been solved, and we have produced a range of prototypes for a new music bibliography.

7.5   To some extent, our experiments with these new media and subject fields overlaps the foreign language experiments. We are working now with an index to documents in the field of the performing arts, including theatre, cinema, opera, the circus, and so on. The collection,

however, is in the Départment des Arts du Spectacle of the Bibliothèque nationale in Paris, and we are now processing their strings,
and producing French output, in regular batches. We are also producing an index of AV materials for EUDISED (the European
Documentation and Information Service for Education) and we are
working on this material simultaneously in three languages, English,
French and German. We also hope to carry out an evaluation exercise shortly, testing indexer consistency when dealing with sociological literature. But the sociologists involved in the project are employed by the Royal Danish Library in Copenhagen, so this is, again,
an international venture.

8 SURVEY OF PRECIS USERS

8.1 This seems to bring us, quite naturally, to the range of different indexing agencies throughout the world which are now involved in PRECIS.
These users fall into the two general categories which are shown in
Figs. 12 and 13:
(1) Figure 12 is a list of agencies which have already adopted the
system, and which now produce PRECIS indexes on either a
regular or an intermittent basis.
(2) Figure 13 shows a list of agencies which are at present involved in
pilot projects, or else have made enquiries which may lead to pilot
projects.
Neither of these lists is complete; we frequently hear of hitherto un-
known projects somewhere or other, many on a modest scale, and
including manually-produced, not computer-assisted, indexes, and all
apparently working to their users' satisfaction. We also receive enquiries on a more official level from government and other institutional
libraries—I would estimate that probably half of the places on the official British Library courses on PRECIS are taken by indexers from outside the British Library itself. We have run our first "exported" full
course for indexers; this was held at Kuala Lumpur in Malaysia in November 1975. We may soon be involved in another—possibly in Pretoria early in 1977.

8.2 The most interesting feature of the organizations listed in these pages
is their sheer diversity. Their variety can be seen from a number of
viewpoints:
(1) the size of the agency, which ranges from a high school library to
two national collections.
(2) varying degrees of subject specialization; the list includes not only
pan-disciplinary indexes (such as those to two national bibliographies), but also specialist indexes in fields such as medicine and
education.
(3) the range of languages in which indexing is being conducted.
(4) the variety of media being indexed.

A)   CATALOGS OF LIBRARIES OR LIBRARY NETWORKS

1.   British Library Reference Division (*formerly British Museum Library*)
        —*(a) COM, cumulating; (b) computer; (c) 2-stage; (d) PRECIS S/H*

2.   East Sussex Public Libraries—*(a) paper; (b) computer; (c) 2-stage;
        (d) DC*

3.   Sheffield College of Education—*(a) card; (b) manual; (c) 1-stage*

4.   Stockwell College of Education (London)—*(a) paper; (b) computer;
        (c) 2-stage; (d) DC*

5.   Polytechnic of Central London—*(a) paper; (b) computer; (c) 2-stage;
        (d) DC*

6.   City of London Polytechnic—*(a) paper; (b) computer; (c) 2-stage;
        (d) DC*

7.   Aurora High School Library (*Ontario, Canada*)—*(a) card; (b) manual;
        (c) 1-stage*

B)   BIBLIOGRAPHIES

1.   *Australian National Bibliography*—*(a) printed & cumulating;
        (b) computer; (c) 2-stage; (d) DC*

2.   *British National Bibliography*—*(a) printed & cumulating; (b) computer;
        (c) 2-stage; (d) DC*

3.   *A/V Materials for Higher Education (British Universities Film Council)*
        —*(a) printed; (b) computer; (c) 2-stage; (d) UDC*

4.   *HELPIS* (A/V materials)—*(a) printed, intermittent; (b) computer;
        (c) 2-stage; (d) DC*

5.   *HELPIS—MEDICAL*—*(a) printed, intermittent; (b) computer; (c) 2-
        stage; (d) DC*

6.   *British Education Index*—*(a) printed & cumulating; (b) computer;
        (c) 2-stage; (d) PRECIS S/H*

Note on symbols: (a)   =   form and/or frequency of output

                       (b)   =   production: computer or manual

                       (c)   =   1-stage or 2-stage index

                       (d)   =   if 2-stage, classification or other address system

Figure 12. Users of PRECIS

A)   CATALOGS OF LIBRARIES OR LIBRARY NETWORKS

1.   S.G.M.E. (*Dept. of A/V Materials, Ministry of Education, Quebec*) *—(a) printed, French; (b) computer; (c) 2-stage; (d) Lamy-Rousseau classification of A/V materials*

2.   Université de Rouen, Section Science*—(a) printed or COM, French; (b) computer; (c) 2-stage; (d) thesis serial number or PRECIS S/H*

3.   Bibliothèque nationale: Départment des arts du spectacle— *(a) printed, French; (b) computer; (c) 2-stage; (d) shelf-mark or PRECIS S/H*

B)   BIBLIOGRAPHIES

1.   *British Catalogue of Music—(a) printed & cumulating; (b) computer; (c) 2-stage; (d) details not settled*

C)   OTHER CATALOGS

1.   National Film Board of Canada*—(a) printed & on-line; (b) computer*

D)   BACK-OF-THE-BOOK INDEXES

1.   Public Record Office (London)*—indexes to calendars etc*

2.   Scottish Record Office (Edinburgh)*—indexes to calendars etc*

3.   *Journal of the Forestry Commission—index to journal articles*

E)   AGENCIES PLANNING PILOT PROJECTS, OR ENQUIRING FOR TRAINING OR PROGRAMS

1.   Malaysian National Library
2.   State Library, Pretoria, South Africa
3.   Bibliotekscentralen, Denmark
4.   Det Kongelige Bibliotek, Copenhagen, Denmark
5.   ONTERIS (Ontario Educational Research Information Service)
6.   British Library (Library Association Library)
7.   Indian Library Science Abstracts
8.   *Bibliothèque nationale du Quebec*
9.   Polytechnic of North London
10.   Preston Polytechnic
11.   London Borough of Hillingdon
12.   University College, Cork, Ireland
13.   Kirklees County Library

Figure 13. PRECIS pilot projects

9 PERFORMANCE DATA AND EVALUATION

9.1   I shall finish this session with a few remarks on performance data and
evaluation. These remarks will have to be brief, at least as far as evaluation is concerned, for the very good reason that we have not, ourselves, attempted any evaluation of PRECIS. Nor do we see how we
can, since any evidence which we, as the designers of the system,
offered to the profession at large would clearly be suspect. We have,
however, gathered quantities of data relating to the characteristics of
PRECIS indexers and indexes, such as the average number of lead
terms per string, and the expected daily output of an indexer. A selection of these data is shown in Figure 14.

1   *Indexing rates*

Indexing rate (i.e. string writing) is approximately 30 documents
per working day of 7¼ hours, i.e. the average time taken to string
a document on a new theme is ca. 18 minutes. Note: This figure
represents "elapsed working time", as opposed to "stop-watch"
time per document; the latter would be 37–50% shorter.

2   *Statistical properties of strings*

	Averages (mean)
Number of strings per document	1
Number of terms per string	2.7
Number of lead terms per string	1.9

3   *Operation of the RIN and SIN systems*

Proportion of documents handled by quoting existing SINs from
three-year-old file
(1971–1973)   55%

Number of terms in thesaurus   33,000

This is now available on 7 microfiches at 42 X reduction

Figure 14. Indexing performing figures collected by British National Bibliography

9.2   Effective evaluation is, of course, a very expensive business, in terms of
both money and manpower. Although we are not prepared to engage
in this ourselves, we are willing to provide material for other people to
evaluate. A small scale evaluation of PRECIS has been conducted at
Liverpool Library School, and some of the figures arising from this
test are shown in Figure 15.

9.3   We have not, ourselves, carried out any experiments on the use of
PRECIS for machine-retrieval or SDI, though we hope to do so during
the next year or so, as soon as we have designed a satisfactory inverted
file structure. However, an SDI experiment is now in progress in the
University of Toronto, and we hope that Prof. Ann Schabas will release

some results within a year or so. Some experiments in the machine-searching of PRECIS strings have also been conducted in Canberra, where it was generally concluded that the contents of the PRECIS field on current MARC tapes consistently gave better results, in terms of the classical measures of recall and precision, than other subject fields such as DC and LC class numbers, titles, and Library of Congress subject headings.

(1) *Test Environment*

Test index = PRECIS index to 584 journal articles in the field of management.

100 questions; 1 relevant document per question; each question searched once only.

28 searchers, mainly students.

(2) *Success Rate of Searches*

Number of successful searches (relevant document retrieved)	83
Number of unsuccessful searches	17
Recall ratio	83%

(3) *Search Times*

Average per question (to nearest 15 secs)

	Mean		Median	
	Mins.	Secs.	Mins.	Secs.
Successful searches	1	30	1	00
Unsuccessful searches	4	00	3	00
All searches	1	45	1	00

Figure 15. Evaluation research at Liverpool Library School

9.4   As a final remark, we take note of user reactions to PRECIS as it appears in *BNB* and similar publications. On the whole, it would seem that PRECIS has been very well received by the users of the national bibliography. The first, and perhaps the most encouraging, reaction actually came from the proof readers who were employed on reading BNB/MARC diagnostics when PRECIS was first introduced in 1971. They learned how to interpret the strings in Field 690, and claimed that, for the first time, they could tell what the documents were about. And that, I believe, is what it is all about!

NOTES

1. British Museum, Department of Printed Books, *Subject Index of the Modern Works Added to the British Museum Library . . .* (London: The Museum, 1902–   ).

2. British Library, *Working Party on Classification and Indexing: Final Report*, London: British Library, 1975. (R&D Report No. 5233)

Multilingual Aspects of PRECIS

Jutta Sørensen
Bibliotekscentralen, Copenhagen, Denmark

1   INTRODUCTION

1.1   An international symposium on the theme "Subject retrieval in the seventies" was held at this library school about five years ago, where one of the speakers, Geoffrey Lloyd, gave the following reasons for developing a subject approach which is neutral with respect to natural language:

". . . the rapidly increasing production, transfer and consumption of scientific information present . . . serious problems of international exchange. . . . The advent of the computer can help us to handle the sheer bulk or mass of information produced, but . . . will not get us any nearer the information heaven than the Tower of Babel, unless we can adopt, maintain and use one standard switching language to control the currents and interconnect the lines of information flow in all their interlingual and interdisciplinary diversity".

1.2   Lloyd's paper dealt specifically with the use of a classification scheme, the UDC, as an interlingual switching language. However, the needs he referred to are as acute today as when the paper was given in 1971: our objectives are still the same; we are still in the seventies; we have not reached that hypothetical "information heaven" of a medium for exchanging information which is neutral with respect to both subject field and language. The quotation from Lloyd therefore seems an appropriate starting point for this paper, even though we are not now concerned with classification in its "library" sense, but with a quite different approach: that is, a technique for alphabetical indexing which appears to have the potential to function as a multilingual system.

2 THE LINGUISTIC BASIS OF PRECIS

2.1 Although PRECIS was originally devised for indexing in English, its syntactical procedures, and the algorithms for entry generation, have also been applied experimentally in other languages, both European and non-European. These experiments began during the early development of the system, and the results seemed to be sufficiently encouraging to justify further research. We can assume, on a purely theoretical level, that a number of different factors will affect the extent to which an indexing language, such as PRECIS, can be applied to more than one natural language. We need to consider whether the procedures for concept analysis and string writing will lead to the production of index entries in non-English languages which a native speaker of these languages would regard as both sensible and unambiguous. These syntactical factors must then be distinguished from the quite different problems associated with the construction of reconciled thesauri covering more than one language. I shall not deal in this paper with the construction of a multilingual thesaurus (this aspect is now being investigated by the International Organization for Standardization), but will concentrate instead on those problems which, in PRECIS terms, are more closely related to syntax. These can be considered from two viewpoints, and the difference between them can be expressed in the form of two questions:

— firstly, is the basic "grammar" of the system, as represented by the schema of role operators (see Figure 1 in Derek Austin's paper on syntax, p. 14) capable of functioning in more than one natural language?

— secondly, can the codes and procedures used for constructing compound terms and phrases, such as the differencing codes and connectives, either be applied as they stand to languages with other conventions, or modified so that they can deal with different languages, without disturbing the logic on which the present system is based? For example, could we devise codes that (a) would lead to the production of acceptable entries in a language such as German, a language which frequently uses inflected forms of terms, and also shows a tendency towards the synthetic construction of single-word compound terms; (b) continue to satisfy the logic on which PRECIS is based?

These questions, taken separately, involve several further problems (certainly enough for another Workshop), and it will not be possible to cover all this ground in the present paper. I shall therefore consider, briefly and at a fairly superficial level, the principal role operators viewed from a multilingual viewpoint, and then move on to consider some of the mechanisms for dealing with compound terms and phrases.

2.2 It is a simple matter to relate the first question to an example which resembles many of the English subjects already considered during this Workshop. A typical demonstration of concept analysis and entry production in English can be seen in Figure 1. We now have to ask ourselves how far the grammatical procedures used in this example, particularly the role operators, will lead to sensible index entries when applied to terms in other languages, such as French, German and Danish. Obviously, we should expect this to be a difficult task if our interpretation of grammar was limited to its traditional sense, that is the context of a particular language. We speak of French grammar, for example, and recognize that this is different from English grammar or German grammar. If our grammatical horizons were still limited in this way, there would probably be little point in searching for a single grammatical framework which would operate successfully in several languages. But, in fact, this is not a hopeless search, for two principal reasons. Firstly, the traditional definition of grammar applies only to literary language, whereas we are concerned with an indexing language: that is, a documentation language in which concepts are expressed in terms selected from natural language, and which uses at least part of the structure of natural language, but is nevertheless subject to logical constraints, and should therefore be regarded as an artificial language. Within these imposed limitations, we should expect a higher chance of success in our search for generalized indexing procedures which will operate successfully in more than one natural language.

(1) *Subject statement*

    Damage of timber by insects

String

    (1) timber
    (2) damage $v by $w to
    (3) insects

(2) *Index entries*

    TIMBER
       Damage by insects
    DAMAGE. Timber
       By insects

(3)   INSECTS
       Damage to timber

Figure 1. Subject analysis and indexing in English

2.3   Secondly, we are supported in these enquiries by several recent advances in the field of general linguistics. Linguists are concerned with certain structural features that appear to be common to all human languages. These structural features are known as linguistic universals. Several theories are emerging in this field; one of these seems to be especially promising from the viewpoint of an indexing system such as PRECIS. This is the recognition of certain deep cases (in a grammatical sense) which clearly specify the role of a given term vis-a-vis the other components of a statement or utterance, regardless of how

that statement is expressed in the surface structure of any particular
language. It is necessary to distinguish clearly between the deep cases,
regarded as linguistic universals, such as agent and patient, and those
surface cases, characteristic of a particular language, such as nomina--
tive, dative and accusative. It is not easy to demonstrate this distinction
in English index entries. Cases appear in their most manifest form in
inflected languages (such as German and the Slavonic family), and
English has generally shed its inflections, except for personal pronouns. We can, however, make the distinction by considering ordinary
sentences instead of index entries. In the following sentence:

> "He caught the bird"

—the pronoun "He" expresses the nominative case, and indicates the
term which functions as the subject of the verb "to catch"; "the bird"
is then in the accusative case. We can also express the same idea in the
form of a passive sentence:

> "The bird was caught by him".

It is now "The bird" which is in the nominative, and "he" has been
changed into "him" to indicate the dative. These distinctions may
seem to be subtle, or even superfluous, to the speaker of a non-inflected
language such as French or English, but they have to be understood, at
a deep intuitive level, by every speaker of an inflected language, such as
German or Polish, since the correct form of every word in a sentence
depends upon its case.

2.4   In the sentences shown above, a word representing a given concept
changed its case from the nominative in the active construction ("He")
to the dative in the passive construction ("Him"). Case changes of this
kind are common at a surface structure level in all natural languages.
Nevertheless, they tend to obscure an obvious fact: the person who
actually caught the bird was logically the same in both sentences, the
person who functioned as the agent of the action "To catch". Linguists are searching for deep cases based on this kind of logic, and a
number of these have been identified. These include cases such as the
location, the agent, various kinds of object, and so on, which clearly
resemble the roles employed in PRECIS. We have already seen, in the
example of subject analysis in Figure 1 how the role operators are used
to achieve an order of terms in an input string which is suited to the
mechanical production of a set of meaningful entries. We should also
note that the order prescribed by the operators does not necessarily
correspond to the order found in a "natural" statement of the subject,
as seen at the top of Figure 1. The natural-sounding expression in
English:

> Damage of timber by insects

—starts with the name of an action, and this is followed by: (i) the object, and (ii) the agent. This should be seen in contrast to the order of
terms in the string, where the object was written before the action, and

the action before the agent. We could say that the operators have
therefore been used to normalize the order of terms: that is, to
organize them into a standard pattern which experience has shown
is suitable for entry generation. This now brings us to the major
question: Will this normalization procedure continue to be effective
when it is applied to terms from other languages?

3   USE OF THE CORE OPERATORS IN FOUR LANGUAGES

3.1   If we now turn to Figure 2 we shall find this subject, i.e. "Damage of
timber by insects", expressed in four different languages: English,
French, German and Danish. In most of these subject statements, the
order of terms is not only different from the order found in a PRECIS
string; it also varies from one natural language to another. The French
statement:

Détérioration du bois d'oeuvre par les insectes

—generally corresponds to the English, since both begin with the name
of an action, followed by an object, and then an agent. In German,
however, a different pattern is found: the natural expression of this
subject:

Nutzholzbeschädigung durch Insekten

—calls first for the construction of a compound term, "Nutzholzbeschädigung", which embodies both the name of the object, "Nutzholz",
and also the name of the action, "Beschädigung", and this is then followed by the name of the agent, "Insekten". The Danish version gives
the closest match with the normalized order of terms in a PRECIS
string, at least as far as their one-to-one relationships are concerned,
despite the fact that the statement:

Insekters beskadigelse af tømmer

—is expressed in the active rather than the passive mood: that is, the
order is agent-action-object rather than object-action-agent.

3.2   At Position 2 of Figure 2 the separate components of these subject
statements have been labelled by operators which indicate their cases,
and the terms have then been organized into normalized "raw strings",
that is, strings which consist of operators plus terms expressed as
nominatives, but still lacking any of the case marking adjuncts of natural language, such as prepositions, differences and inflections, and
even, occasionally, articles and pronouns. These adjuncts are added to
the raw string by the indexer, and as we might expect, they vary from
one language to another, depending upon the conventions which are
characteristic of a given language. At Position 3 in Figure 2 we can see
the strings which would be produced after these adjuncts have been
added. In English, we can complete the input string quite simply by
adding two prepositions, "by" and "to", introduced by connectives.

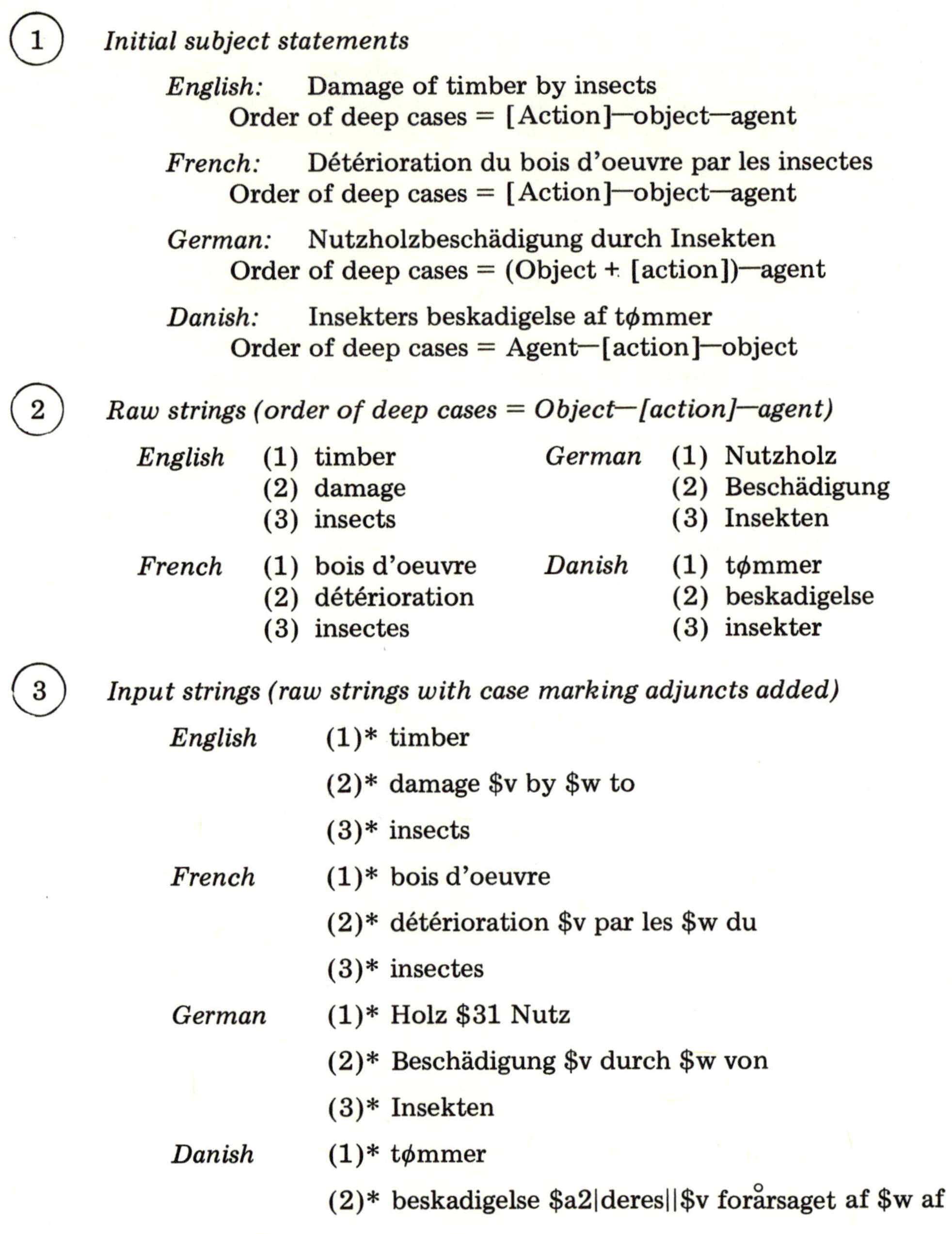

Figure 2. Subject analysis in four languages

This string would give rise to the entries seen at Position 1 in Figure 3.
The French raw string would be handled in much the same way as the
English, though the conventions of this language call for the addition
of definite articles attached to prepositions, so that "de" becomes "du",
and "par" becomes "par les". The output of the final string is seen at
Position 2 in Figure 3. The German string also resembles the English,
at least as far as connectives are concerned, but it differs in the treatment of the name of the object, coded as key system. The term
"Nutzholz" is, in fact, a compound which literally means "Useful
wood"; it consists of two separate elements, the focus "Holz" (wood),
and the difference "Nutz". The difference has been prefixed by one of
a new range of differencing codes which will be considered later. It
just happens that, in this particular example, none of the terms is subject to an inflectional change, but this problem will also be considered
later. The output of the German string can be seen at Position 3 in
Figure 3.

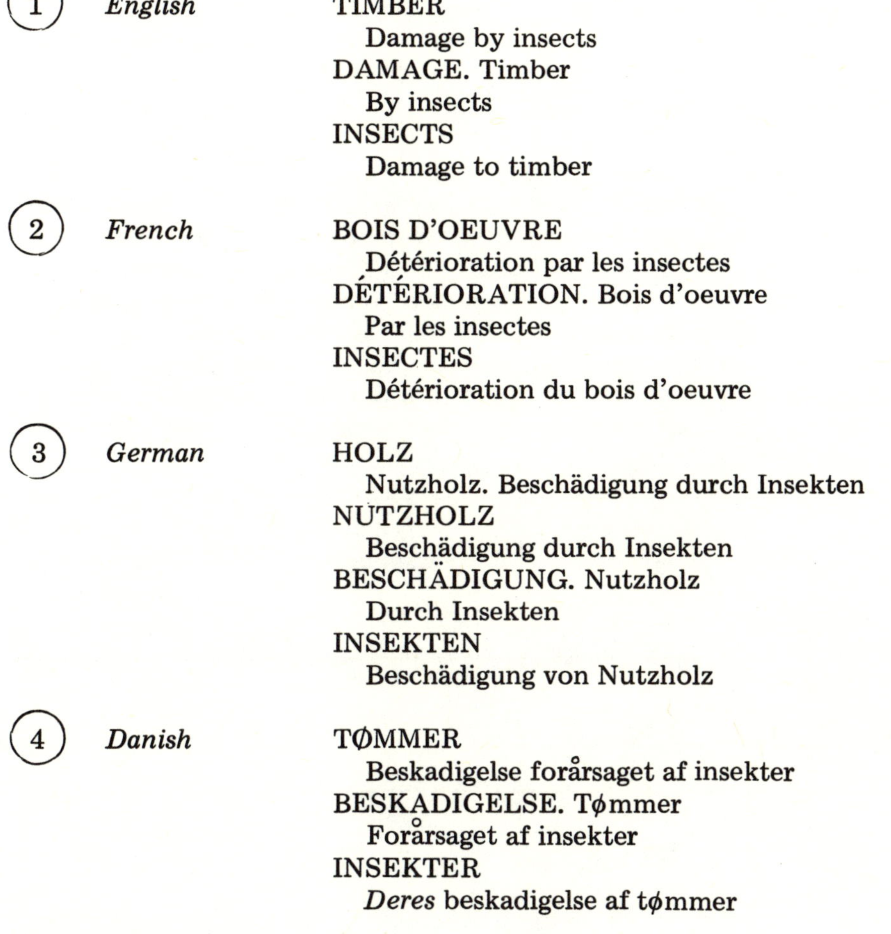

Figure 3. Generation of entries in four languages

3.3   At first glance, we might expect few problems when indexing in
Danish, since the order of terms in the original Danish statement was
simply a mirror image of the order required in PRECIS. Nevertheless,
this language introduces special difficulties for the indexer, due to the
fact that Danish does not possess the full range of expressive prepositions found in the other three languages. For example, the English
prepositions "of" and "to" both translate into the single preposition
"af" in Danish. For obvious reasons this could lead to latent ambiguities in index entries, especially when handling subjects such as "Attitudes *of* students *to* teachers". In order to deal with this and similar
problems, the indexer has to adopt some of the surface structure conventions which resolve these ambiguities in literary Danish. This involves a range of extra codes which have now been specified, such as
the code $a2 which is attached to the action term in the Danish string
at Position 3 in Figure 2. This code ensures that a possessive pronoun,
"deres" ("their"), is inserted into certain entries to resolve the ambiguity—as shown in the third of the Danish entries in Figure 3.

4   CODES FOR HANDLING INFLECTIONS

4.1   The code which introduced the possessive pronoun into the third of
the Danish entries was chosen from one of a number of categories of
new codes which have recently been added to PRECIS to allow the
system to handle the surface features of a range of non-English languages. One of these categories, which is shown in Figure 4, contains
codes for dealing with inflections. These codes, which are recent developments, are not described in the PRECIS *Manual.* They allow the
indexer to specify up to four different inflected versions of a term in
addition to the lead itself, which should always be expressed in its

	Not target of a connective	*Target of a connective*	*Standard: print whether connective present or not*
"Not up" inflection	$s1	$s2	$s3
"Not down" inflection	$t1	$t2	$t3

Figure 4. Codes for handling inflections

① *Polish subject statement:* Szkodzenie drzewa budowlanego przez owady

   Order of deep cases: [Action]—object—agent

   English translation: Damage of timber by insects

   Raw string:
- (1) drzewo budowlane
- (2) szkodzenie
- (3) owady

② *Input string:*
- (1)* drzewo budowlane $t2 drzewa budowlanego
- (2)* szkodzenie $v przez $w
- (3)* owady

③ *Entries:*

Drzewo budowlane
   Szkodzenie przez owady
Szkodzenie. Drzewo budowlane
   Przez owady
Owady
   Szkodzenie drzewa budowlanego

Figure 5. Demonstration of inflection codes

nominative form. The experiments carried out so far indicate that this range of codes should be enough to handle any syntactical situation which would call for a change of inflection in an indexing situation. German is recognized as a member of the class of inflected languages, but in the example considered earlier it happens that none of the terms requires a visible change of inflection. However, an inflection would be needed if we indexed this subject in Polish. This can be seen in Figure 5, where a Polish subject statement is first analyzed in terms of the deep cases of its components, and these are then organized into a raw string. This leads, in its turn, to an input string (at Position 3) which contains an inflection attached to the key system "Drzewo budowlane" ("Timber"). Consequently, this term appears in its nominative form only in the first two entries; in the phrase in the last entry (the one with the lead term "Owady") it is automatically printed in its accusative version, "Drzewa budowlanego".

5   EXTENDING THE DIFFERENCING CODES AND PROCEDURES

5.1   We can now consider another group of codes which have been developed especially to deal with non-English languages. These are new differencing codes which will allow the indexer to handle languages, such as German and Danish, in which complex concepts are frequently expressed in the form of single-word compounds constructed by synthesis out of their separate parts. In Figure 6 we can see a typical English compound term at Position *A*. This is the term "Reinforced concrete bridges", which can be broken down fairly simply into the

(A) *English example*

1   *Term:*   Reinforced concrete bridges

2   *Input:*   (1)* bridges $i concrete $m reinforced

3   *Entries:*   BRIDGES
                   Reinforced concrete bridges
               CONCRETE BRIDGES
                   Reinforced concrete bridges
               REINFORCED CONCRETE BRIDGES

(B) *German example*

1   *Term:*   Eisenbetonbrücken

2   *Input:*   (1)* Brücken $31 Beton $32 Eisen

3   *Entries:*   BRÜCKEN
                   Eisenbetonbrücken
               BETONBRÜCKEN
                   Eisenbetonbrücken
               EISENBETONBRÜCKEN

Figure 6. Coding of compound terms

focus, "Bridges", the direct difference "Concrete", and the indirect difference "Reinforced". Each of these functions can be expressed exactly by the codes seen at Position 2, and the output is shown at Position 3.

5.2   This concept is expressed in German by the term "Eisenbetonbrücken", which consists of a single word, but is nevertheless amenable to exactly the same kind of analysis as its English counterpart: that is to say, we can identify a focus ("Brücken"), a direct difference ("Beton"), and an indirect difference ("Eisen"). An indexer may select any of these parts of the word as a lead, just as the individual words in the English term might also be chosen as leads.

5.3   This can now be achieved in PRECIS by using a range of generalized differencing codes and procedures which have recently been added to the system. These new codes were used in the German input seen at Position B-2 of Figure 6, and it can be seen that the new codes consist of a dollar sign followed by two numbers, instead of the dollar sign followed by a single letter in codes such as $i and $m. These new codes do not invalidate the differences described in the *Manual* and shown on the list of operators. However, the new codes are more generalized and flexible than the previous codes; they can do all that the previous codes allowed, plus a great deal more. The computer can, in fact, handle both the old and the new differencing codes with equal ease.

5.4 The increased range of options allowed by these codes has been achieved by a process known as "unstacking". If we consider the structure of one of the standard codes, we can see that the letter which follows the dollar sign actually conveys three stacked instructions to the computer:

(1) firstly, it indicates that the following element is either a direct or an indirect difference. We can put this another way, and say that the code specifies the "level" of the difference, or its semantic distance from the focus. A direct difference therefore has a semantic distance of "one", an indirect difference has a semantic distance of "two", and so on.

(2) secondly, the code indicates whether or not a lead should be constructed under the difference.

(3) thirdly, the code instructs the computer to leave a space between the difference and the following word.

Some of these instructions have been separated or unstacked in the new differencing codes. The first of the two numbers which follow the dollar sign is selected by the indexer from the Table shown in Figure 7. This number specifies whether the difference which follows the code is needed in the lead, and whether it should be followed by a space (as in English adjectives), or should close-up to the next part of the term (as in some German words). It does not indicate the level of the difference: that is, whether the difference is direct or indirect. This is indicated separately by adding another number to the code which specifies the exact semantic distance or level within the range from one to nine. This means that a direct or first level difference would be indicated by 1, an indirect difference by the figure 2, and so on.

	Space-generating	*Close-up*
Non-lead	0	1
Lead	2	3

Figure 7. Meaning of first number in generalized differencing codes

5.5 At first sight it may appear that this system based on numbers is more complex than the letter codes which were developed for English. Experience has shown, however, that the new system is easier to remember and apply than the old, perhaps because a smaller number of decisions are involved at each step. In any case, the new system will map on to the old exactly; a table of equivalence between the old and the new codes is shown below:

$h	=	$01	$k	=	$02
$i	=	$21	$m	=	$22

5.6   These new differencing codes and procedures were developed in the first place as extra options to ensure that PRECIS could handle those single-word compounds which are common in German and similar languages. Examples taken from these languages can be seen in the first two positions of Figure 8. Position *A* shows a Danish term, "Træbygninger" ("Timber buildings") which contains one first-level close-up difference. Position *B* shows the German term "Gedackte Holzpfeifen" (a technical term, "Closed wooden pipes", in the field of organ building), which includes both a close-up and also a space-generating difference, each at "level one". In a case like this, the printing of correct upper-case initials on German nouns will be handled by a special subroutine in the program. It should be stressed at this point that although these codes were devised as the result of experiments with German and similar languages, the use of these codes will not be limited to the Germanic languages. Similar situations also occur in English, even though they are less common. Owing to what we can only call an orthographic accident, English terms such as "Dining rooms" and "Soup spoons" are written as adjectival constructions in the usual two-word form, whereas terms such as "Bedrooms" and "Teaspoons" have developed into single words. Nevertheless, these words still contain recognizable foci (that is, "Rooms" and "Spoons"), and also logical differences ("Bed" and "Tea"). Consequently, the new codes will have immediate value for indexers working in English. They will not only allow the indexer to deal with single-word compounds, but also with terms containing differences on a level which exceeds the capacity of the earlier system. Each of these situations is illustrated in Figure 8. Position *C* shows the coding of the term "Re-upholstered armchairs" which contains one space-generating difference ("Upholstered"), and also two close-up differences ("Arm" and "Re-"). Position *D* shows the coding of a term which contains a third-level difference, "Arc-": that is, a difference which qualifies an indirect difference. These situations are not uncommon in indexing technical reports, and had to be handled by somewhat unorthodox methods before these new codes had been developed.

6   **CONCLUSION**

6.1   This kind of immediate feedback from research to practical indexing has been typical of all the experiments carried out so far into the multilingual aspects of PRECIS. In this paper I have been able to mention only some of the new procedures which are now being developed by cooperative research in various centres in Europe. I would now like to consider, quite briefly, some implications of this research.

6.2   Firstly, and as we might expect, contact with indexers working in non-English languages led to a general re-appraisal of the theoretical premises on which PRECIS is based, particular attention being paid to its underlying linguistic principles. This led to the study of case gram-

(A) *Danish example*

    Concept: Træbygninger ("Timber buildings")

    Input: (1)* bygninger $31 træ

    Entries: BYGNINGER
        Træbygninger
    TRÆBYGNINGER

(B) *German example*

    Concept: Gedackte Holzpfeifen ("Closed wooden pipes")

    Input: (1)* Pfeifen $31 Holz $21 Gedackte

    Entries: PFEIFEN
        Gedackte Holzpfeifen
    HOLZPFEIFEN
        Gedackte Holzpfeifen
    GEDACKTE PFEIFEN
        Gedackte Holzpfeifen

(C) *English example*

    Concept: Re-upholstered armchairs

    Input: (1)* chairs $31 arm $21 upholstered $12 re-

    Entries: CHAIRS
        Re-upholstered armchairs
    ARMCHAIRS
        Re-upholstered armchairs
    UPHOLSTERED CHAIRS
        Re-upholstered armchairs

(D) *English example*

    Concept: Arc-welded steel containers

    Input: (1)* containers $21 steel $22 welded $33 arc-

    Entries: CONTAINERS
        Arc-welded steel containers
    STEEL CONTAINERS
        Arc-welded steel containers
    WELDED STEEL CONTAINERS
        Arc-welded steel containers
    ARC-WELDED STEEL CONTAINERS

Note: * = focus as lead

Figure 8. Examples showing use of generalized differences

mar as a possible explanation of the working of the system, at least at
the level of the raw strings which were seen in some of the earlier examples. It was always realized that this swing towards explicit linguistic
explanations might reveal a need to re-think parts of the established
English-language system, but, in fact, experience has shown that this
will not be necessary. On the contrary, these contacts with other languages have tended to confirm, rather than undermine, the general
premises on which the system has been based since it was re-designed
in 1973.

6.3   Obviously, these contacts with other languages revealed a need to
develop extra codes and procedures to enable the indexer to deal with
those surface features which are characteristic of a given language or
group of languages, such as inflections and so on. These are the codes
which the indexer adds to his raw strings to produce input strings which
are capable of generating acceptable output in his own language. Several
of these new codes and procedures have now been specified, and only
a selection could be described in this paper. Work is now being conducted into procedures for dealing with prepositional phrases in French
and other Romance languages. These, too, will be of obvious benefit to
English indexers, since English possesses many structural characteristics
of these languages.

6.4   One interesting point has already emerged from these enquiries. This
is the fact that the PRECIS *Manual* no longer describes the total system.
The English-language version described in the *Manual* will continue to
be effective, and all the existing files can be left intact. We saw an example of this when we considered the new differencing codes, when it
was seen that codes such as $i will continue to operate, and can be
matched exactly by equivalents in the revised system. Nevertheless,
many of the procedures now being developed will have little, if any,
value for English indexers. This means that the present version of the
Manual will strictly describe an English sub-grammar extracted from a
more generalized macro-grammar. Indexers working in other languages, such as Danish, will be able to extract their own lcoal grammars from this generalized system, and these local grammars will not
necessarily be the same as English at the surface structure level.

6.5   In time we can visualize a series of local sub-grammars which will
allow indexers in different language communities to work successfully in their native languages, without necessarily contacting indexers
working in other languages. PRECIS has, in fact, already been applied
independently in this way to various European languages. Figure 9
shows part of a page from an index in French to scientific theses held
in the University of Rouen in France. This kind of independent working is what I mean when I refer to PRECIS as a multilingual system. I
wish to conclude by making a clear distinction between two concepts:
(1)   firstly, multilingual indexing: that is, the independent use of a
general system in more than one language.

Atmosphère
Voir aussi
   Air
Auchénorhynques. Languedoc. France
   Parasites: Dryinidae & Strepsiptères. Etude systématique,
     biologique & écologique   T313(1971)9
Aucoumea klaineana. Plantations. Gabon
   Racines. Anastomose. Etude morphologique
     T414(1973)45
Autofécondation. Lombriciens
   Etude expérimentale   T103(1963)3
Auxines. Graines. Pisum sativum
   Auxines & gibbérellines. Rôle au cours du développement
     des graines   T413(1964)1
Avoine. *Matériel d'étude*
   Végétaux. Croissance, développement & métabolisme.
     Influence de la vernalisation   T403(1951)4
Azote
Voir aussi
   Composés azotés
Azote. Aspergillus repens
   Nutrition   T403(1925)1
Azote. Constituants. Bacillus megaterium
   Métabolisme. Rôle de l'acide glutamique   T413(1974)8
Azote. Constituants. Caryopses. Sorgho
   Evolution au cours de la germination   T508(1973)1
Azote. Constituants. Feuilles. Végétaux
   Métabolisme *en relation avec la* respiration — *Matériel*
     d'étude: Phaseolus multiflorus, Polygonum fagopyrum,
     Rumex acetosa & Triticum vulgare   T413(1949)1
Azote. Constituants. Gamétophytes femelles & sporophytes.
   Dicranum majus & Dicranum scoparium
   Métabolisme. Evolution au cours du développement
     T508(1970)15
Azote. Constituants. Stictacées
   Métabolisme   T508(1970)19

Bacillus megaterium
   Constituants: Azote. Métabolisme. Rôle de l'acide
     glutamique   T413(1974)8
   Sporulation. Régulation. Rôle de la glutamine
     T413(1974)8
Bactéries
Voir aussi
   Bacillus megaterium
   Diplococcus pneumoniae
   Escherichia coli
   Rhodopseudomonas spheroides
Bactéries. Contaminants. Elevage de larves de bivalves
   Détermination   T118(1974)2
Bactériochlorophylle. Rhodopseudomonas spheroides
   Biosynthèse. Régulation. Rôle de l'ALA synthétase
     T413(1973)31
Bactériophages
   Lysogénie   T403(1954)3
Bactériophages lambda
   Constituants: ADN. Réplication. Régulation
     T413(1973)32
Basidiomycètes
Voir aussi
   Coprinus radiatus
Basidiomycètes. Seine-Maritime. France
   Répartition géographique, *1864-1968*   T518(1970)1/1-1/2
Bicyclus. Afrique   TU413(1971)2
Biologie
Voir aussi
   Anatomie
   Biométrie
   Botanique
   Ecologie
   Entomologie
   Ethologie
   Génétique
   Morphologie
   Physiologie
   Rythme biologique
   Taxonomie
   Zoologie

Biosynthèse. Vitellus. Oeufs. Poules
   Rôle des acides gras alimentaires & des acides gras du
     tissu adipeux   T413(1973)37
Bivalves
Voir aussi
   Mytilus edulis
Bivalves
   Byssus. Sécrétion. Etude anatomique & physiologique
     T508(1969)30
Bivalves marins
   Larves. Elevage. Contamination par les bactéries —
     Matériel d'étude: Mytilus edulis   T118(1974)2
Blabera craniifer
   Embryon. Développement. Etude morphologique
     T228(1968)7
Blé
Voir aussi
   Triticum vulgare
Blé
   Coléoptile. Elongation *en relation avec l'* activité
     enzymatique des isopéroxydases   T78(1972)24
   Coléoptile. Isopéroxydases. Activité enzymatique *en*
     relation avec l' élongation du coléoptile   T78(1972)24
   Graines. Constituants: Glucides. Evolution au cours de la
     maturation   TU253(1970)1
   Graines. Maturation. Evolution du taux des glucides
     TU253(1970)1
Bordeaux. *Régions étudiées*
   Air. Pollution par spores d'Epicoccum nigrum. Etude
     quantitative — *Régions étudiées: Bordeaux & Pau,*
     1957-1963   T103(1964)4
Bore. Végétaux
   Nutrition   T403(1963)6
Botanique
Voir aussi
   Végétaux
Bryophyllum daigremontianum
   Feuilles. Constituants: Acides aminés. Biosynthèse.
     Influence de la lumière   T403(1959)5
Bryophytes
Voir aussi
   Dicranum majus
   Dicranum scoparium
   Mnium
   Sphaignes
Buthus occitanus. *Matériel d'étude*
   Arachnides. Comportement sexuel *en relation avec la*
     nutrition   T508(1972)19
Byssus. Bivalves
   Sécrétion. Etude anatomique & physiologique
     T508(1969)30

Calcaire. Constituants. Sol
   Effets sur le développement & le métabolisme de Lupinus
     albus — *Régions étudiées: Ardèche & Montagne Noire*
     T563(1971)10
Calyptorhynques
   Embryon. Développement   T413(1972)18
   Reproduction & développement embryonnaire
     T413(1972)18
Cameroun
   Africains. Sang. Sérum. Constituants: Cuivre, fer &
     prot´ eines — *Matériel d'étude: Individus sains &*
     malades   T413(1971)9
Capparidaceae
   Chimiotaxonomie   T413(1973)21
Carcinus maenas
   Croissance & mue. Rôle de l'organe Y   T413(1957)6
   Organe Y. Rôle dans la croissance & le déclenchement de
     la mue   T413(1957)6
Carence. Magnésium. Constituants. Feuilles. Pommiers.
   Vergers. Ille-et-Vilaine
   Symptômes — *Variétés étudiées: Golden Délicious &*
     Reine des reinettes   T508(1969)3
Carex. Massif Armoricain. France
   Etude systématique   T508(1967)17

Figure 9. Extract from index in French to scientific theses in Rouen University

(2)   secondly, translingual indexing: that is, indexing a document in
        one source language, submitting the input string to a computer,
        and expecting the machine to translate this string into a differ-
        ent version in another target language, so that this new string
        can be manipulated by a standard program into acceptable entries
        in the target language.

6.6   Obviously, this goal of a translingual indexing system is more ambi-
        tious, and far more difficult, than working independently in any one
        language. However, the benefits are obvious when we consider that
        Europe is now establishing a MARC-based bibliographic exchange sys-
        tem, and that certain countries, such as Belgium and Canada, have legal
        obligations to provide subject indexes to their national bibliographies
        in more than one language. This is therefore an appropriate time to
        report that the British Library has set up a research project to examine
        the feasibility of adding a translingual component to PRECIS. At the
        moment it is too early to speculate on the outcome of these experi-
        ments, but at least it can be reported that the problems do not appear
        to be insoluble. This work, which takes us literally to the present
        frontiers of information science, is beginning to look promising.

6.7   I cannot yet report on the technical aspects of translingual indexing,
        but I would at least like to explain our motivation. Work of this kind
        must clearly involve a considerable investment in terms of both human
        resources (i.e. the intellectual efforts of indexers, linguists, systems
        analysts and programmers), and the costs of equipment and computer
        time, especially during the experimental stages. Faced by the present
        economic climate, we have examined our own motivation, asking how
        we can justify so much effort when international networks are already
        operating on a monolingual basis. I believe that these efforts are
        justified, and I would suggest two reasons, the first economic and the
        second cultural.

6.8   It is not difficult to identify the economic factors. We are still faced
        by the information explosion, and in some fields it appears that the
        number of new documents is rising exponentially. This development
        represents the output of considerable human intellectual effort, and
        as such we have to regard it as one of our most valuable economic re-
        sources. Much of this work is in foreign languages. If we are to make
        the optimum use of this resource, we must avoid, as far as possible,
        duplication of effort in bibliographic control This applies especially
        in the context of the newly emerging international networks. In sim-
        ple terms, there should be no need for an indexer working, say, in
        France, to carry out the subject analysis and description of docu-
        ments (in the widest sense) which have already been handled in their
        country of origin, such as the United States or Britain. If we can
        develop an effective switching routine, and given that this could then
        be accepted as a standard procedure at the network level, we could

accept country-of-origin indexing in much the same way that we shall increasingly accept country-of-origin descriptive cataloging. After all, this is the motivation which underlies MARC and other related systems. However, there would be one major difference in the subject approach—each country would receive output, and submit input, in its own language. This would mean that smaller countries, such as Denmark, could most effectively contribute their material to an international exchange network, and also receive output from that network, without having to pay the price of giving up their own languages when indexing their own national output.

6.9   This brings us naturally to the cultural factors. These are more difficult to define, but they are nevertheless real and important. In our field of information science, language is surely our most important tool. Language serves as the communication link between one scientist and another, and between the makers and users of information. At the interface between these different communities, we must be sensitive to the matter of language. Within that context, we need to realize that a person's natural language is an intrinsic part of his cultural identity. To a large extent, language reflects our patterns of thought and our systems of ideas. The imposition of one working language upon the members of an international network must entail the surrender of some part of the cultural identity of certain members. This applies not only at the international level, but also within certain countries in which different communities speak different natural languages. The same problems can be found within a single natural language community; if we can achieve switching between one natural language and another, we could apply the same procedures to the automatic switching of index data between, say, scientist's English and layman's English, or between different varieties of "ordinary" English, such as American, Australian and British.

6.10   Until the translingual switching mechanisms have been developed and made available, much of this aspect of our work may seem as castles in the air. No doubt we shall encounter formidable problems, but we have found no evidence yet that these goals are unattainable, and the prospect appears promising; we would not feel justified in giving up these goals before we have even tried. At its deepest level, this whole question is concerned with two fundamental rights. The first is the right to be different, which is the only true equality. In our field, that means the right to retain our identities as represented by our own languages. The second is the right to demand that modern technology should serve people as they really are; it should not be necessary to force different language communities into a monolingual mold simply because that gives easier answers from the computer's point of view.

II. Research Projects and Comparative Studies

PRECIS Compared with Other Indexing Systems

Phyllis A. Richmond
School of Library Science, Case Western Reserve
University

PRECIS is such an interesting indexing system that obviously the first thing to compare it to is the Library of Congress subject headings (LCSH). The other type of indexing to be considered here is Keyword-in-Context (KWIC). The reason I have included KWIC is that when I asked one of my Information Science colleagues if he had seen PRECIS, his reply was that it was just another form of KWIC indexing. So, in case anyone *else* should suffer from that delusion, I included a KWIC sample for every heading where it was possible to do so.

This study is a *comparison*. (An *evaluation* is being performed at Wollongong University in Australia as a full-scale study dealing with relevance-pertinence-recall-precision-fallout in retrieval. It is basically a user study which attempts to measure retrieval effectiveness. It began in January 1975 and is to be finished by January 1977. It was begun before Rowena Swanson's rather devastating critique of evaluation studies and their shortcomings.[1] I do not know to what extent it will overcome the weaknesses of earlier evaluation studies with regard to methodology.)

The present study is not made in such depth. It is rather more impressionistic. Since the number of entries in KWIC indexing depends on how many words there are in the title, I have not included this form of indexing in the quantitative section. I began with the preconceived notion that PRECIS was going to be a big improvement on LCSH. I think that the logical and linguistic features of PRECIS and the versatility allowed the indexer lead to that impression. Therefore, my working hypothesis was that, quantitatively and qualitatively, PRECIS should make subject material more accessible than the LCSH.

DATA BASE

In order to test this hypothesis, I took a sample consisting of those works published in both the United Kingdom and the United States, gleaned from a single issue of the *British National Bibliography* (*BNB*), the weekly list issued on December 31, 1975.[2] This issue contained a total of 648 separately numbered entries. Of these, 78 were published in both countries. Sixty were analyzed, and the remaining 18 were omitted because they were exactly the same as the ones used. I did not see much sense in listing ten American plays, each of which had exactly the same PRECIS entries. So, only one is represented in the qualitative analysis, but all are covered in the quantitative section. There were some additional books issued by presses, such as the Oxford University Press, which publish in both countries. Where there was no specific information in either the imprint or the notes to the effect that an American edition existed, I omitted such items. In some cases, American titles varied from British titles, for reasons best known to author and publisher, but in most cases the title was the same in either edition.

METHODOLOGY

The methodology in gathering data to make the comparison was simple. First, all entries in the issue of the *BNB* were scanned, looking for information on an American edition. The whole issue was looked over several times to be sure nothing was omitted. Americans will be interested to note that in at least two cases the same work had two different class numbers. There was, however, only one I. D. number representing the physical item.

After collecting all of the Anglo-American imprints, I then checked each one in the Subject index of *BNB* to find the PRECIS entries. This process was greatly facilitated by the fact that in every case directly following the Dewey number by which the whole *BNB* is arranged, there is a class description. This class description is almost always the same as the PRECIS string describing the work. It is different just often enough to keep things interesting. For example, one may have the *BNB* entry:

658.4 — EXECUTIVE MANAGEMENT

658.403. Business firms. Management. Decision making.

Book: Bridge, John.
  Managerial decision making.

The PRECIS entries for this item are:

Business firms
  Management. Decision making

Management. Business firms
  Decision making

Decision making. Management. Business firms

A class designation like this makes it rather easy to find the PRECIS index terms for the item. Where the class designation is different, it is usually because part of the designation is a cross-reference or it is too broad to be of much use. At least one can use it as a point of departure in searching the Subject index. The designations in the Dewey schedules (18th edition) for the same classes are:

658.4   Principles of management. Executive management.

               Principles: planning, organizing, directing, coordinating,
               reporting, communication

658.403   Decision making.

               Information analysis, sources of information, problem
               solving, techniques of analysis

Dewey would not have led me to the PRECIS index terms.

Two more comments on searching: first, not all of the terms one could use from a string are in the index. The indexer controls the content so that parts which seem superfluous may be in the string but not used as headwords in the subject index list. Second, sometimes one runs into terms used for other books which would seem on the surface to be usable with the one being examined. Specifically, for the book *Women's Liberation in the Twentieth Century* the PRECIS entry

     WOMEN. United States
       Role in society, 1900-1975

was not applied, although there is an entry of this type attached to a British book on the subject.[3]

After getting the PRECIS entries and listing them, the *National Union Catalog* (*NUC*) was used to find the American entries for the same works. Most of the time, this was not a great problem, even though on the day I set aside to search my sixty titles the computer at the Ohio College Library Center (OCLC) was not functioning and I had to search most of them the hard way—in the unbound *NUC* issues for 1975 and 1976. Not one of the items listed in the December 31, 1975 issue of *BNB* was in the January-March *NUC* cumulation for 1976. A very few turned up in bound volumes for earlier years, in those few cases where the American edition had been published before the British. After this day-long search, I had about twenty problem children. I returned and looked for them when the OCLC was working, aided by an eager beaver student. Eventually, after considerable trial and error, all the entries were found. A goodly number turned up under editor instead of title, and the one entry not on the MARC tape was found under editor in a re-search of the unbound *NUC* catalogs. The student was horrified that the entry was not under title as in *BNB*, having learned her current rules pretty well in the beginning cataloging courses. But, of course, these works probably had been cataloged before that specific rule change came through, or came under undesuperimposition. The changes in American and British titles caused some pain because the search code does not make allowance for a different title, and the little green gremlins came back with the equivalent of "never heard of it." At this point the student became excited, but we tried various variations and eventually OCLC came across.

When the LC entry in MARC format was called up, it was a simple matter to take down the subject headings. No added entries (Roman numeral type) were included, since they are not subject headings. For both PRECIS and LCSH, I did not make use of cross-references in the file, though sometimes I noted them for my own information, along with a few snide comments.

Since I had copied down the entry to the end of the imprint date (sometimes adding series and notes if pertinent), I also had sufficient information to make my Keyword-in-Context index as well. This was made for the title, no matter how the item was entered and the only problem encountered here was the kind of title used. Some were too short, although probably they would be helpful in a full index. Others were so long that an identification number of some kind certainly would have been needed. I did not use more than seventy-six columns, and in many cases considerably less. The problem titles, notably for literary works, were omitted for obvious reasons. What can one do with titles like *Creeps, Too many rabbits, My fat friend, By a stroke of luck, Divorce me, darling,* or *A flea in her ear?*

This kind of indexing, in its Keyword-out-of-Context (KWOC) version, wherein the rotation is removed, works well in literary usage for concordances, and it certainly would be an improvement for some titles,[4] but since my colleague called PRECIS a rotated index I thought it would be more to the point to show the difference.

QUANTITATIVE ANALYSIS

The total number of entries in the *BNB* weekly list was 648. Of these, 78 were used for quantitative purposes. The proportion of the whole which had both American and British imprints for the identical work was 12.04%. The proportion used for qualitative purposes was 9.57% or 60 works.

For the 78 works, there were 173 PRECIS entries and 97 LCSH. In other words, there were almost twice as many PRECIS entries. This figure, however, can be deceptive. In the first place, for novels, plays and other individual literary works, the Library of Congress does not assign a subject heading, only an added entry for title. This affected some 23 items in the total list. Exceptions occurred in 7 instances. These were almost always collections, anthologies, diaries, autobiographies—materials not basically creative in the same sense that a poem, novel or play is creative. Thirty of the 78 books published on both sides of the Atlantic were literary in form.

A different type of breakdown was made to get a closer approximation of the ratio of PRECIS to LCSH. Four divisions were made according to certain measurable situations:

Group 1. Number of LCSH exceeds number of PRECIS
Group 2. Both equal in number
Group 3. PRECIS exceeds LCSH by 1
Group 4. PRECIS exceeds LCSH by 2+

This type of grouping determined how I originally sorted the documents, since half of my hypothesis assumed a quantitative difference in favor of PRECIS. The figures support this hypothesis:

Group 1. LCSH exceeds PRECIS 11
Group 2. Both equal 19
Group 3. PRECIS exceeds LCSH by 1 24
Group 4. PRECIS exceeds LCSH by 2-5 24

Thus, the PRECIS entries exceed the number of LCSH in 48 out of 78 cases, or 61.54% of the time. There are, however, 14 literary works in Group 3 and 12 in Group 4. If these are removed, the PRECIS advantage for Groups 3 and 4 combined drops to 22. If LC should suddenly decide to throw a general subject heading on each literary work as PRECIS does, the spread would change to:

```
Group 1.  LCSH exceeds PRECIS . . . . . . . . . . . . . . . . . . . . . 11
Group 2.  Both equal  . . . . . . . . . . . . . . . . . . . . . . . . . . . . . 33 (19+14)
Group 3.  PRECIS exceeds LCSH by 1 . . . . . . . . . . . . . . . . 22 (24−14+12)
Group 4.  PRECIS exceeds LCSH by 2-5 . . . . . . . . . . . . . . 12 (24−12)
```

Since neither of these things actually is the case, however, quantitatively the advantage clearly is with PRECIS.

To round out the picture, the *rate* of difference in assigning LCSH in Group 1 was 1.27 terms per document, whereas the PRECIS rate in Groups 3 and 4 averaged 2.58 terms per document, which is a shade over double. Thus the overall advantage of PRECIS quantitatively so far as *rate* is concerned is 1.31%, or 13 more terms per 1,000 documents. In other words, PRECIS would by no means overload the index.

Finally, it remains to compare the two systems by subject, using the appropriate Dewey class for each Group (see Figure 1). From this table it may be seen that the three most significant fields in this issue of *BNB* were literature, social sciences and fine arts. Even if the items in Group 1 are subtracted, this pattern still holds for the remaining three groups. In Group 1, however, the three leading subjects are social sciences in first place, with science and technology tied for next place. In Group 2, where LCSH and PRECIS are equally represented, the top subjects are fine arts in first place, technology and literature in second and social sciences in third. The dominant overall pattern is set primarily by Groups 3 and 4.

No Bradford distribution could be determined, although in a much larger sample such a possibility might occur, especially since PRECIS is so much stronger on the literary side.

If more is better, then PRECIS wins quantitatively. The effects on the qualitative side, however, are probably of greater interest.

DEWEY CLASS NUMBER

	000	*100*	*200*	*300*	*400*	*500*	*600*	*700*	*800*	*900*
Group 1	1	0	0	5	0	2	2	1	0	0
Group 2	0	0	1	3	0	1	4	5	4	2
Group 3	0	1	1	2	0	1	2	3	14	0
Group 4	0	0	0	6	0	1	1	4	12	0
TOTAL	1	1	2	15	0	5	9	13	30	2

Figure 1. Summary of Dewey Decimal Classification numbers for each group.

QUALITATIVE ANALYSIS

On quality, certainly the Wollongong University experiment will provide
important evidence. The results will appear as a measure of the retrieval factors
being studied. However, the actual *values* which determine the degree to which
an item is relevant to a user have not yet been fully identified. Nicholas Rescher,
in his *Introduction to Value Theory*,[5] gives an indication of what such values
may be. The number of variables is somewhat staggering.

Therefore, in this case, I propose to concentrate on what PRECIS offers
that is not offered anywhere else. All examples in Standard Format will be eliminated, not because they are just like KWIC indexing in using the method of rotation, nor because they use approximately the same terms as subject headings
in a goodly number of cases, but because, in order to show where PRECIS is different, I would like to assume that the methodology and terminology are *constants* which the Standard Format in PRECIS shares with the other systems.

CASES

The Inverted Format in PRECIS has been represented only by three examples. In no case, was the operator (6), which calls for this format, tagged for use
as a headword, in the Lead, so there is no actual inversion. In one case, where
operator (4), viewpoint-as-form, might have been used under different circumstances, an example is made to show what the PRECIS entry would be like.

The other seven examples demonstrate some, but by no means all, of the
unique features of this form of indexing. They are given herewith, with the format of the strings which produced them. The features include operator (3), sub-
stitutions, the special (1) (2) (1) grouping that produces reciprocal entries, and
the (s) operator as role definer, indirect agent and indirect action. The reader
should look at all of the examples carefully, noting where they differ and where
they overlap or reinforce each other. The unique features of PRECIS are in some
instances marked with an arrow, but readers should not have much trouble identifying them. The format of the strings has been checked at *BNB*.

Salajan, Ioanna.   *Zen comics.*

PRECIS string:
       *(1) Cartoons $1 strip $1 humorous $1 American
       (6) collections from individual artists

      (The asterisk in this and following strings indicates that the term is
        wanted in the lead.)

PRECIS: **Cartoons**
       American humorous strip cartoons—*Collections from individual
        artists*

       Strip cartoons
       American humorous strip cartoons—*Collections from individual
        artists*

Humorous cartoons
American humorous strip cartoons—*Collections from individual artists*

American cartoons
American humorous strip cartoons—*Collections from individual artists*

LCSH: ——

KWIC: ——

Ferry, Anne Davidson.   *All in good time: love poetry of Shakespeare, Donne, Johnson, Marvell.*

PRECIS string:
     *(1) poetry in English $d 1558-1702
     (p) special subjects
     *(q) love
     (6) critical studies

PRECIS: **Poetry in English**
     1558-1702. Special subjects: Love — *Critical studies*

     Love. Special subjects. Poetry in English, *1558-1702* ←— *Location*
     — *Critical studies*   *of date*

LCSH: Love poetry, English — History and criticism

       English poetry — Early modern, 1500-1700 — History and criticism

KWIC: love poetry of   Donne, Johnson, Marvell. All in g
         poetry of   Johnson, Marvell. All in good time
        Marvell. All in   love poetry of Shakespeare. Donne
        Shakespeare, Donne   Marvell. All in good time: love poe
        All in good time;   poetry of Shakespeare, Donne, Joh
        good time; love   Shakespeare, Donne, Johnson, Mar

Merkl, Peter Hans   *Political violence under the Swastika: 581 early Nazis.*

PRECIS string:
     *(0) Germany
     *(1) political parties
   (sub 2) (1)
     *(q) Nationalsozialistische Deutsche Arbeiter Partei
     *(2) membership
     *(2)
     *(3) psychosocial aspects
     *(6) case studies

PRECIS: **Germany**
Political parties. Nationalsozialistische Deutsche Arbeiter Partei.
Membership. Psychosocial aspects—*Case studies*

Political Parties. Germany
Nationalsozialistische Deutsche Arbeiter Partei. Membership.
Psychosocial aspects—*Case Studies*

Nationalsozialistische Deutsche Arbeiter Partei.
Membership. Psychosocial aspects—*Case studies*

Membership. Nationalsozialistische Deutsche
Arbeiter Partei
Psychosocial aspects—*Case studies*

Psychosocial aspects. Membership. Nationalsozialistische Deutsche Arbeiter Partei
—*Case studies*

*"Germany.
Political
parties"
blanked out*

LCSH: Nationalsozialistische Deutsche Arbeiter Partei—History
National socialism—Biography
Germany—Politics and government—1918-1933

KWIC:
Political violence under the Swasti
Swastika. Political violence under
violence under the Swastika. Politi

Allen, Edward Henry. *Handbook of energy policy for local governments.*

PRECIS string:
  (0) United States
*(1) energy resources
*(2) management $v by $w of
*(3) local authorities
  (6) manuals

PRECIS: **Energy Resources.** United States
Management by local authorities—*Manuals*

Management. Energy resources. United States
By local authorities—*Manuals*

Local authorities. United States
Management of energy resources—*Manuals*

*Rearrangement
when agent is
lead term*

LCSH: Energy policy—United States—Handbooks, manuals, etc.

KWIC: Handbook of   energy policy for local government
  policy for local   governments. Handbook of energy
  governments.   Handbook of energy policy for loc
  policy for   local governments. Handbook of e
  of energy   policy for local governments. Hand

Ghez, Gilbert R. *The allocation of time and goods over the life cycle.*

PRECIS string:
        *(1) families
        *(p) resources
        *(2) allocation
    (sub 3) (2) allocation of family resources
        *(2) decision making
         (2)
        *(3) life cycle factors

PRECIS: **Families**
      Resources. Allocation. Decision making. Life cycle factors

      Resources. Families
      Allocation. Decision making. Life cycle factors

      Allocation. Resources. Families
      Decision making. Life cycle factors

      Decision making. Allocation of family resources
        Life cycle factors

      Life cycle factors. Decision making. Allocation of
        family resources

                                                              Substitute phrase

LCSH: Consumers—Mathematical models

        Consumption(Economics)—Mathematical models

KWIC: life cycle. The   allocation of time and goods over
          over the life   cycle. The allocation of time and g
          of time and   goods over the life cycle. The alloc
          goods over the   life cycle. The allocation of time a
          allocation of   time and goods over the life cycle.

Luza, Radomir. *Austro-German relations in the Anschluss era.*

PRECIS string:†
        *(1) Austria
        *(2) foreign relations $v with $w with
        *(1) Germany $d 1918-1945

---

†For a *classified* catalog, such as *BNB*, two strings are required, viz.:

  *(1) Austria   *(1) Germany
  *(2) foreign relations $v with   *(2) foreign relations $v with
   (3) Germany $d 1918-1945   (3) Austria $d 1918-1945

Note the change in the third term (to agent). The documents are thus classed simultaneously under each country, but in the two classes required.

PRECIS: **Austria**
      Foreign relations with Germany, *1918-1945*

    Foreign relations. Austria
      With Germany, *1918-1945*   *Full*

    Foreign relations. Germany   *reciprocal*
      With Austria, *1918-1945*   *relationships*
                                      indicated

    Germany
      Foreign relations with Austria, *1918-1945*

LCSH: Austria—History—1938-1945

       Anschluss movement—1918-1938

       Austria—Politics and government—1918-1938

       Nationalism—Germany

       Schirach, Baldur von, 1907-

KWIC: Anschluss era. Austro-German rela
                             Austro-German relations in the An
                             relations in the Anschluss era. Aus

Anderson, Irvine H.   *The Standard-Vacuum Oil Company and United States East Asian Policy, 1933-1941.*

PRECIS string:
      *(1) United States
       (2) foreign relations $v with $w with
      *(1) Far East
    (sub 3) (2) foreign relations between Far East & United States
       (s) role $v of the $w in
      *(3) Standard-Vacuum Oil Company $d 1933-1941

PRECIS: **United States**
    Foreign relations with Far East. Role of the
      Standard-Vacuum Oil Company, *1933-1941*

    Far East   *Reciprocal*
    Foreign relations with United States. Role of   *relationships*
      the Standard-Vacuum Oil Company.
      1933-1941

    Standard-Vacuum Oil Company   *Agent as*
    Role in foreign relations between Far East and   *lead term,*
      United States, *1933-1941*   *substitution*

LCSH: Standard-Vacuum Oil Company

          Corporations, Foreign—Indonesia

          United States—Foreign relations

KWIC: United States East   Asian Policy. Standard-Vacuum Oi
          and United States   East Asian Policy. Standard-Vacuu
          Standard-Vacuum   Oil Company and United States Ea
          States East Asian   Policy. Standard-Vacuum Oil Com
          Asian Policy.   Standard-Vacuum Oil Company an

Fisher, Louis. *Presidential spending power.*

PRECIS string:
          *(1) United States
          *(2) government
          *(2) budgeting
     (sub 2) (2) government budgeting
          (2) control $v by $w of
          *(3) presidency $d 1789-1975

PRECIS: **United States**
          Government. Budgeting. Control by presidency, *1789-1975*

          Government. United States
          Budgeting. Control by presidency, *1789-1975*

          Budgeting. Government. United States
          Control by presidency, *1789-1975*

          Presidency. United States   ⟵——— *Agent as lead term*
          Control of government budgeting   ⟵——— *role defined*
             1789-1975

LCSH: United States—Appropriations and expenditures

          Budget—United States

          Finance, Public—United States

KWIC: power. Presidential spending
                                       Presidential spending power
                                       spending power. Presidential

Esslinger, Dean Robert.   *Immigrants and the city; ethnicity and mobility in a*
nineteenth-century midwestern community.

PRECIS strings:

    (x)(1)* Indiana
    (y)(p)* South Bend
    (y)(2)* urbanization
    (y)(2)   effects of migration of European immigrants $d ca 1850—ca
             1880

    (x)(0)   Indiana
    (y)(p)   South Bend
    (y)(1)* immigrants $i European
    (y)(2)* migration
    (y)(2)   effects on urbanization $d ca 1850—ca 1880

PRECIS: **Indiana**
          South Bend. Urbanization. Effects of migration of European immi-
              grants, ca 1850—ca 1880

          South Bend. Indiana
          Urbanization. Effects of migration of European immigrants, ca
              1850—ca 1880

          Urbanization. South Bend. Indiana
          Effects of migration of European immigrants, ca 1850—ca 1880

          Migration. European immigrants. South Bend. Indiana
          Effects on urbanization, ca 1850—ca 1880

          Immigrants. South Bend. Indiana
          European immigrants. Migration. Effects on urbanization, ca 1850—
              ca 1880

          European immigrants. South Bend. Indiana
          Migration. Effects on urbanization, ca 1850—ca 1880

LCSH: South Bend, Indiana—Foreign population

          Urbanization—South Bend, Indiana

          Social mobility—South Bend, Indiana

KWIC: century midwestern community.   city: ethnicity and mobility in a 19
          ethnicity and mobility in a   community. Immigrants and the ci
          community. Immigrants and the   ethnicity and mobility in a 19th ce
          mobility in a 19th century   Immigrants and the city: ethnicity
          city: ethnicity and mobility   midwestern community. Immigran
          community. Immigrants and the   mobility in a 19th century midwes
          Immigrants and the city: 19th century midwestern commun

CONCLUSION

For my qualitative analysis, I made no attempt to compare PRECIS index entries with either the *terminology* of LCSH or book titles, or with *rotational manipulation of terms* in titles in the KWIC procedure. Assuming arbitrarily that terminology and rotation were constants, I then removed all PRECIS indexing made with the Standard Format (20 items) and all but three samples of potentially Inverted Format (31 items). With the remaining nine examples from my group of sixty, I concentrated on the refinements associated with the Predicate Transformation Format induced by operator (3), the (1) (2) (1) sequence, the role definer operator (s) and a few other unique features which allow PRECIS to make the most elegant use of its context-dependency basis. The indexing produced in these operations cannot be duplicated in either LCSH or by Keyword-in-Context methodology or even with both used together. Therefore, on this basis alone, I believe that the second part of my hypothesis—that PRECIS is a qualitative improvement—has been demonstrated.

The question may be raised that nine cases out of sixty—equivalent to 15% or 150 per thousand—are not a tremendous advance. One must remember, however, that aside from differences in the terminology used to convey concepts, which may be as much a matter of taste as of customary usage, the two greatest problems in all indexing are ambiguity and semantic confusion occasioned by inadequate context accompanying terms of dubious ancestry. These terms include homonyms, homographs, metaphor, allusion, neologisms and, of course, public words with private meanings. Lack of context in subject headings and the general unwillingness to add clarifying terms to titles in the various processes of indexing by title ensure the continuation of both problems. PRECIS stops them dead in their tracks.

NOTES

1. Rowena Swanson, "Design and Evaluation of Information Systems," *Annual Review of Information Science and Technology* (Washington, DC: American Society for Information Science, 1975), v. 10, pp. 43-101; idem, "Performing Evaluation Studies in Information Science," *Journal of the American Society for Information Science*, v. 26 (May-June 1975), pp. 140-156.
2. *British National Bibliography*, no. 1357 (December 31, 1975), B75-30801-B75-31449.
3. Ibid., p. 72 of the Subject Index.
4. The University of Bath Comparative Catalogue Study—as reported to Philip Bryant, *Catalogue & Index*, no. 41 (Summer 1976), pp. 6-8—indicated that its experimental KWOC catalog was rather well received and further experimentation will be carried out with this and similar formats. "It was developed quite deliberately as an enhanced Title catalogue as it was felt that, used purely as a subject catalogue, a derived KWOC listing could be highly misleading." It could, however, be used for a "supplementary subject approach." The examples comparing PRECIS, LCSH and KWIC entries for the

same title also would support the view that these supplement rather than supplant each other. The problem comes with the notion that one and only one should be sufficient. A smaller study made at the Liverpool Polytechnic Department of Library and Information Studies has been reported by K. G. B. Bakewell, "The PRECIS Indexing System," *The Indexer*, v. 9, no. 4 (October 1975), pp. 160-166. The need for feedback from user to indexer was suggested by the study's results.

5. Nicholas Rescher, *Introduction to Value Theory* (Englewood Cliffs, NJ: Prentice-Hall, 1969).

APPENDIX

Contents of Groups 1 to 4 summarized in text.

Group 1

Cases where there are more LCSH than PRECIS entries

Author or title	LCSH	PRECIS	Difference	DC Class number
1. Antigens	2	1	1	574
2. Drug abuse	3	2	1	362
3. Gibbs	3	2	1	016
4. Luza	5	4	1	327
5. McCall's	2	1	1	745
6. Matras	3	1	2	301
7. Natural history	3	1	2	616
8. Rey	2	1	1	523
9. Turner	4	2	2	323
10. Women's liberation	2	1	1	301
11. Leboyer	2	1	1	618
	31	17	14	

Number of works by DC main class

5	300
2	500
2	600
1	700

(No literary works)

1. *The Antigens*

PRECIS: **Antigens**

LCSH: Antigens and antibodies

       Immunochemistry

KWIC: Antigens

2. *Drug abuse control: administration and politics*

PRECIS: **Drug abuse.** United States
        Social control

       Social control. Drug abuse. United States

LCSH: Drug abuse—United States—Addresses, essays, lectures

      Drug abuse—Treatment—United States—Addresses, essays, lectures

      Narcotic laws—United States—Addresses, essays, lectures

KWIC: | politics. Drug | abuse control: administration and |
control:	administration and politics. Drug a
politics.	Drug abuse control: administration
and politics.	politics. Drug abuse control: admi

3. Gibbs, Donald A.   *A bibliography of studies and translations of modern Chinese literature, 1918-1942.*

PRECIS: **Chinese literature**
      1912— Translations into English language—*Bibliographies*
      1912— Western criticism—*Bibliographies*

LCSH: Chinese literature—20th century—History and criticism—Bibliography

      Chinese literature—Translations into English—Bibliography

      English literature—Translations from Chinese—Bibliography

KWIC: | modern Chinese | bibliography of studies and transla |
of studies and	Chinese literature, 1918-1942. A b
studies and	literature, 1918-1942. A bibliograp
studies and	modern Chinese literature. A bibli
literature	studies and translations of modern
1918-1942.	translations of modern Chinese lite

4. Leboyer, Frederick.   *Birth without violence.*

PRECIS: **Childbirth**

LCSH: Childbirth

      Childbirth—Psychology

KWIC: | | Birth without violence |
| | violence. Birth without |

5. Luza, Radomir. *Austro-German relations in the Anschluss era.*

PRECIS: **Austria**
    Foreign relations with Germany, *1918-1945*

    Foreign relations. Austria
    With Germany, *1918-1945*

    Foreign relations. Germany
    With Austria, *1918-1945*

    Germany
    Foreign relations with Austria, *1918-1945*

LCSH: Austria—History—1938-1945

    Anschluss movement—1918-1938

    Austria—Politics and government—1918-1938

    Nationalism—Germany

    Schirach, Baldur von, 1907-

KWIC: Germany in   Anschluss era. Austro-German rela
                                        Austro-German relations in the An
                                        relations in the Anschluss era. Aus

6. *McCall's Golden do-it book*

PRECIS: **Handicrafts**
    —Manuals—Juvenile literature

LCSH: Handicraft

    Art—Study and teaching

KWIC: book. McCall's Golden do-it
                                      do-it book. McCall's Golden
                                      Golden do-it book. McCall's
                                      McCall's Golden do-it book

7. Matras, Joseph. *Social inequality, stratification and mobility.*

PRECIS: **Social classes.** United States

LCSH: Social classes

    Equality

    Social mobility

| KWIC: | Social
and
mobility.
inequality | inequality, stratification and mobil
mobility. Social inequality, stratifi
Social inequality, stratification and
stratification and mobility. Social |

8. *The natural history of rabies*

PRECIS: **Rabies.** Man

LCSH: Rabies

       Rabies—History

       Rabies virus

| KWIC: | | history of rabies. Natural
Natural history of rabies
rabies. Natural history of |

9. Rey, Hans Augusto.   *The stars: a new way to see them.*

PRECIS: **Constellations**

LCSH: Constellations

       Stars

KWIC: ——

10. Turner, Robert Phillip.   *Up to the front of the line: Blacks in the American political system.*

PRECIS: **Negroes.** United States
         Political aspects

         Political aspects. Negroes. United States

LCSH: Negroes—Politics and suffrage

       Negroes—Civil rights

       Negroes—History

       Slavery in the United States

| KWIC: | the line: Blacks
front of the line
Blacks in the
the American | American political system. Up to t
Blacks in the American political sy
political system. Up to the front of
system. Up to the front of the line |

11. *Women's liberation in the twentieth century*

PRECIS: **Feminism.** United States
     1898-1972—Readings from contemporary sources

(could also have used:

Women. United States
     Role in society, *1898-1972*

because the same kind of entry is found under "Great Britain.")

LCSH: Feminism—United States—Addresses, essays, lectures

United States—Social conditions—Addresses, essays, lectures

KWIC:

twentieth	century. Women's liberation in the
Women's	liberation in the twentieth century
in the	twentieth century. Women's libera
century.	Women's liberation in the twentiet

Group 2

Cases where LSCH and PRECIS entries are equal

Author or title	PRECIS	LCSH	Difference	DC class number
1. Anderson	3	3	0	327
2. Best	1	1	0	823
3. Current dermatologic	2	2	0	616
4. Evans	1	1	0	797
5. Fox	2	2	0	621
6. Ferry	2	2	0	821
7. Fluid	3	3	0	612
8. Gallion	1	1	0	711
9. Goldwasser	1	1	0	951
10. Kane	2	2	0	770
11. Kanury	1	1	0	541
12. Kurtz	1	1	0	930
13. Paz	1	1	0	809
14. Penfield	2	2	0	612
15. St. Erkenwald	1	1	0	821
16. Smith	3	3	0	770
17. al-Suhrawardi	1	1	0	297
18. Theories	1	1	0	301
19. [Michals] *	2	2	0	770
	31	31		

*Deleted except for counting purposes

Number of works by DC main classes

1	200
2	300
1	500
4	600
5	700
4	800 (literary works)
2	900

Ratio of nonliterary to literary works is 15:4

1. Anderson, Irvine H.   *The Standard-Vacuum Oil Company and United States East Asian Policy, 1933-1941.*

PRECIS: **United States**
  Foreign relations with Far East. Role of the Standard-Vacuum Oil Company, *1933-1941*

  Far East
  Foreign relations with United States. Role of the Standard-Vacuum Oil Company, *1933-1941*

  Standard-Vacuum Oil Company
  Role in foreign relations between Far East & United States, *1933-1941*

LCSH: Standard-Vacuum Oil Company

  Corporations, Foreign—Indonesia

  United States—Foreign relations

KWIC: United States East   Asian Policy. Standard-Vacuum Oi
  and United States   East Asian Policy. Standard-Vacuu
  Standard-Vacuum   Oil Company and United States Ea
  States East Asian   Policy. Standard-Vacuum Oil Com
  Asian Policy.   Standard-Vacuum Oil Company an

2. *The best American short stories**

PRECIS: **Short stories in English**
  1900-   —Texts

LCSH: Short stories—American

---

*LC entered under Foley, Martha, ed.

KWIC: American short stories. Best
                                               Best American short stories
                                               Short stories. Best American
                                               Stories. Best American short

3. *Current dermatologic management*

PRECIS: **Integumentary system.** Man
             Therapy—*Reviews of research*

         Therapy. Integumentary system. Man
             —*Reviews of research*

LCSH: Skin—Diseases

         Skin diseases—Therapy

KWIC: Current dermatologic management
                                               Dermatologic management. Curren
                                               Management. Current dermatologi

4. Evans, George Heberton.   *Canoeing the wilderness.*

PRECIS: **Canoeing**
             —*Manuals*

LCSH: Canoes and canoeing

KWIC: Canoeing wilderness waters.
                                               Waters. Canoeing wilderness
                                               Wilderness waters. Canoeing

5. Fox, Robert W. *Practical triac-SCR projects for the experimenter.*

PRECIS: **Electronic equipment**
             Thyristor circuits

         Thyristor circuits. Electronic equipment

LCSH: Thyristors

         Transistor circuits

KWIC: for the   experimenter. Practical triac-SCR
         experimenter.   Practical triac-SCR projects for the
         triac-SCR   projects for the experimenter. Prac
         Practical   triac-SCR projects for the experim

6. Ferry, Anne Davidson.   *All in good time; love poetry of Shakespeare, Donne, Johnson, Marvell.*

PRECIS: **Poetry in English**
      1558-1702. Special subjects: Love—*Critical studies*

   Love. Special subjects. Poetry in English. *1558-1702—Critical studies*

LCSH: Love poetry, English — History and criticism

   English poetry — Early modern, 1500-1700—History and criticism

KWIC: love poetry of   Donne, Johnson, Marvell. All in go
         poetry of   Johnson, Marvell. All in good time
         Marvell. All in   love poetry of Shakespeare, Donne
         Shakespeare, Donne   Marvell. All in good time; love poe
         All in good time;   poetry of Shakespeare, Donne, Joh
         good time; love   Shakespeare, Donne, Johnson, Ma

7. *Fluid environment of the brain*

PRECIS: **Brain.** Man
      Cerebral fluids. Physiology—*Conference proceedings*

   Cerebral fluids. Man
      Physiology—*Conference proceedings*

   Physiology. Cerebral fluids. Man
      —*Conference proceedings*

LCSH: Brain — Congresses

   Cerebrospinal fluid —Congresses

   Choroid plexus—Congresses

(NLM substitutes "Blood-brain barrier" for the first LCSH heading.)

KWIC: brain. Fluid environment of the
                                 environment of the brain. Fluid
                                 fluid environment of the brain.

8. Gallion, Arthur B. *The urban pattern: city planning and design.*

PRECIS: **Town planning**
      to 1974

LCSH: Cities and towns—Planning

KWIC: pattern: city planning and design. The urba
         and   design. The urban pattern: city pla
         urban   pattern: city planning and design.
         city   planning and design. The urban pa
         The   urban pattern: city planning and d

9. Goldwasser, Janet. *Huan-ying: workers' China.*

PRECIS: **China**
         Social life—*Personal observations*

LCSH: China—Description and travel—1949-

KWIC: China. Huan-ying: workers'
                                           workers' China. Huan-ying

10. Kane, Art. *The persuasive image.**

PRECIS: **Photography**
         Kane, Art—*Critical studies*

         Kane, Art. Photography
         —*Critical studies*

LCSH: Photography, Artistic

         Kane, Art

KWIC: image. The persuasive
                                           persuasive image. The

11. Kanury, Anjaneya Murty.   *Introduction to combustion phenomena: (for
                                   fire, incineration, pollution and energy
                                   applications)*

PRECIS: **Combustion**

LCSH: Combustion

KWIC: Introduction to   combustion phenomena.
         to combustion   phenomena. Introduction

———————————
*LC enters under John Poppy, who wrote the text.

12. Kurtz, Seymour.   *The world guide to antiquities.*

PRECIS: **Antiquities**
           —*Encyclopedias*

LCSH: Antiquities—Dictionaries

KWIC: antiquities. The world guide to
                                                   guide to antiquities. The world
                                                   world guide to antiquities. The

13. Paz, Octavio.   *Children of the Mire: modern poetry from Romanticism to
                      the avant-garde.*

PRECIS: **Poetry**
           ca 1900—ca 1970—Critical studies

LCSH: Poetry, Modern—History and criticism

KWIC: poetry from   avant-garde. Children of the Mire:
         garde. Children of   modern poetry from Romanticism
         Children of the   poetry from Romanticism to the a
         the Mire: modern   Romanticism to the avant-garde. C

14. Penfield, Wilder.   *The mystery of the mind: a critical study of conscious-
                          ness and the human brain.*

PRECIS: **Mind**
           Neurophysiological aspects

         Neurophysiological aspects. Mind

LCSH: Brain

         Consciousness

KWIC: of consciousness and the   brain. Mystery of the mind: a criti
         of the mind: a critical   consciousness and the human brai
         brain. Mystery of the   critical study of consciousness and
         study of consciousness   human brain. Mystery of the mind
         the human brain. Mystery   mind: a critical study of conscious
         consciousness and the   mystery of the mind: a critical stu
         Mystery of the mind: study of consciousness and the hu

15. St. Erkenwald

PRECIS: **Poetry in English**
        1066-1400—Texts

LCSH: Erkenwald, Saint, Bp. of London, d.693—Legends

KWIC: Erkenwald, Saint
                                               Saint Erkenwald

16. Smith, John Frederick.   *Photographing women**

PRECIS: **Photography**
        Special subjects: Women. Smith, John Frederick—*Critical studies*

        Women. Special subjects. Photography
        Smith, John Frederick—*Critical studies*

        Smith, John Frederick. Women. Special subjects. Photography
        —*Critical studies*

LCSH: Photography of women

         Photography, Erotic

         Smith, John Frederick

KWIC: Photographing women.
                                          women. Photographing

17. al-Suhrawardi, Abu al-Najib.   *A Sufi rule for novices.*

PRECIS: **Sufi life**
        —*Early works*

LCSH: Sufism—Early works to 1800

KWIC: novices. A Sufi rule for
                                          rule for novices. A Sufi
                                          Sufi rule for novices. A

---

*American title: *Photographing sensuality.* Entered under text author: Sean Callahan)

18. *Theories of group processes*

PRECIS: **Group dynamics**
         Theories

LCSH: Group relations training—Addresses, essays, lectures

KWIC: group processes. Theories of
processes. Theories of group
Theories of group processes

Group 3

Cases where PRECIS entries exceed LCSH by 1

Author or title	LCSH	PRECIS	Difference	DC class number
1. Brock	1	0	1	823
2. Clinic	2	1	1	362
3. Devlin	2	1	1	581
4. Evers	3	2	1	759
5. Feydeaux	1	0	1	842
6. Gippius	2	1	1	891
7. Laurence	1	0	1	822
8. Louise	2	1	1	641
9. Nabokov	1	0	1	891
10. Ornstein	2	1	1	153
11. Orr	2	1	1	746
12. Parish	1	0	1	823
13. Principles	2	1	1	617
14. Weiler	3	2	1	232
15. World	2	1	1	810
16. Fisher	4	3	1	353
17. Zimmerman	5	4	1	770
18. [Cleary] *	1	0	1	823
19. [Hintze] *	1	0	1	823
20. [McCollough] *	1	0	1	823
21. [Rhodes] *	1	0	1	823
22. [Wilcox] *	1	0	1	823
23. [Wolitze] *	1	0	1	823
24. [Mitchell] *	1	0	1	823
	43	19	24	

*Deleted except for counting purposes.

Number of works by DC main classes

1	100
1	200
2	300
1	500
2	600
3	700
14	800 (literary works)

Ratio of nonliterary to literary works is 10:14

1. Brock, Rose. *Tarn house.*

PRECIS: **Fiction in English**
       1900-   —Texts

LCSH: ——

KWIC: ——

2. *The clinic and information flow: educating the family planning client in four Latin American countries*

PRECIS: **Latin America**
       Family planning services—*Reports, surveys*

       Family planning services, Latin America
       —*Reports, surveys*

LCSH: Family planning—Latin America

KWIC: clinic and information flow. The
                          flow. The clinic and information
                          information flow. The clinic and

3. Devlin, Robert. *Plant physiology*

PRECIS: **Plants**
       Physiology

       Physiology. Plants

LCSH: Plant physiology

KWIC: Physiology. Plant
                          Plant physiology.

4. Evers, Carl G. *The marine paintings of Carl G. Evers.*

PRECIS: **Paintings**
     American marine paintings. Evers, Carl G.—*Illustrations*

     American paintings
     American marine paintings. Evers, Carl G.—*Illustrations*

     Evers, Carl G. American marine paintings
     —*Illustrations*

LCSH: Evers, Carl G.

         Ships in art

KWIC: Carl G.   Evers. the marine paintings of
           The   marine paintings of Carl G. Evers.
           marine   paintings of Carl G. Evers. The

5. Feydeau, Georges. *A flea in her ear: a farce-comedy in three acts.*

PRECIS: **Drama in French**
     1848-1900—English texts

LCSH: ——

KWIC: ——

6. Gippius, Zinaida Nikolaevna. *Between Paris and St. Petersburg: selected diaries of Zinaida Gippius.*

PRECIS: **Poetry in Russian**
     Gippius, Zinaida Nikolaevna—*Diaries*

     Gippius, Zinaida Nikolaevna. Poetry in Russian
     —*Diaries*

LCSH: Gippius, Zinaida Nikolaevna, 1869-1945—Diaries

KWIC: ——

7. Laurence, Charles. *My fat friend: a comedy in 2 acts.*

PRECIS: **Drama in English**
     1945-   —Texts

LCSH: ——

KWIC: ——

8. Louise, Mattie.   *Meatless recipes.*

PRECIS: **Vegetarians**
         Food—*Recipes*

         Food. Vegetarians
         —*Recipes*

LCSH: Vegetarianism

KWIC: Meatless recipes.
                                               recipes. Meatless

9. Nabokov, Vladimir.   *Tyrants destroyed, and other stories.*

PRECIS: **Fiction in Russian**
         1917-   *—Texts (including translations)*

LCSH: ——

KWIC: ——

10. Ornstein, Robert Evans.   *The psychology of consciousness.*

PRECIS: **Consciousness**
         Psychological aspects

         Psychological aspects. Consciousness

LCSH: Consciousness

KWIC: consciousness. Psychology of
                                               Psychology of consciousness.

11. Orr, Jan. *Now needlepoint: a joyous approach to creative designing.*

PRECIS: **Embroidery**
         Needlepoint—*Manuals*

         Needlepoint. Embroidery
         —*Manuals*

LCSH: Canvas embroidery

KWIC: a joyous   approach to creative designing. No
         approach to   creative designing. Now needlepoin
         to creative   designing. Now needlepoint: a joyo

12. Parish, Peggy. *Too many rabbits.*

PRECIS: **Children's stories in English**
        1900-   —Texts

LCSH: ——

KWIC: ——

13. *Principles and practice of operative dentistry.*

PRECIS: **Dentistry**
        Surgery

        Surgery. Dentistry

LCSH: Dentistry, Operative

KWIC: operative   dentistry. Principles and practice o
        practice of   operative dentistry. Principles and
        Principles and   practice of operative dentistry.
        dentistry.   Principles and practice of operative

14. Weiler, Eugen. *Jesus, son of God: encounter and confession of faith.* *

PRECIS: **Christ**
        Names: son of man

        Names: Christ
        Son of man

        Son of man. Names. Christ

LCSH: Jesus Christ—Person and offices

       Christian life—1960-

KWIC: God: encounter and   confession of faith. Jesus, son of
        Jesus, son of God: encounter and confession of faith.
        and confession of   faith. Jesus, son of God: encounter
        faith. Jesus, son of   God: encounter and confession of
        confession of faith.   Jesus, son of God: encounter and

---

*LC entered under Lessing, Erich—photographer.

15. *The world turned upside down: prose and poetry of the American Revolution.*

PRECIS: **English literature**
American writers, *1607-1830—Anthologies*

American writers. English literature
1607-1830—Anthologies

LCSH: American literature—Revolutionary period, 1775-1783

KWIC: poetry of the
Prose and
Revolution.
American

American Revolution. Prose and
poetry of the American Revolution
Prose and poetry of the American
Revolution. Prose and poetry of th

16. Fisher, Louis. *Presidential spending power.*

PRECIS: **United States**
Government. Budgeting. Control by presidency, *1789-1975*

Government. United States
Budgeting. Control by presidency, *1789-1975*

Budgeting. Government. United States
Control by presidency, *1789-1975*

Presidency. United States
Control of government budgeting, *1789-1975*

LCSH: United States—Appropriations and expenditures

Budget—United States

Finance, Public—United States

KWIC:

power. Presidential spending
Presidential spending power
spending power. Presidential

17. Zimmerman, John. *Photographing sport.**

PRECIS: **American photography**
Special subjects: Sports. Kauffman, Mark, Leifer, Neil & Zimmerman, John—*Critical studies*

Sports. Special subjects. American photography
Kauffman, Mark, Leifer, Neil & Zimmerman, John—*Critical studies*

---

*LC enters under Sean Callahan who wrote text.

Kauffman, Mark. Sports. Special subjects. American photography
Kauffman, Mark, Leifer, Neil & Zimmerman, John—*Critical studies*

Leifer, Neil. Sports. Special subjects. American photography
Kauffman, Mark, Leifer, Neil & Zimmerman, John—*Critical studies*

Zimmerman, John. Sports. Special subjects. American photography
Kauffman, Mark, Leifer, Neil & Zimmerman, John—*Critical studies*

LCSH: Photography of sports

Zimmerman, John

Kauffman, Mark

Leifer, Neil

KWIC: Photographing sport.
sport. Photographing

Group 4

Cases where there are 2-5 more PRECIS entries than LCSH

Author or title	PRECIS	LCSH	Difference	DC Class number
1. Allen	3	1	2	352
2. Barris	6	1	5	791
3. Barron	3	1	2	327
4. Benchley	4	1	3	791
5. Cooper	4	1	3	629
6. Current topics	7	2	5	574
7. [Edwards] *	4	1	3	791
8. Eshleman	2	0	2	811
9. Esslinger	6	3	3	301
10. Freeman	2	0	2	812
11. Ghez	5	2	3	329
12. Goldstein	4	1	3	345
13. [Gottlieb] *	2	0	2	812
14. [O'Morrison] *	2	0	2	812
15. [O'Neill] *	2	0	2	812
16. [Sawyer] *	2	0	1	812
17. [Sheiness] *	2	0	2	812
18. [Spitzer] *	2	0	2	812
19. [Tasca] *	2	0	2	812
20. [Terry] *	2	0	2	812
21. [Weller] *	2	0	2	812
22. Salajan	4	0	4	741
23. Stewart	3	1	2	818
24. Merkl	5	3	2	329
	80	18	62	

*Deleted except for counting purposes

Number of works by DC main class

6	300
1	500
1	600
4	700
12	800 (literary works)

Ratio of nonliterary to literary works is 12:24 = 1:2

1. Allen, Edward Henry.   *Handbook of energy policy for local governments.*

PRECIS: **Energy resources.** United States
    Management by local authorities—*Manuals*

    Management. Energy resources. United States
      By local authorities—*Manuals*

    Local authorities. United States
      Management of energy resources—*Manuals*

LCSH: Energy policy—United States—Handbooks, manuals, etc.

KWIC:
Handbook of	energy policy for local government
policy for local	governments. Handbook of energy
governments.	Handbook of energy policy for loc
policy for	local governments. Handbook of e
of energy	policy for local governments. Hand

2. Barris, Alex.   *Hollywood's other men.*

PRECIS: **California**
    Los Angeles. Hollywood. Cinema films. Acting. Male supporting actors, *1937—ca 1970*

    Los Angeles. California
      Hollywood. Cinema films. Acting. Male supporting actors, *1937—ca 1970*

    Hollywood. Los Angeles. California
      Cinema films. Acting. Male supporting actors, *1937—ca 1970*

    Cinema films. Hollywood. Los Angeles. California
      Acting. Male supporting actors, *1937—ca 1970*

    Acting. Cinema films. Hollywood. California
      Male supporting actors, *1937—ca 1970*

    Male actors. Acting. Cinema films. Hollywood. Los Angeles. California
      Male supporting actors, *1937—ca 1970*

LCSH: Moving-picture actors and actresses.

KWIC:
Hollywood's other men.
men. Hollywood's other
other men. Hollywood's

3. Barron, John. *KGB: the work of Soviet secret agents.*

PRECIS: **Soviet Union**
      Secret services: Komitet Gosudarstvennoĭ Bezopasnosti, *to 1973*

      Secret services. Soviet Union
      Komitet Gosudarstvennoĭ Bezopasnosti, to *1973*

      Komitet Gosudarstvennoĭ Bezopasnosti
      to 1973

LCSH: Russia (1923-   ) Komitet Gosudarstvennoĭ Bezopasnosti

KWIC:
                                       agents. KGB: the work of Soviet se
                                       KGB: the work of Soviet secret ag
                                       secret agents. KGB: the work of So
                                       work of Soviet secret agents. KGB:

4. Benchley, Nathaniel. *Humphrey Bogart.*

PRECIS: **American cinema films**
      Acting. Bogart, Humphrey—*Biographies*

      Acting. American cinema films
      Bogart, Humphrey—*Biographies*

      Bogart, Humphrey. Acting. American cinema films
      —*Biographies*

      Cinema films
      American cinema films. Acting. Bogart, Humphrey—*Biographies*

LCSH: Bogart, Humphrey, 1899-1957

KWIC: ——

5. Cooper, Henry S. F. *Moonwreck: 13, the flight that failed.**

PRECIS: **Moon**
      Manned space flight. Apollo 13

      Manned space flight. Moon
      Apollo 13

      Space flight. Moon
      Manned space flight. Apollo 13

---

*American title: Thirteen, the flight that failed.

Apollo 13. Manned space flight. Moon

LCSH: Project Apollo

KWIC: ——

6. *Current topics in membranes and transport.*

PRECIS: **Organisms**
    Cells. Membranes. Pathology

    Cells. Organisms
      Membranes. Pathology

    Membranes. Cells. Organisms
      Pathology

    Pathology. Membranes. Cells. Organisms

    Organisms
      Membranes. Transport phenomena—*Reviews of research*

    Membranes. Organisms
      Transport phenomena—*Reviews of research*

    Transport phenomena. Membranes. Organisms
      —*Reviews of research*

LCSH: Cell membranes—Collected works

      Biological transport—Collected works

KWIC: Current topics in membranes and t
membranes and transport. Current
topics in membranes and transport
transport. Current topics in membr

7. Eshleman, Clayton.   *Portrait of Francis Bacon.*

PRECIS: **Poetry in English**
    American writers, *1945-*   —*Texts*

    American writers. Poetry in English
      1945-   —*Texts*

LCSH: ——

KWIC: ——

8. Esslinger, Dean Robert. *Immigrants and the city: ethnicity and mobility in a nineteenth-century midwestern community.*

PRECIS: **Indiana**
    South Bend. Urbanization. Effects of migration of European immi-grants, *ca 1850—ca 1880*

    South Bend. Indiana
    Urbanization. Effects of migration of European immigrants, *ca 1850—ca 1880*

    Urbanization. South Bend. Indiana
    Effects of migration of European immigrants, *ca 1850—ca 1880*

    Immigrants. South Bend. Indiana
    European immigrants. Migration. Effects on urbanization, *ca 1850—ca 1880*

    European immigrants. South Bend. Indiana
    Migration. Effects on urbanization, *ca 1850—ca 1880*

    Migration. European immigrants. South Bend. Indiana
    Effects on urbanization, *ca 1850—ca 1880*

LCSH: South Bend, Indiana—Foreign population

    Urbanization—South Bend, Indiana

    Social mobility—South Bend, Indiana

KWIC:

century midwestern community	city: ethnicity and mobility in a 19
ethnicity and mobility in a	community. Immigrants and the ci
community. Immigrants and the	ethnicity and mobility in a 19th ce
mobility in a 19th century	Immigrants and the city: ethnicity
city: ethnicity and mobility	midwestern community. Immigran
community. Immigrants and the	mobility in a 19th century midwes
Immigrants and the city:	19th century midwestern commun

9. Freeman, David E. *Creeps: a play in one act.*

PRECIS: **Drama in English**
    American writers, *1945-*   *—Texts*

    American writers. Drama in English
    1945-   *—Texts*

LCSH: ——

KWIC: ——

10. Ghez, Gilbert G.   *The allocation of time and goods over the life cycle.*

PRECIS: **Families**
Resources. Allocation. Decision making. Life cycle factors

Resources. Families
Allocation. Decision making. Life cycle factors

Allocation. Resources. Families
Decision making. Life cycle factors

Decision making. Allocation of family resources
Life cycle factors

Life cycle factors. Decision making. Allocation of family resources

LCSH: Consumers—Mathematical models

Consumption(Economics)—Mathematical models

KWIC: life cycle. The   allocation of time and goods over t
over the life   cycle. The allocation of time and g
of time and   goods over the life cycle. The alloc
goods over the   life cycle. The allocation of time a
allocation of   time and goods over the life cycle.

11. Goldstein, Joseph.   *Criminal law: theory and process.*

PRECIS: **United States**
Criminal law. Justice. Administration

Criminal law. United States
Justice. Administration

Justice. Criminal law. United States
Administration

Administration. Justice. Criminal law. United States

LCSH: Criminal justice, Administration of—United States—Cases

KWIC: Criminal law: theory and process.
law: theory and process. Criminal
process. Criminal law: theory and
theory and process. Criminal law:

13. Merkl, Peter Hans.   *Political violence under the Swastika: 581 early Nazis.*

PRECIS: **Germany**
Political parties. Nationalsozialistische Deutsche Arbeiter Partei.
Membership. Psychosocial aspects—*Case studies*

Political parties. Germany
    Nationalsozialistische Deutsche Arbeiter Partei. Membership.
        Psychosocial aspects—*Case studies*

Nationalsozialistische Deutsche Arbeiter Partei
    Membership. Psychosocial aspects—*Case studies*

Membership. Nationalsozialistische Deutsche Arbeiter Partei
    Psychosocial aspects—*Case studies*

Psychosocial aspects. Membership. Nationalsozialistische Deutsche
    Arbeiter Partei
    —*Case studies*

LCSH: Nationalsozialistische Deutsche Arbeiter Partei—History

       National socialism—Biography

       Germany—Politics and government—1918-1933

KWIC: Political violence under the Swasti
                                   Swastika. Political violence under t
                                   violence under the Swastika. Politi

14. Salajan, Ioanna.   *Zen comics.*

PRECIS: **Cartoons**
        American humorous strip cartoons—*Collections from individual*
           artists

        Strip cartoons
        American humorous strip cartoons—*Collections from individual*
           artists

        Humorous cartoons
        American humorous strip cartoons—*Collections from individual*
           artists

        American cartoons
        American humorous strip cartoons—*Collections from individual*
           artists

LCSH: ——

KWIC: ——

15. Stewart, Donald Ogden. *By a stroke of luck!: an autobiography.*

PRECIS: **English literature**
    American writers. Stewart, Donald Ogden—*Autobiographies*

    American writers. English literature
    Stewart, Donald Ogden—*Autobiographies*

    Stewart, Donald Ogden. American writers. English literature
    —*Autobiographies*

LCSH: Stewart, Donald Ogden, 1894- —Biography

KWIC: ——

PRECIS in a University Library

Valentina de Bruin
University of Toronto Library

The title of this paper might imply that there has been an exciting break-through and that a large Canadian university library has abandoned LC subject headings (LCSH), and is actually using PRECIS. Let me clarify the situation: we are not using PRECIS—yet. What will be examined in this paper is the possibility. Perhaps by this time next year, the words "Use of" will be able to precede the title of another paper.

In this paper, I will attempt to describe the factors influencing acceptance or non-acceptance of PRECIS as they pertain to our institution, and how we are going about creating an atmosphere among staff and other users, which may tip the scales in favour of acceptance.

In our university, the major factor militating against the acceptance of PRECIS, or any other new subject approach for that matter, is the sheer over-whelming size of the collection: over one million titles, all with LC subject headings. When faced with a number of this magnitude, the immediate and understandable reaction is to throw up one's hands, close one's mind, and utter, with feeling, one word: "Impossible!"

Another negative influence is what might be called the "hibernation syndrome". We're comfortable, safe, and cozy in our warm familiar burrow and, baby, it's cold outside. Change is uncomfortable, it takes a lot of effort, and besides, it can be rather messy. It's not fashionable to be thought of as resisting change per se, and I would not describe anyone in our institution thus. However, all too often, reasoning might go something like this: . . . The contemplated change or innovation must be proven to be a "good thing", and must not be too disruptive. Even though we really think and believe that this change actually could be an improvement (if only our special circumstances were different), we're not sure, because we're getting along fine now just as we are, and what's even more important, we and our users are accustomed to things as they are. We can think of many more very good reasons, reasons which will be very difficult to refute, why things should remain as they are. It's all right for people who are just making a fresh start, but we have too much behind us to make this change possible . . .

I wonder, at this point, what happened to all those who had a vested interest in prop planes when jet planes were the innovation on the market? Is

there somewhere some airline with a retrospective inventory of prop planes,
limping along, serving some customers as well as they have become accustomed
to expect, and others not at all? I realize that this is an analogy that invites cries
of "not relevant", but I mean to be simple, and brutal.

A more serious deterrent to the consideration of the application of PRECIS
to all currently-cataloged materials in our case, and at this time, is the economic
reality. We rely to a great extent, as do most large university libraries in North
America, on Library of Congress cataloging, both in print and in machine-
readable form. In our case, we also use National Library of Canada machine-
readable records (CAN/MARC). As long as LC and our national library do not
supply PRECIS strings as well as LC subject headings (as UK MARC does), we
would be faced with additional expense in applying PRECIS strings to records
which come to us with perfectly good LC subject headings. In these times of
budget cuts, we obviously cannot afford to do that. Compounding this state of
affairs is the fact of our participation in the UNICAT/TELECAT network, composed of university and other libraries in Ontario and Quebec, who also supply
only LCSH to their "original" cataloging. The alternative of using LCSH for
material with LC or other copy as available, and applying PRECIS to material
where no copy of any sort is available, is illogical, disorderly, and practically in-
conceivable. A possible approach could be to apply PRECIS to a well-defined,
logically-separable subset of material.

The three major factors, then, against PRECIS in our university library are:
a huge retrospective file, some very real resistance to change, and the favorable
economic aspects of continuing to use LCSH.

What then, are the factors predisposing us to accept PRECIS? I will not go
into the very obvious merits of PRECIS itself, which have been so ably proven
by my fellow seminar participants. Rather, I'd like to start with the word "impossible", which has such a familiar ring to me. It was heard loud and clear and
often, when the decision was made in the Spring of 1975 to close our public
card catalogs on July 1, 1976, and institute a system of COM microform catalogs. Despite impassioned pleas, no postponement of the July 1976 date was
allowed. As it happened, on July 1st the card catalogs were indeed closed, and
the microform alternates were in place shortly thereafter. The period in-between
was marked by the gradual, and difficult task of orienting and educating staff to
the new catalog environment. As a matter of fact, acceptance by most staff of
the radical change did not come about until the microcatalogs were actually
in use. Contrary to expectations, the library did not come apart at the seams,
there were no riots in the streets, and personnel at the catalog information desk
were not attacked. User acceptance was immediate, and much to our surprise,
user remarks on the new catalog environment were almost without exception
complimentary.

I mention the foregoing event because I believe it has brought about a
climate of acceptance of change, and has allayed to some extent the unex-
pressed fear of change. I believe that these factors will have a direct bearing
on the possibility of introducing PRECIS into our system. (Simplistically put,
it's a matter of striking while the iron is hot.)

Other plus factors which augur well for the adoption of PRECIS, at least
to some extent, in our situation, are, in no particular order:

- The bulk of our records are in machine-readable form. We have an integrated MARC data base.

- We have accepted the principle of "normalized" and "non-normalized" name and subject headings. "Normalized" in the case of subject headings refers to *LCSH*, and in the case of names refers to an authoritative form as established in our official catalog, either as used by LC, or, in the case of newly established headings, according to *AACR*. In our microcatalogs, we have interfiled what we call our "old" and "new" catalogs. "Old" is a home-grown cataloging and classification scheme discontinued in 1958, with "non-normalized" names and subjects, e.g. inverted forms of government subdivisions: Labour, Dept. of instead of Dept. of Labour. "New" is strictly according to LC and *AACR*, all "normalized". In the card catalogs, these records were filed in different banks of drawers labelled "old" and "new" classification.

- Growing dissatisfaction among the staff with LC subject access, especially since it is realized that in a machine-readable environment we are tied to subject headings that resist change simply because they were not designed in the first place to be machine-readable and machine-manipulable. (Here I would like to acknowledge our great debt to *LCSH*, which, manifestly, has done a great job through the years. Gratitude, not denigration, is the keyword.)

- PRECIS programs have been written for the computer installation at UTLAS. These were done for the College Bibliocentre, and arrangements can be made for their use.

- Although most of our staff has had little or no exposure to PRECIS, there are some of us who know what it's all about, and are convinced that PRECIS will provide better subject access and that it is a disservice to our users, if, knowing this, we do nothing about it.

What are we doing about either accepting or rejecting PRECIS? As long ago as last winter, a committee was formed to look into PRECIS as a means of providing subject access to uncataloged theses and technical reports. Of necessity (because of the tremendous amount of work associated with the initial production of the microcatalogs) this committee became dormant after meeting twice, once to hear a lucid and convincing presentation on PRECIS by C. D. Robinson. It is now time to revive this committee. We know that it is folly to expend time and money on developing machine-readable subject authority files for *LCSH*, which was never designed for machine-manipulation. We also know that PRECIS was designed, in the first instance, to be totally machine-manipulable, and therefore instantly responsive to change. We know these things, but how can we convince the rest of the staff, and thereby the users? It is a process of education, exposure, and even infiltration in the manner of a benevolent "fifth column".

How is this being done? As a partial effort and a small beginning, I prepared three subject indexes, intended for informal evaluation by reference staff in our Science & Medicine Library and Humanities & Social Sciences Library. A "hard" subject, medicine, was chosen in the first instance. In order to be as random and as objective as possible, records were chosen and indexes constructed as follows:

(1) *BNB* cumulations for January to August 1975 in Dewey class numbers
613.8 to 619 were matched against our card catalog. The result was
246 matches. Photocopies of our catalog cards were taken and consecutively numbered.

(2) PRECIS strings, as supplied by *BNB* were used to construct a PRECIS
index, called Index B. Relevant references as supplied in the *BNB* subject index were used.

(3) LC subject headings as found on the catalog cards were used to construct the LC index, called Index C. Relevant *"see"* and *"see also"*
references were taken from the 8th edition of *LCSH*. This was necessary because, though our card catalog has *"see"* references, it has
never had *"see also"* references.

(4) Index A is a paired keyword index, and, rightly or wrongly, it is not in
context with the title at each access point. Only words identified by
subfield $a in the MARC format were chosen, capitalization was re-
tained, and words (other than initial articles) omitted by reason of
their presence on a stop-list are indicated by periods. For example, the
title: *The drug, the nurse, the patient* results in the following entries:

      drug. nurse
      nurse. patient
      patient

I realize that this approach to keyword indexing is neither KWIC nor KWOC.
It is intended as a two-step approach, in order to parallel the two-stage approach
taken with *LCSH* and PRECIS for the purposes of this evaluation.

The three indexes were duly constructed, referring to the consecutively num-
bered records. Copies of the indexes were left with the reference staff of the
Science and Medicine Library, and with the reference staff of the Robarts Library
(Humanities and Social Sciences Library). There was no formal questionnaire.
Rather, there was the suggestion that one look up natural language subjects, like:
Back trouble, Children's diseases (including mental problems), Diagnosis of coro-
nary diseases, Effect of drugs on the brain, Relation of intelligence and mental
illness in old people, Diseases of newborn babies, Fat children, Pollutants of the
environment, of food, Action of drugs, Blood disorders in children, etc., etc. They
were also asked to evaluate the three indexes in terms of: ease of use, relevancy
of chosen access words to literary warrant and records retrieved, incidence of obsolete terminology, usefulness of *"see also"* and *"see"* references, and, in the final
analysis, as always, personal preference.

After four weeks, comments were collected. There were only 7 in all: 3 from
the Science and medicine librarians and 4 from the Humanities and social sciences
librarians. 6 of these replies were overwhelmingly on the side of PRECIS. (The
indexes were identified only as A, B, and C, but, of course, this was an informed
audience, and they readily identified them as LC, "funny" keyword, and "something else".)

Here are some of the comments on the three indexes:

Comments on Index A: (no context paired keyword)

- No *see* or *see also* references.
- Some peculiar headings used, e.g. Disturbed mentally. Childhood *and* Children.
- No consistent pattern for subdividing main headings.
- It is an easy enough index to use, but it is often misleading; there must be a high percentage of irrelevant material . . . This type of index . . . looks like it was done by someone who did not know anything about the subject . . .
- A disaster—frightening to think it could be used in a field like medicine.
- Not good for chosen subjects, specific topics, many false drops.
- Titles . . . a bad choice. Librarians used to apply logic . . . would need a thesaurus and even that wouldn't be adequate.
- Search is quick, but compared to the other indexes you miss a lot and/or get irrelevant items.
- Keyword headings give better coverage than LC—but headings like "Diseases" are useless.

Comments on Index B (PRECIS)

- Prefer over keyword—categories are grouped under main concepts in one place . . . able to pick up more . . . Index will be very lengthy if large collection is being considered, probably not feasible; one wants to keep consistency in large collection.
- I liked PRECIS best—"*see also*" references helpful—no "*see*" references, but LC has too many.
- PRECIS easiest to use—most familiar terms.
- . . . PRECIS the most rewarding index to use—not the easiest. Nothing is easier than a KWIC index, but you can never find anything in it . . .
- . . . The closest to what I would expect fo find in an index. It has more logic to it . . .
- The best of the lot to me—best for works in chosen subjects such as "*see also*" references under topics like "Drugs"—good for specific topics, vocabulary generally good and up-to-date.
- No "*see*" reference from "carcinoma" to "cancer" . . . from "Levodopa" to "L-Dopa".
- Heavy use of [qualifier] "Man" might offend women's lib . . .
- Generally the best—items entered under current terminology—both specific and general terms used. Groupings very useful for relational purposes. Cross references ("*see also*") fairly adequate. I would prefer more.

Comments on Index C (Library of Congress Subject Headings)

- Outdated terminology mixed with more modern—logic of relational structure has been destroyed. Would this become a problem for index B (PRECIS) at a later date? . . . Large number of cross references get you there in the end, but after an annoying process.
- Some books have no available categories.
- Much longer than the other two . . . Outdated vocabulary.

— May seem good, simply because it's larger than the other two [indexes].
— Terminology odd, e.g., Dentistry, Operative Corpulence.
— Seems to have most complete list of terms and fullest authority structure, therefore most satisfactory to use.
— Has more obsolete terms and the most awkward reference structure.
— Plus for LC: we are used to it.
— Very cumbersome to use due to "*see*" and "*see also*" . . . least useful. It looks like something I know very well: LC!

Six replies favoured PRECIS, and one favored *LCSH*. *LCSH* was rated second by six respondents, and Keyword by one. The person who rated *LCSH* third had some rather devastating comments about it: "The "*see*" references are crippling any possible value of this index . . . terms used can be obsolete or baffling, e.g. Morons, *see* Mentally handicapped, Paw, *see* Hand, Animal fluids and humors, *see* Body fluids, Melancholia.

One reply graded Keyword, PRECIS, and *LCSH* for retrieval relevance with the following results:

Keyword: 17 "so-so" and 8 "bests"
PRECIS: 13½ "so-so" and 28 "bests"
LCSH: 20½ "so-so" and 12 "bests"

Keyword was awarded 16½ stars, PRECIS 35½ stars, and *LCSH* 22 stars.

A quantitative analysis of index entries for the 246 records yielded the following results:

	LCSH	*PRECIS*	*Keyword*
Number of entries	332	406	555
Entries per record	1.35	1.65	2.26
Number of unique lead terms *	261	238	416
Unique lead terms per record	1.06	0.97	1.69
Number of "*see*" references			
To one other term	349	1	n/a
To two other terms	9	—	n/a
Number of "*see also*"			
To 1 other term	51	27	
To 2 other terms	19	10	
To 3 other terms	6	2	
To 4 other terms	6	—	
To 5 other terms	1	1	
To more than 5 terms	7	4	
Total "*see also*"	90	44	
Total number of terms referred to by "*see also*"	185	97	

---

*For LCSH, lead term is considered to be the word or words preceding a subheading. For Keyword, the first word.

Mutuality of terminology between Keyword, PRECIS, and *LCSH* was also
briefly examined. The stem of the first word was considered, with the following results:

Keyword, PRECIS, *LCSH* word the same: 101
PRECIS, *LCSH* word the same: 124
Keyword, *LCSH* word the same: 133
Keyword, PRECIS word the same: 150
Word exclusive to Keyword: 152
Word exclusive to PRECIS: 30
Word exclusive to *LCSH*: 173 (114 of these are *"see"* references from
words not used in Keyword or PRECIS)

In this sample, there is a higher degree of mutuality between Keyword and
PRECIS than between Keyword and *LCSH*. Also, *LCSH* uses more words which
are not used either by Keyword or PRECIS.

Where do we go from here? I would like to continue the process of exposure,
and do comparisons on more "hard" subjects, e.g. engineering, mathematics,
and on "soft" subjects such as sociology, philosophy. I would like to have more
librarians, as well as students and faculty do evaluations of the resulting indexes.
I realize that such comparisons have been done before, and are being done now
by others, but I believe that this redundancy is well justified because of its
immediacy. These will be indexes to items in *our* collection, and will be evaluated
by *our* staff and users. In the process, we are being educated. This has more
impact than reading reports of similar studies done elsewhere. This is a benevolent redundancy which aids and abets the honorable process of infiltration.

Our subcommittee on handling uncataloged theses and technical reports
has been re-activated and I hope that by the end of the year we can prepare a
firm proposal to apply PRECIS to this material, with a short bibliographic
description and sequential numbering. We hope to prove that this can be done
more economically than full cataloging with LC classification and subject headings, and with more satisfactory results.

And—we'll go on from there. Nothing is impossible.

Machine Searching of UK MARC on Title, Library of Congress Subject Headings, and PRECIS for Selective Dissemination of Information

Ann H. Schabas
Faculty of Library Science, University of Toronto

My attention was first drawn to PRECIS in 1969 when I spent a year in England studying at the University of London. My major interest that year was PRECIS which was then in the final months of gestation. This interest has continued since my return to Canada and has led to this project.

I have set up and am operating a selective dissemination of information service (SDI) for the express purpose of comparing retrieval from searches on PRECIS strings with retrieval from searches on other subject indexing systems, namely Library of Congress subject headings (LCSH) and Title. I will talk mainly about my experiences with profile revision during the test phase of the project, from January through August of this year, but first a brief description of the service.

The data base being searched is UK MARC. To be more precise, I am searching the weekly tapes from the British Library restricting my search to those bibliographic records appearing for the first time, i.e. those records which have an *n* in the leader of the MARC record, and which do not contain a Juvenile or a Fiction indicator in the 008 control field. The net number of records searched through each week averages approximately 550.

The users of this SDI service were recruited especially for this project a year ago. My criteria for selecting a user group were that its range of interests be wide and that it have a good representation of multidisciplines. Each interest should be clearly defined, not overly broad, answerable to some extent with monographs, and have at least as much permanence as the project (12-18 months). One further point: the users would have to be relied upon to sustain the feedback in the form of relevance judgements week after week. A tall order. To a great extent these criteria have been met.

In a mailing in October, 1975, the members of the Toronto Chapter of the Special Libraries Association, numbering about 450, were invited to join the project. Fifty-nine people responded of whom 50 became users when the service began in January, 1976. The other nine were contacted but withdrew their names by mutual agreement for a variety of reasons.

I met with each prospective user and worked out tentative profiles. The group had the wide range of interests (subjects) I was seeking: New Towns, Urban Transportation, Alternative Work Patterns, Police and the Community, Immigrants and the Community, Drug Addiction, Recycling of Wastes, Ombudsmen, Energy Crisis, Crime, Noise Pollution, Human Stress, Women and Employment, Safety, to name a few. Users with more than one interest were encouraged to set up more than one profile. In several cases very similar profiles were worked out for two different users. Other pairs of profiles are closely related but have some distinct difference. In all, 84 profiles were negotiated.

The profile logic uses the Boolean operators: OR, AND and NOT. Complex logic can be accommodated but it has been found that fairly simple structures are most effective. A profile expression consists of words or phrases "ORed" together in "OR-groups", and these groups are "ANDed" or "NOTed" together. A profile may be made up of several such expressions. Profile size is not limited, nor are the number of profiles. Limitations relate to the total number of profile words (500) which can be accommodated in one tape run. In actual fact, the shortest profile is one word long (on Metrication) and the longest one (on Veterinary Science) has 56 words, in two expressions. The average length of a profile is just over 14 words.

Five different searches are performed for each profile. The profile words are matched in turn against words from each of the three MARC fields, Title, *LCSH*, and PRECIS (one-field searches) and against words from two combined fields, namely Title combined with *LCSH*, and Title combined with PRECIS (two-field searches). These two-field searches were included to measure the degree to which one field enriches the other and to identify possible noise that could result from falsely associating words from different contexts. Adjacency of post-coordinated words may be reduced when two fields are involved.

A hit occurs when there is a match between the profile and the bibliographic record for at least one of the searches. The output supplied to the user consists of a bibliographic reference for each hit, in card image format, with a "tear-off" section to be returned with a relevance judgement. If a citation is a hit on more than one search, only one copy of the citation is supplied to the user. For the user's response, three levels of relevance are provided on the printout: "definitely useful," "possibly useful" and "not useful." The user is also asked to indicate if he had prior knowledge of the item from some other source.

The test phase of the project started at the end of January, 1976, and continued for 30 weeks. During the early months of testing a number of software modifications were made. Space requirements within the computer needed to be adjusted, overflow checks incorporated, and output and output formats improved. Actual output for each profile was generated and mailed from the start, but the software changes made the early data quite unreliable.

It was clear from the start that the natural language profiles formulated during the initial interviews with the users would need considerable revision in most cases. The aims of the test phase were to optimize recall and precision and to identify and reduce to a minimum any obvious bias towards one or other of the indexing languages represented. What to do? One procedure would have been to leave the profiles in their original natural language form; but this would have implied that the profiles were adequate, which they were not. It would also have meant a probable bias to the more familiar *LCSH* terminology. Another procedure would have been to structure the profiles by consulting the authority lists for both indexing languages; but there was no PRECIS thesaurus available comparable to the one for *LCSH*. I finally decided to make profile modifications based, as much as possible, on information gleaned from the data base itself. Only with this dynamic approach would both indexing languages be contributing equally to profile editing.

Several techniques were used. Wordlists were generated each week for each profile. These lists consisted of words, other than a small set of "stop" words, which were present in the Title, *LCSH* and PRECIS fields of records containing at least one profile word. Stating it another way, these words were those which occurred in records with a user's profile words. The lists varied greatly in length. Most contained between one and two hundred words a week. Some were very short. A few were closer to five hundred words long. Most could be scanned quite quickly and easily to identify candidate words for the profile for which they had been generated. As the profiles became enriched, these lists became less useful; and they were stopped after a few months.

The frequencies of occurrence of profile words were cumulated from week to week. Words which did not occur in the data base over many weeks were considered for deletion. Words which occurred too frequently were suspected of producing unwanted hits, or noise.

The third and most useful profile editing technique was the examination of the hits themselves along with the relevance judgements from the users. For this it was necessary to wait for a number of weeks until enough feedback had accumulated. For any one profile, the citations were grouped by the three levels of relevance. The "not useful" group was first examined to see which words were causing the unwanted hits. If an examination of the other groups showed that the offending words were not contributing wanted citations, they were considered for deletion. Much depended on the overall volume of output for the profile and the user's tolerance for noise. One user is interested in BOOKS but the word BOOKS was finally dropped from his profile because of the noise it produced, and this after many attempts to control the problem with "NOT logic" and other adjustments to the profile. Another user is interested in "words." He is living with the noise of the false drops because of a particularly appropriate hit which could only have been retrieved by the term "words." Other common words giving similar problems to other profiles are "economic," "social," "organization" ("organisation"), "environment," "planning," "region," "community," "illustration" and "power," to name a few. In a number of cases reasonable precision has only been achieved at the expense of recall.

In some cases a problem term occurs less frequently, and the noise it generates can be tolerated. "Stress" is one such term. It applies both to humans and to materials. It is not always possible to sift out the unwanted citations, but their number is low.

The "definitely useful" and "possibly useful" groups were studied to identify candidate words with which to enrich the profile. This was the most helpful way to minimize any bias towards either of the indexing languages. The profile on "Marine Ecology" is a case in point. The *LCSH* heading "Seashore ecology" was providing some good hits. These same citations were being missed on the PRECIS search because the comparable PRECIS expression is "Coastal ecosystems". "Ecosystems" was added to the profile. This worked both ways. The "Safety" profile was missing on *LCSH* searches until "Accidents" was added to it.

During the early weeks of the service, I experimented with left truncation

which yielded some amusing results. The word "Trial" in a Criminology profile
was retrieving hits on "Industrial." "Culture" in another profile was hitting "Ag-
riculture." "Mother" in "Chemotherapy" baffled us for a while. There were
many unpredictable situations like this, until left truncation was eliminated except when explicitly asked for.

During the test phase the profiles were reviewed thoroughly three times, in
April, June and August. The wordlists from the early runs were scanned once, in
April. Profile revision is far from an exact science, as others have observed before
me. It is a little like indexing: an iterative process which is usually terminated
not because one arrives at a satisfactory result but because a point of diminish-
ing returns is reached. I realized this point had been reached in August when I
found myself contemplating adding words to profiles which had been tried and
rejected earlier in the test period. In a real SDI system profiles should probably
never be frozen. The research nature of my project, however, calls for this and
the profiles were frozen towards the end of August.

I should like to say a few words about the human element in the project,
the users. They have, to date, been quite remarkable regarding feedback. The
record shows better than 95% of citations are reported on within four weeks of
the search which generated them. I believe this pattern will continue for the re-
mainder of the project. On the other hand, with a few exceptions, the users have
shown little interest in profile revision. The wordlists generally were not scanned
by the users. Very rarely, and not at all for several months, has a request been
received to change a profile, even slightly. Noise tolerance varies widely. The
"Words" profile has large output and low relevance, about 14%, but the user is
satisfied because of the occasional gem he receives. Other users, fortunately only
one or two, seem irritated by every false drop.

Relevance judgements, the choice between "definitely useful" and "possibly useful", vary understandably between users. Some seem reluctant to say
anything is "definitely useful" without the book in hand. Others are very liberal
with their "definitely useful" judgements. One user puzzled me because every
citation was coming back "definitely useful". When I finally inquired, I found
out that he had, without realizing it, slipped into the routine of checking up on
the mechanics of a hit, in effect checking up on the computer. If the hits were
mechanical hits — and they always were — he would check the "definitely useful" box without thinking, and then add the comment "not really". This was
the only occasion when I questioned a user's relevance decisions.

There are some puzzling "NOT logic" conflicts with users. Because the
"NOT logic" may affect some but not all searches, a citation with a "NOT
word" may well be sent to the user as a hit. Sometimes when this has occurred,
the citation comes back marked "definitely useful!"

A word about the other question on the feedback slip, about prior knowledge of the citation. Although I have no quantified data on this as yet, I am sur-
prised how few users have heard of the citations I send them. Only one user answers yes to that question most of the time.

A number of the profiles have been far from successful. After the first review of profiles in April, I dropped seven users and 13 profiles. Either the profile
could not be satisfied with monographs, or the user was too busy to send back
the feedback slips. Of the 71 profiles remaining, two have had no hits in the past
15 weeks. Six others have had fewer than five in the same time period. A few

others have had a number of hits, but none have been relevant. Certainly if there were a cost for this SDI service, these users would have withdrawn long ago. Because it is free and a research project, no one has dropped out since May.

There have been no changes in profiles since late August, 1976. Of the eight weekly tapes searched since then, fairly complete feedback has been received on the first five and partial feedback on the sixth. The collection of data will continue for another six months. It is too early to quote results. The following is a preliminary report only.

There are about 3.5 hits on the average for each profile each week, ranging for any one profile from none to over 20. A little more than half of the hits from all searches are judged relevant. Precision is very similar for each of the three one-field searches, slightly over 60%. For the two two-field searches precision is likewise similar but slightly lower, probably because words are more often falsely post-coordinated when two fields are involved.

A "pseudo-recall" for each search can be worked out by comparing the number of relevant hits from one search with the number of relevant hits when the searches are pooled. In this respect, the searches depart more from one another. As is to be expected, the Title field recall is the lowest, not much better than 50%. Recall for the other two one-field searches, *LCSH* and PRECIS, fall in the 70-80% range. Recall for the two two-field searches, Title with *LCSH* and Title with PRECIS, fall in the 80-90% range. In both these latter cases, there appears to be a noticeable difference in favor of PRECIS. Obviously, it is premature to say more on this point now.

It is clear that monograph indexing cannot exploit the detail of indexing possible with PRECIS. I had hoped, at the outset of my project, that profiles could be refined in some cases to use at least some of the PRECIS manipulation coding, but as feedback started to come in, and the results were examined, it became evident that the profiles should stay at the verbal level. The profile modifications suggested during the test phase tended to broaden and blunt the profiles, not sharpen them. There is still much to be done to study machine searching of PRECIS for non-monographic publications.

III. Practical Applications

Manual Application of PRECIS in a High School Library

Audrey Taylor
PRECIS Project, Aurora High School Library, Aurora,
Ontario, Canada

The first library in Canada to use PRECIS for subject access to its collection
was a school resource centre. The decision was made in 1971 to apply PRECIS
manually to a one-stage card index in the library of Aurora High School, under
the York County Board of Education, a jurisdiction in Ontario immediately
north of Metropolitan Toronto. The fact that a school library undertook such an
innovation should not come as a surprise. The magnitude and accelerated pace
of change experienced by all segments of our society have impinged particularly
upon educators. The needs of students, teachers, parents, school administrators
and politicians have increased the demands made on the information systems of
our schools and their libraries. Customary left-to-right, step-by-step methods of
finding and dealing with information have been overtaken by instant information patterns released by electronic technology. The Olympic Games, space exploration, war and violence have long been instantaneous and universal events
shared by millions round the world. The learning rhythms of our students have
been shaped by this electronic culture; indeed, they appear to "march to a different drummer". The technology for information systems instantly responsive
to our students is now available; it remains for those who have the temerity to
organize learning systems to initiate change.

I would like to share with you the reasons I consider PRECIS to be significant to the development of the information system so urgently required in both
our elementary and secondary school libraries, as well as how we initiated the
first stage of this system in one particular school.

Since occasional reference to automation will be made throughout this
paper, I should state here that as of July 1, 1976, we entered the second stage of
our PRECIS project, the automation of the catalog. This phase has been made
possible by a two-year research grant awarded by the Ontario Ministry of Education.

A review of the educational climate in Ontario in the 60's might be helpful
in understanding the decision taken. A growing emphasis on individualized learning, independent study and research and de-emphasis of the textbook as the
only source of information, led to a rapid growth of resource centres in the
schools. Since the mid-sixties, small classroom libraries have expanded into areas
designed to house multi-media collections supporting a diverse and complex cur-

riculum. Yet, despite ample evidence of acute need for a better system of subject access to information in these multi-media collections—any practicing school librarian can speak at length about personal experiences and frustrations—school libraries have not been able to take advantage of new technology and developments in the fields of library and information science. This has not been a priority item with school administrators or politicians. In fact, there has been a general tendency in the last few years to cut back library staff and funds.

In York County, as early as 1969, both administrators and librarians were concerned about the limited use of school libraries, in particular the card catalogs provided at considerable expense of time and money. One administrator had made the provocative suggestion that the card catalog be abandoned, the materials be shelved in any convenient manner and let the devil take the hindmost in the search for information! This deliberate challenge had to be answered.

In the Spring of 1971, Irene McCordick, Master Teacher of Libraries for the York County Board, and I found that we shared a concern to find ways of improving access to library materials through redesigning the card catalog and use of a more appropriate method of subject indexing. We agreed that the major problem was lack of adequate subject access.

My experience in secondary schools, where there was a need to mine relatively small collections—8,000-10,000 titles—had led me to the use of analytics in a desperate attempt to identify information buried within individual titles. This effort could not overcome the problems inherent in the subject headings, whether they were taken from *Sears' List of Subject Headings* or from *Library of Congress Subject Headings (LCSH)*, namely the lack of specificity in the terminology and a structure which concealed terms desirable as access points in an index. A short research study which I undertook at the School of Library and Information Science at the University of Western Ontario in 1970, indicated that content analysis of curriculum materials produces terminology more suited to the information needs of students and teachers than terms drawn from standard lists. Despite revisions, the *Sears* and *LCSH* lists of subject headings remain, to a great extent, out of touch with the thought and language of today's users.

Irene McCordick had had recent experience in elementary schools where she had observed acute inadequacies at this level as well. Of necessity, cataloging had to be purchased commercially. The quality of the work was inconsistent and the subject headings taken from *Sears* were inappropriate for younger children. Much of the subject heading work needed to be redone to reflect the curriculum and to meet the expectations of pupils and teachers; teacher-librarians rarely had time to accomplish this.

We were also aware of other obstacles preventing intelligent and fruitful use of resource materials; the card catalog is an unwieldy and frustrating tool; the Dewey Decimal classification scatters information related to one curriculum topic; "see" and "see also" references are often inadequate or altogether absent.

Not all the problems could be solved simultaneously. The opportunity to experiment with alternatives came with my appointment effective September, 1971, to the library of Aurora High School due to open in September, 1972. I submitted two proposals to the Administrative Committee of the York County Board of Education, advocating an innovative approach to the cataloging and classification of materials for the new school. In the second proposal, I recommended that PRECIS be used as the method for subject indexing. The Committee gave its approval to the implementation of an innovative card catalog which would address itself to the goal of "increased ease, efficiency and speed in gaining access to information within the collection." Three specific areas of need were identified: depth and specificity in indexing; terminology drawn from the library materials and curriculum guidelines; collocation of Dewey notations on individual subject cards in order to counter the scattering of information by the classification scheme.

After investigating different indexing systems, it was clear that PRECIS was the most likely method to satisfy our needs. Numerous features were in its favour: the conceptual approach to knowledge; selection of terminology from the content analysis of the documents; the concept of an open-ended vocabulary allowing terms encountered in the literature to be admitted freely to the index; multiple access points derived from a single string of terms; and a syntax providing the context-establishment of terms within a natural language order. While recognizing the fact that PRECIS had been designed to produce a printed subject index from machine-held files, I was convinced that it could be adapted to a manual system, a one-stage card index.

Initial information about PRECIS came from two papers.[1,2] The two documents served as the source both of information and inspiration for the subject index at Aurora High School. Subsequent consultation with Ann Schabas and with Gordon Wright, then Director of the College Bibliocentre, who was planning to use PRECIS, confirmed my decision to adopt PRECIS. The desirability of later conversion to a machine-readable format was never lost from sight. It was clear that we could not implement the full potential of PRECIS in a manual system, given our small staff and working conditions.

From January, 1972 to June, 1976, more than 7000 titles have been classified, cataloged and indexed using PRECIS; these include fiction and non-fiction, print and non-print items. While this might appear to be a modest accomplishment, a number of facts should be kept in mind. The implementation of PRECIS and the designing of an innovative card catalog took place in the context of the development and operation of a new school library with one professional librarian in charge. The normal staff complement of a high school library in York County is one teacher-librarian and a secretary. Because of the special nature of the Aurora project, we were assigned, in addition, a library technician to assist with the classification and descriptive cataloging of the materials. Commercial cataloging could not provide the style of card required for the innovative character of the Aurora catalog.

During the early stages, the intellectual task of indexing was literally a matter of "learning by doing". The authority files built slowly, as there was no access to other PRECIS files. My formal education in the PRECIS method started with a course offered by C. Derek Robinson at the College Bibliocentre in July, 1974. The definitive *PRECIS Manual*[3] became available at the same time. I was unable to implement the changes that had occurred in PRECIS since its early developmental stages until September, 1975. Despite the fact that the catalog was begun when only a limited amount of information about PRECIS was available, the final product has not diverged in any essentials from the principles of the system. I was given this assurance by Derek Austin during discussions we had in July, 1975. His enthusiasm for the project encouraged us to pursue the work in spite of internal pressures and problems encountered along the way.

It should be noted, however, that the building of the semantic part of the system was postponed. The subject catalogs do not contain a reference structure in the true sense. Rather, in many instances, terms belonging by definition in the reference structure were built into the strings. As a result, we have a pragmatic rather than a pure PRECIS index. Automation of the system has provided the opportunity to construct a proper RIN file.

A number of decisions were made in regard to the structure of the new catalog. The aim was to design a tool which would assist students in the location of information, directing them to shelf locations where they could browse through the materials immediately available. There was a need to reduce the bulk of the catalog—students seldom look beyond the first card in the traditional subject catalog in order to obtain a location number. As a result, they overlook information pertinent to their search. In order to accomplish this, one of our most radical decisions was to omit citations in the non-fiction subject file until automation of the system could provide a different form of catalog, i.e. a book catalog. The author/title files would provide brief citations—call number, author, title and date of publication. Full bibliographic data were recorded on the shelf list. We have observed that in recent years students are being trained to record bibliographic information when the material is in hand.

The resulting public catalog contained six separate files: subject indexes for fiction and non-fiction. The author and title files did not become part of the public catalog until the second year of operation, as we attempted to evaluate, informally, student use of the PRECIS subject indexes. Authority files and control files were developed for staff use.

Work on the subject index began in late January, 1972, with the fiction collection. The lack of subject access to fiction had long been a source of personal frustration to me, both as a library user and a librarian. As the 18th edition of the Dewey schedules was not then available, there was no alternative but to start subject indexing in this unexplored area. This turned out to be more of a challenge than I had foreseen. I was forced to learn, simultaneously, the methodology for PRECIS and techniques for the concept analysis of novels. I literally battled my way through the writing and manipulation of strings after identifying concepts, values, historical events and subjects of general interest to our future readers. During our first year of operation, the English department requested that I index the entire fiction collection for the four basic concepts used in the literature courses: tragedy, comedy, satire and irony, and romance. At their request, each title was to be assigned only one concept. I attempted this for a year-and-a-half, but found it an impossible task. Some books defied classification. Teaching staff, when consulted, rarely agreed among themselves on the appropriate choice. I would like to attempt this exercise again, under different circumstances, as students frequently ask me to find them a novel that fits one of the prescribed concepts. Such a request seldom brings forth an immediate response from me!

Because fiction is not classified by Dewey in a school library, the format of the subject catalog differed from that planned for non-fiction. The PRECIS string was typed on the appropriate number of cards, one for each access point in the string. Behind these were filed individual citations for each novel to which the string had been applied. The PRECIS cards were color-coded by an orange band across the top, in order to distinguish them from the citations. As the subject catalog developed, we found that the filing of citations for strings already in the catalog presented a problem for the filing clerk. This was solved by providing with the citations for each title the P slip on which was recorded the appropriate strings and their manipulations. Figure 1 is an illustration of the Fiction Subject Catalog:

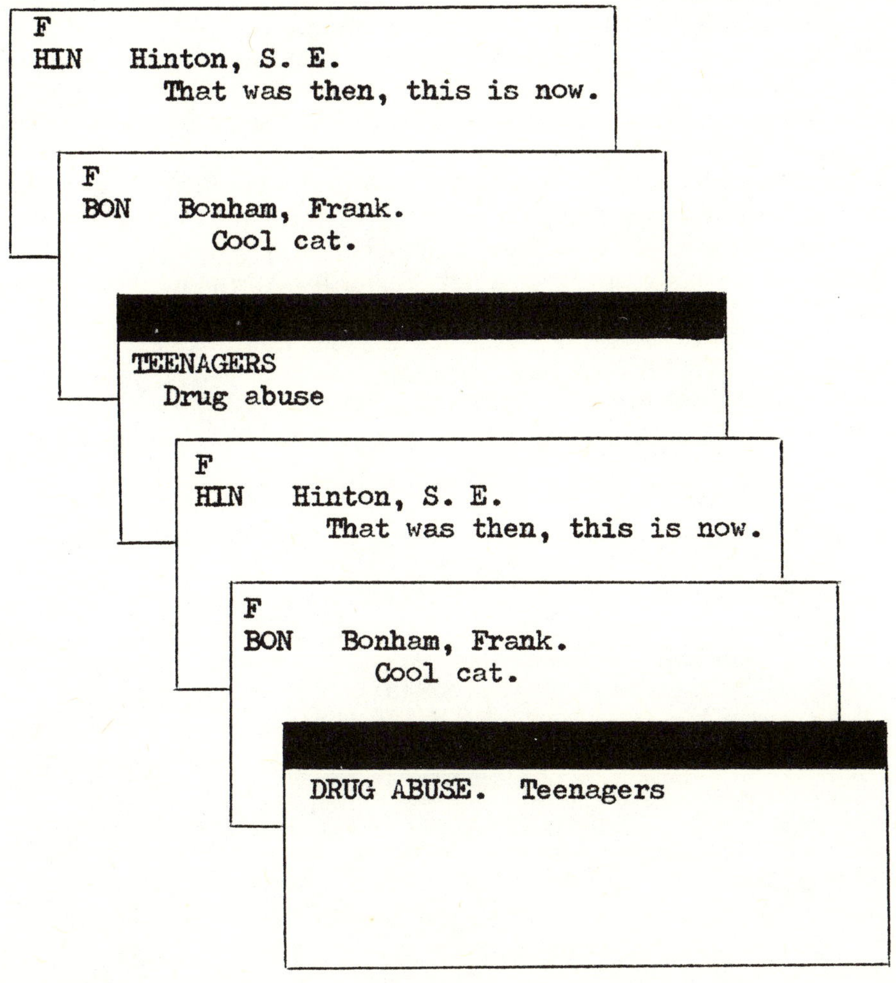

Figure 1

Two control files were maintained, one by the indexer, the other by the typist. Each card contained a PRECIS string in its first position and information regarding the terms to be used in the lead position. The cards were filed alphabetically by the first term in the string. The files were checked, one against the other, three or four times a year in order to catch and eliminate errors.

In April, I began to index the non-fiction collection. As the teaching staff had not yet been hired, the work proceeded on the basis of knowledge gained from my eleven years' experience as a high school librarian, and the content analysis of the materials. A few general course outlines were also helpful. I made every effort to incorporate in the index strings the vocabulary, concepts and emphases of school curricula. Subsequent interaction with students and staff was reflected in the increasing responsiveness of the index to their needs.

The format of the non-fiction catalog was dictated by needs referred to earlier: to provide a browsing tool which would lead the user quickly and easily to the shelves; to decrease the size and complexity of the files; to overcome the scatter of information inherent in the use of the Dewey classification. In order to fulfill these needs, the following decisions were made:

(1)   to write as many strings as considered necessary to retrieve pertinent information contained in a single title.

(2)   to omit citations, using only location numbers, i.e. Dewey notations on the "subject cards".

(3)   not to follow the BNB practice of restricting each string to a single classification number, but rather to let each string attract information, i.e. all the applicable Dewey numbers.

As a result, we have produced a radically different subject index as shown in Figure 2:

```
GOVERNMENT
   Theories of Trudeau, Pierre Elliott

327.71
971.404
```

```
TRUDEAU, PIERRE ELLIOTT
   Theories of government

327.71
971.404
```

Figure 2

As new materials were added to the collection, and indexed with strings already in use, they were noted in the subject index only if the classification numbers differed from what had already been recorded on the subject cards. Thus, these cards began to cumulate an array of Dewey numbers indicating to the user the different shelf locations where information could be found.

As with fiction, two control files were kept in order to check for human error and to provide authority listings. They served a third function—control for updating in the public catalog. As new materials flowed through the system, they were classified and cataloged by the technician, before coming to the indexer. In the case of a new string being written, it was entered on a card, and the classification number of the book for which it was used was noted. The card was then flagged to alert the typist that this string, its shunts and the list of location numbers must be typed for the public catalog. In the case of an old string being assigned to a title with a classification number not already recorded, the new notation was added to the card. The cards for strings already in use were flagged in a different color to alert the typist to the fact that new information had to be added to the strings in the public catalog. Updating was done once every two months—five times a year.

The subject files described are already being overtaken by automation. The new system will enable us to produce a complete one-stage subject index linking the PRECIS strings to short records as in Figure 3:

```
GOVERNMENT
  Theories of Trudeau, Pierre Elliott

327.71 THO    Trudeau and foreign policy.  Thordarson, Bruce.  1972
971.404 TRU   Approaches to politics.  Trudeau, Pierre Elliott.  1970

GOVERNMENT.  Canada
  Policies on corporations

338.971 LEW   Louder voices: the corporate welfare bums.  Lewis, David.
                 1972
```

Figure 3

The author/title files in the public catalog use a brief citation—call number, author, title and date of publication. It has been our observation that long bibliographic entries in the traditional card catalog are disregarded by most of our users. The short record is sufficient for the location of materials, the primary function of the catalog.

We have become aware of other libraries following a similar pattern. The Bath University Comparative Catalogue Study has recently published a series of reports concerning catalog format and the use of short records.[4] The microfiche subject index at Ryerson Polytechnical Institute, Toronto, uses a short citation. More recently, the Robarts Library, University of Toronto, has closed its card catalogs and provides on both microfiche and microfilm a variety of indexes. The complete bibliographic files are organized in shelf list order by classification number; author, title and subject files offer short entries.

We have not had time or staff to evolve appropriate criteria of adequacy for measuring either the performance of the manually constructed index or user attitudes. Reaction has been assessed through informal questioning of staff and students. We have had such comments as, "it's easy to use", "don't have to worry about all that title stuff", "yes, I can find what I'm looking for". The students appear to experience no difficulty in working with the PRECIS format. They seem to find the collocation of Dewey numbers in the subject index useful to their search.

While it is interesting to hear about new developments and special projects in the fields of library and information science, one always thinks, "There must be problems. What are they?" The problems which I will identify must be considered in the context of a particular library: a school resource centre with a small staff; pressure to build a collection in a short period of time; and lack of full documentation on the PRECIS method.

One of the greatest difficulties encountered was simply to find blocks of time for analysis of the materials. There was a lack of understanding on the part of the teaching staff as to the nature and goals of the project. Their chief concern focused on the quantity of materials on the shelves—accessibility was of little significance to them. At one point, we were forced to process some 300 titles without indexing them. Some 150 of these still remain without any form of access.

In time, however, as use of the new catalog was put to the test for research projects, the significance of the usefulness of PRECIS and the time required to produce the index became more visible. One history teacher assigned a senior class, as part of its research, the task of listing terms and concepts missing in the index which would have been pertinent to the search. The response was unanimous—the students had experienced no problems in locating the information required. While this exercise did nothing to relieve the pressures of producing the index, it made clear an important point—the time taken to analyze the materials was justified.

The most overwhelming of the internal problems inherent in any indexing system is control of the vocabulary. The control files already described gave access to the first terms in the strings. The only complete record available was the public catalog. Constant search of the public files was onerous yet essential. An attempt to keep an alphabetical list of terms used both as leads and non-leads was abandoned in the second year because of lack of time. As a result, redundant terms occurred with some frequency. The most glaring errors have been corrected. A complete cleaning of the strings and terminology is now under way as part of the automation process.

The fact that we began to build the subject index using the early form of PRECIS presented an internal problem later when we switched to the definitive form in September, 1975. The early strings seldom contained more than four terms; we used the straightforward rotation of the elements coming successively into the lead position. A simple method for identification of lead terms was devised for the typist. The new coding system of PRECIS II, with its added flexibility and complexity in the shunting procedure, required a different approach. At this point in the history of the project, the secretary had been reduced to half-time in the library. In order to facilitate the typing of the new strings, the indexer's control file displayed on the back of each card the full manipulation of the individual string. This reduced speed in the indexing process, but proved helpful to the typist.

Some problems in the collocation of terms in the catalogs resulted from the switch to PRECIS II, but we chose to ignore this aspect. Students did not appear to experience any difficulty and continued to use the catalog with the same ease.

An orientation program is offered to the first-year students, at the beginning of each school year. Through the use of transparencies and handouts, students are led through the process of using the catalogs. It is a matter of explaining the differences they will encounter in the catalog format, rather than a full exposition of PRECIS. I am convinced that students are oblivious to the two-line entry—they simply access the file at the term they choose, read the information given in the entry, decide whether or not it is applicable to their search, identify the location number or numbers and proceed to the well-labelled stacks. We are still confronted with the well-worn question, "Where can I find something about. . . ?" A trial run through the catalog is generally sufficient to remind a student that this catalog is different from others he has used. Such experiences serve to lend credence to my conviction that we need a different kind of tool for searching, one in a format that can be more quickly and easily scanned than cards.

New developments in the Ontario library scene began to impinge upon the project. The implementation of on-line, computer-based cataloging support services from the University of Toronto Library Automated System (UT/LAS)[5] became a significant factor in our awareness of the need for a new information system for school libraries. A proposal for a Canadian materials network was submitted to government agencies by Gordon Wright and a committee of concerned librarians and teachers.[6] PRECIS had been adopted by the College Bibliocentre for the indexing of audiovisual materials. The Ontario Ministry of Education, in cooperation with the Metropolitan Toronto School Board, had funded a project to make accessible research documents in the field of education. Known as ONTERIS (Ontario Educational Research Information System), this project has a computer-produced PRECIS index as one of several approaches being tested for subject retrieval of documents. Ann Schabas had begun work on comparing the machine-retrieval capabilities of PRECIS and Library of Congress subject headings for the purpose of an SDI service.

In the Spring of 1975, Irene McCordick and I began to lay the ground work for extending the PRECIS project beyond the confines of Aurora High School. Dialog with individuals from other school jurisdictions explored the need to develop a network for schools which could provide machine-readable cataloging with PRECIS indexing. While considerable interest was expressed, it became obvious that the production of an automated model was necessary as the first step in the development of such a network.

We also initiated discussions with a number of people within our own School Board, aware that something new had to be introduced on a number of different levels. Irene McCordick, in her role as Master Teacher, organized an in-service seminar called, "Word relationships and their relevance for students searching a subject index." This seminar was held in response to an earlier series of workshops which had presented a developmental model employing word association in introducing younger students to learning through individual inquiry. The later seminar explored further the nature of language skills students require for success in the search for materials and the assessment of their relevance. Both teachers and librarians, in an indirect fashion, had their first encounter with PRECIS. I presented examples of PRECIS strings and selections from the reference section of the PRECIS manual to illustrate various word relationships. The results were electrifying! Teachers were struck by the syntactic and semantic structures of PRECIS; they felt that the constant use of a PRECIS index might well be a potent factor in developing students' skills in investigation and ability to use language with precision.

Kenneth A. Stanley, an Area Superintendent with our Board, stated that he found exciting "the probability that the learner will have brought to his attention sources and directions of enquiry that he would not have thought of himself."

In schools, a PRECIS index may conceivably be more than a finding device; it appears to have potential as a learning tool. Only in-school research can fully assess this potential of PRECIS and demonstrate how best to make it available to students.

We feel strongly that schools are likely to accept PRECIS and the type of catalog we intend to produce, only if the future users are well informed about it. We have conducted PRECIS workshops, both last Spring and again this Fall, in order to acquaint librarians and teachers with the nature of PRECIS and the advantages it can bring both to them and to their students. Attendance at the workshops has been gratifying, with participants coming both from York County and other educational jurisdictions. Irene McCordick and I published an article addressed to school administrators in the journal, *Education Canada*.[8] A longer article appeared in *Canadian Library Journal*.[9]

Early this year, Irene McCordick and I submitted a proposal[10] requesting funds to the Ontario Ministry of Education's Grants In Aid of Educational Research program. Acceptance of the proposal and the granting of research funds for a two-year period were announced in May, and work on the new project began in July.

The intent of the project is to take advantage of the technology now available to link the PRECIS subject index to computer-stored bibliographic records and produce a model catalog in Computer Output Microform (COM). This will be accomplished through the facilities of the University of Toronto Library Automated System (UT/LAS) which already provides cataloging services to a variety of users, and houses the PRECIS computer program. The resulting working model will serve as a base to determine future developments of a network for school libraries.

The potential for the development of manual PRECIS indexes is obvious because of the acute need for improved subject access to information in library collections. The librarians of the Simcoe Composite School, also in Ontario, are planning to implement a manual card index in January, 1977. This index is likely to be confined to one or two subject areas. This should be a useful and interesting experience as we will have the opportunity to develop a process for the sharing of information of mutual concern and benefit. We may be able to identify areas to be explored and directions to be taken in the building of the network.

Individual undertakings are not practicable unless the intent is to develop a centralized system capable of dissemination to others. PRECIS has the potential for a shared endeavor through the automation process, providing the building blocks necessary for the information system so urgently required for elementary and secondary school libraries.

NOTES

1. Ann Schabas, "Trends in Indexing," *Ontario Library Association, Proceedings of the 69th Annual Conference, London, Ontario, May 14-16, 1971* (Paper given to the Special Libraries Special Interest Group of the Ontario Library Association, May 15, 1971.) (London, Ontario: Ontario Library Association, 1971).
2. Derek Austin, "A Conceptual Approach to the Organization of Machine-held Files for Subject Retrieval," *Conceptual Basis of the Classification of Knowledge: Proceedings of the Ottawa Conference On the Conceptual Basis of the Classification of Knowledge, October 1-5, 1971*, Ed. Jerzy A. Wojciechowski (Munich: Verlag Dokumentation, 1974), pp. 371-98.
3. Derek Austin, *PRECIS: A Manual of Concept Analysis and Subject Indexing* (London: Council of the British National Bibliography, 1974).
4. University of Bath, Library, *Bath University Comparative Catalogue Study*, final report (Bath, England: The Library, 1975).
5. Ralph E. Stierwalt, "Cooperative Library System for Ontario Universities," *Ontario Library Review*, v. 58 (June 1974), pp. 83-89.
6. Canadian Materials Network Group, *A Canadian Materials Bibliographic Network for Education*, ed. G. H. Wright (Toronto: The Group, 1974).
7. Barbara Beardsley, *ONTERIS: Primary Development of a Documentation System for Educational Research; Report on Phase I, November 1, 1974-October 31, 1975* (Toronto: Metropolitan Toronto School Board, 1975).
8. Audrey Taylor and Irene McCordick, "Finding Information Made Easier in the School Library," *Education Canada*, v. 16, no. 1 (Spring 1976), pp. 45-46.
9. Audrey Taylor and Irene McCordick, "PRECIS Can Revolutionize Subject Access to Information in School Resource Centres," *Canadian Library Journal*, v. 33, no. 6 (1976), pp. 523-28.
10. *A Computer-based Catalogue Linking the PRECIS Indexing System to School Library Materials: Building a Model for an Ontario-wide Information Network for School Libraries Using PRECIS; a Developmental Research Project* (Aurora, Ontario: York County Board of Education, March 1976).

ADDITIONAL REFERENCES

1. Austin, Derek, "The Development of PRECIS: A Theoretical and Technical History," *Journal of Documentation*, v. 30, no. 1 (March 1974), pp. 47-102.
2. Hunt, Roslyn, et al., "WUSCS; Wollongong University Subject Catalogue Study," first interim report (March 1975).
3. Lamy-Rousseau, Françoise, *Traitement Automatisé des Documents Multimedia avec les Systèmes ISBD Unifié, Lamy-Rousseau et PRECIS: Propositions S.I.L.P.* (Montreal: Ministère de l'Education du Quebec, Service Général des Moyens d'Enseignement, 1974).
4. Robinson, C. "Indexing the Film Catalogue: With Comparisons Between

LCSH and PRECIS Entries," *College Bibliocentre Newsletter*, v. 8 (June 1973), pp. 7-13.

5. Shifrin, Malcolm, *Information in the School Library: An Introduction to the Organization of Non-Book Materials* (London: Bingley, 1973).

Indexing Nonbook Materials by PRECIS

C. Derek Robinson
College Bibliocentre, Ontario

This is neither a research report nor a theoretical study, but a personal account of a working indexer's activity in a particular field and for a particular organization. I have therefore concentrated on the *minutiae* of indexing while attempting to draw general conclusions from specific instances.

For over three years, intensive indexing of nonbook materials by PRECIS took place at the College Bibliocentre, Ontario. This was by no means an intentional experiment in the application of a new subject indexing system to a comparatively new kind of material, but a reflection of the limitations of a working situation. The Bibliocentre was established as a central agency for the acquisition, cataloging and processing of learning materials. Originally intended to serve the Colleges of Applied Arts and Technology, it now also serves many schools of nursing, 99 campuses in all, spread across Ontario. During the period under review, 1973–1976, the workflow amounted to about 100,000 items per annum; the data base has now grown to well over 250,000 records.

In 1973 the then Director, Gordon Wright, following the recommendation of the Canadian MARC Task Force, set up a PRECIS system. In view of the size of the workflow, and certain financial constraints, the resources available could not possibly cope with indexing 100% of the flow or with retrospective indexing of records already in the data base. What was possible was to isolate an area which could be indexed completely. Eventually, two areas were chosen: all items in the disciplines of medicine and nursing; and all nonbook materials. Nonbook materials accounted for about 9% of the workflow; they were easily separable; and there was some dissatisfaction about their treatment by conventional subject methods. We were able from the start to work with a "pure" PRECIS; that is, the entries were not linked to class numbers, but to documents.

PRECIS at the Bibliocentre began rather primitively. I had to adjust from PRECIS 1 to PRECIS 2, indexers had to be trained, and we had to begin with a manual system.[1] Nevertheless, in 1973 we produced a catalog of films which included the first non-experimental standard PRECIS index to appear. Using the *British National Bibliography*'s flowcharts, we wrote our own programs for the Sigma 7 computer at the University of Toronto. These are now being used by Aurora High School and by the ONTERIS Project. In 1974 we published a PRECIS index as direct computer print-out.[2] In addition to two cumulated film

catalogs, we also produced supplements and an authority file containing 6,000
SINs and 2,950 RINs, together with the entries and references they generated.[3]
Unfortunately, the College Bibliocentre's financial problems, always present
but aggravated by inflation on the one hand and by education ceasing to be a
fashionable area for government spending on the other, led to the abandonment
of PRECIS and a number of other services in 1976.

Although we are supposedly in the electronic generation, nonbook materials
are still a comparatively novel mode of instruction and are sometimes regarded
with suspicion. I had no previous experience with them when I joined the Bibliocentre, and I approached them with an open mind. My experience during the
last three years does not contradict Derek Austin's claim that the medium *per se*
makes no difference to the indexing,[4] although I would rephrase this to say that
the medium makes no difference to subject representation by PRECIS. The overall indexing process may differ because of the inherent differences between nonbook materials and monographs, but this is not insuperable.

The indexing process can be divided into subject analysis and subject representation. There is little literature on the subject approach to nonbook materials, and even less on subject analysis. I define subject analysis as the process by
which the subject of a document is discovered, recognized and defined: the
foundation of indexing, classifying and subject heading work. The indexer must
recognize and identify the subject, often with the aid of reference tools or even
outside experts; then, the subject must be defined in a statement so that the
indexer can say, "This book is about the Boer War", or "This phonotape is about
industrial relations in hospitals in Ontario", etc. Once such a subject statement
has been formulated, it has to be represented by index entries or class numbers.
This second process is normally controlled by precedent and by such guides as
classification schedules and printed lists of headings. For an experienced indexer,
all these activities proceed simultaneously in a heuristic way and are not completely conscious.

I have described these familiar phenomena at such length because they are
familiar primarily through the handling of monographs by conventional subject
methods. PRECIS has no list of approved (and inevitably out-of-date) headings;
the authority file grows as the system grows, and can be edited at any time. The
Manual will guide you, but not relieve you of the responsibility of establishing
your own precedents. The subject approach to monographs relies on established
techniques for subject analysis and on traditional reference points: title page,
contents, introduction, etc. . . . Nonbook materials require the use of special
equipment to recover the information they contain. Few organisations which are
central processing agencies can afford the capital investment in such equipment,
let alone pay the salaries of sufficient subject analysts to screen every film and
play every tape. In our particular situation there was the further complication
that only two out of three nonbook items actually passed through the Bibliocentre. We were thrown back on data sheets for some of our work; and we decided that playing the item was the last resort. We relied primarily on abstracts
as the raw material for analysis. These abstracts may have been prepared by a
cataloger at the Bibliocentre or at one of the colleges, or they might be taken
from a distributor's catalog. The latter were usually more reliable; abstracts prepared by catalogers were frequently drawn from only part of the document—
the first few minutes of a sound tape, for example—as we discovered in checking.

Using such available textual sources saved time and money. Thus, although the subject analysis of nonbook materials might present some problems, we could always arrive at a subject statement which could be transformed into a PRECIS string.

There is one more problem that can be considered administrative rather than technical: form divisions. A greater proportion of nonbook materials are retrieved by form than is the case with monographs: recordings of music and several categories of film—abstract, animated, experimental—for example. Should the subject index carry this information? It would help the user who required certain information in a certain format, or who possessed only some items of audiovisual equipment. Many subjects were recurrent, however, and to write many strings which differed only in the form division would be expensive and time-consuming. To some extent, we avoided this difficulty by deciding to issue catalogs limited to a single medium. We did use form divisions when index-ing transfers from one medium to another, using a number of strings of this nature:

    $z 11030 $a   fiction in English
    $z 60030 $a   radio adaptations
    $z 60030 $a   sound tape recordings

That is, the item itself was a tape recording of a radio play which was an adap-tation of a novel. Again, for reasons of economy, we rarely used form divisions as lead terms.

We had few technical difficulties, but the most obvious again relates to differences between monographs and nonbook materials. The great general schemes of subject representation, such as the Dewey Decimal Classification (DC) and Library of Congress subject headings, possess tremendous inertial force: they just keep rolling along. They also possess one great disadvantage when applied to nonbook materials: they were designed for use with mono-graphs. The subject headings do not seem completely efficient in that field; although, DC is less specific than PRECIS in the case of 85% of the books included in the *British National Bibliography*.[5] In my experience, many non-book items—perhaps the majority—deal with subjects that either do not appear or have not appeared as yet in monographs or are much narrower in range and more specific. A filmloop, for example, may be of a few minutes' duration. Some subjects are more suited to a nonbook medium than to print. Some typical examples are:
(1)   Know-alls (i.e. "Smart Alecs");
(2)   A comparative study of size, ranging from atomic nuclei to galaxies;
(3)   Indifference to injustice;
(4)   Individual theorems in geometry;
(5)   Film interpretations of individual poems;
(6)   A sound disc anthology of popular ballads about the enfranchisement of American women.
We were often dealing, therefore, with subjects unlikely to appear in mono-graphs or with self-contained fragments of knowledge. From this I concluded that the use of subject indexing schemes designed for monographs is usually inappropriate and frequently unhelpful when dealing with nonbook materials.

Form divisions are often lacking, so that an experimental film may have to be assigned the heading:

Photography—Experiments

Subject headings are often too broad and provide too few access points. Under these circumstances, it is not surprising that media people have welcomed PRECIS,[6] which can provide clear and specific entries for such subjects.

But was not PRECIS also designed for monographs? How can it cope with nonbook materials more usefully than the traditional schemes? The answer is that PRECIS is based on totally different principles. It is not a finite schedule or a limited list of approved headings on whose Procrustean bed the results of subject analysis have to be stretched or compressed. It is a set of procedures based on the foundation of linguistics. Nowhere is this difference more clearly expressed than in Austin's explanation that no citation order proved satisfactory "until we had overcome the librarian's natural tendency to set terms down in an order which reflects their relative importance as indicators of shelf position."[7] When a subject statement has been formulated, it does not have to be wholly or partially translated into a different and limited retrieval language, but undergoes a less violent transformation into a string which generates index entries. The example cited earlier, "Industrial relations in hospitals in Ontario", becomes

$z 01030 $a   Ontario
$z 11030 $a   hospitals
$z 21030 $a   industrial relations

which the computer will turn into the entries

Ontario
Hospitals. Industrial relations
Hospitals. Ontario
Industrial relations
Industrial relations. Hospitals. Ontario

Nothing has been forced or awkwardly expressed. The linguistic foundation is as suited to nonbook materials as to monographs. In addition, PRECIS offers the advantages of an open-ended vocabulary: terminology can be kept up-to-date and responsive to the user, especially if there is user-indexer feedback. There is no arbitrary limit on the depth of subject analysis or the clarity and specificity of subject representation: an invaluable merit when the indexer is wrestling with "Participation of citizens of Little Burgundy in urban renewal" or "A comparative study of news reports, editorials and columns in newspapers". There is no reason why PRECIS cannot be used to index individual sequences in films; that is, there are no technical reasons, although there may be financial ones. Certainly, we can easily be this specific:

Quebec province
Montreal. Little Burgundy. Urban renewal
Participation of citizens
Montreal
Little Burgundy. Urban renewal. Participation of citizens

Little Burgundy. Montreal
     Urban renewal. Participation of citizens
Urban Renewal. Little Burgundy. Montreal
     Participation of citizens
Participation. Citizens. Little Burgundy
          Montreal
     In urban renewal
Citizens. Little Burgundy. Montreal
     Participation in urban renewal

I can think of only one case in which we departed from the principles of the *Manual*; and since this resulted from our experience with nonbook materials it should be explained. The concept "flow in pipes" is usually regarded as a prepositional difference.[8] This concept will not often occur in a subject statement derived from the analysis of a monograph, but we were suddenly exposed to more than fifty films on fluid dynamics. These had such subjects as "Flow of fluids past towed obstacles" and "Flow of fluids in tee-elbows". The effect of this saturation was to convince me that an equally good case could be made for regarding 'flow' as a directional property.[9] It is unlikely that this would have occurred in different circumstances. We therefore composed such strings as

$z1 1030	$a	reservoirs
$zp 1030	$a	ducts $w from
$zs 1030	$a	flow $v of $w into
$z3 1030	$a	fluids $i incompressible

and created such entries as these:

Reservoirs
     Ducts. Flow of incompressible fluids
Ducts. Reservoirs
     Flow of incompressible fluids
Flow. Incompressible fluids
     Into ducts from reservoirs
Fluids
     Incompressible fluids. Flow into ducts from reservoirs
Incompressible fluids
     Flow into ducts from reservoirs

It need scarcely be added that, although good index entries are the primary goal, such divergence from orthodoxy is, and should be, extremely rare.

I conclude with another example of a complicated subject: a feminist study of Judaeo-Christian attitudes to women. All that was provided for this in *LCSH* was:

(1)   Women in Christianity
(2)   Women and religion

The PRECIS entries were rather more useful:

Women
     Attitudes of Christian Church—*Feminist viewpoints*
     Attitudes of Judaism—*Feminist viewpoints*
Attitudes. Christian Church
     To women—*Feminist viewpoints*

> **Attitudes. Judaism**
> To women—*Feminist viewpoints*
> **Christian Church**
> Attitudes to women—*Feminist viewpoints*
> **Judaism**
> Attitudes to women—*Feminist viewpoints*
> **Feminist viewpoints**
> Judaeo-Christian attitudes to women

The advantages of clarity, specificity and access are achieved with PRECIS. It is true that the number of entries has increased, but strings of this length are the exception rather than the rule. An internal survey revealed that each film required an average of 1.48 LC subject headings; with PRECIS, each film required an average of 2.38 index entries: 1.86 entries under lead terms plus 0.52 references.[10] This is not a high price to pay for specificity and access.

My conclusion is that PRECIS is unrivalled as a subject retrieval system for nonbook materials, mainly because its underlying philosophy is neutral in regard to the format of the document indexed.

NOTES

1. C. D. Robinson, "Indexing the Film Catalogue: With Comparisons Between LCSH and PRECIS Entries," *College Bibliocentre Newsletter*, v. 8 (June 1973), pp. 7-13.
2. *Film Catalogue: A Union List of Films, Videotapes and Filmloops Used in the Ontario Colleges of Applied Arts and Technology*, 2d ed. 1st suppl. (Don Mills, Ontario: College Bibliocentre, 1974).
3. C. D. Robinson, *PRECIS Authority File* (Don Mills, Ontario: College Bibliocentre, 1975).
4. Derek Austin, "The Development of PRECIS: A Theoretical and Technical History," *Journal of Documentation*, v. 30 (1974), p. 97.
5. Ibid., p. 80.
6. Ibid., p. 97.
7. Derek Austin, *PRECIS: A Manual of Concept Analysis and Subject Indexing* (London: Council of the British National Bibliography, 1974), p. 13.
8. Ibid., pp. 88 and 210.
9. Ibid., p. 233.
10. "CB Film Catalogue—Second Edition," *College Bibliocentre Newsletter*, v. 11 (March 1974), pp. 13-14.

The National Film Board of Canada Project

Mary Dykstra
School of Library Service, Dalhousie University,
Halifax Nova Scotia, Canada

Early in 1975 I was invited to the National Film Board (NFB) of Canada to discuss the Board's intention of developing an information retrieval system for the films it distributes. The eventual goal was described as a system for all non-print media in Canada. The developed system was to be compatible with library practice, so that it could interface with already developed national and international systems for print materials. If possible, it was also to be developed in coordination with an automated on-line booking/control system being implemented as a pilot project in the Atlantic Regional Office. There were no other restrictions or pre-conceived configurations. I was told that $3000 was available for research, with a view to the provision of specific recommendations and a concrete proposal. This was the first time in its history that the Film Board had ever attempted to contract for the services of a professional librarian or a person from the "academic sector". The contract was awarded to the Dalhousie University School of Library Service, with myself as principal investigator.

The objectives for the research project were divided into two categories: short term, having to do with the recommendation of a system for NFB itself; and long term, concerning a system for all non-print materials in Canada. The understanding was that I bear in mind the long term objectives but concentrate on those in the short term category. For my own working formula I began to see the project as an exploration of existing studies, systems, and practices in media information storage and retrieval, with a view to culling from them those features which, when consolidated into a single system, would be most likely to satisfy the needs of the National Film Board and its users today and tomorrow.

Two constraints had been given:

(1) existing systems of cataloging and classification, together with existing data bases and networks organized according to these systems;

(2) the on-line Booking/Control System designed by Dymaxion Research Ltd. in Halifax, N. S.

To these constraints I added two more. As a librarian, I hold two basic interrelated tenets which I saw as being very much in line with the objectives:

(1) An information system is never a work of art or technology or expediency designed as an end in itself, but at all times it must be viewed as a tool to assist in the process of delivering to the user the resources

he or she requires. An out-moded system is also inadequate. The best
information system is one which can be most effectively used.
(2) Because the design of an information system is primarily not a tech-
     nical but a user service, the only place to begin and end is with the user.
I saw the users of this system as being both the National Film Board itself,
and the Canadian people who view or show its films.

The National Film Board of Canada was established as an agency of the
Federal government on May 2, 1939, under the direction of John Grierson. A
short time earlier Grierson, internationally known for his work in documentary
film, had been invited from Great Britain to co-ordinate and centralize film activities in Canada.[1] Today the National Film Board has a Head Office in Montreal,
six Regional Offices across Canada and several Offices abroad: three in the United
States, two in Europe, and one each in South Asia and Japan. There are several
Branch Offices under each Regional Office. The film catalogs are produced in the
Head Office; much, though by no means all, of the film production takes place
there. Also located in the Head Office among the various administrative units
are a large film reference library and the film archive.

Approximately 1,500 National Film Board films are currently available in
English. Several of these are also available in French; other films are available in
French only. Some films have been released in other languages as well, especially
in the Toronto area with its large ethnic concentrations. Both an English *Film
Catalogue* and a French *Catalogue des films* are issued every two years. One hundred to two hundred new films are produced annually, including English versions
of French films and vice versa. The Film Board also produces a *Media Catalogue*
listing its film loops, film strips, kits, cassettes, and other materials. Several films
are produced by the Film Board under contract for other government departments, such as the Department of Labour. From time to time special projects are
undertaken; for instance the beautiful and expensive volume *Between Friends/
Entre Amis*[2] was produced by the Film Board as a gift from Canada for the American Bicentennial.

Each Regional Office and Branch Office maintains a film library from which
films are booked locally. Also the Regional Office libraries and most Branch libraries contain one or several prints of the films currently available. All new films
are released to the regions from the Head Office in Montreal; a film number is assigned to each film upon release. Films in each film library are physically arranged
according to these numbers, which indicate among other things the length of the
film and consequently the size of the container. All films are released to the Regional Offices with "promo" sheets and any other relevant material. The excellent
NFB film annotations, however, are not included with the film at this point. Booking staff and film users alike must wait up to three years for new films to be listed
in the *Catalogue*, where these annotations appear.

Presently, users of NFB films have available to them the film catalogs from
which they may make their choices. The 1,500 or so films in each catalog are
listed in a broad subject arrangement. Several of the headings in the English
Film Catalogue are as follows:

Feature Films

Canada—The Land
Earth Sciences and Physical Geography

Social Geography
Environment—Conservation—Pollution
The North

Canada—Past and Present
History Films
The Eskimo
The Indian
Portraits—Lifestyles—Institutions
National Defence
Regional Films

Sports and Recreation
Sports
Recreation

Of Special Interest to Women

The World Around

To pick one example, under the heading "Regional Films," seventy-one films are listed, representing almost as many regions. These headings (about forty in all) are the only means of subject access.

Included in each *Catalogue* is a title index and an index of producers and directors. The catalogs are glossy, well-designed, and profusely illustrated. Although they are out of date from the day they appear, they are nevertheless among the most beautiful film catalogs on the market. They are intended to provide information, but their main purpose is to sell films.

Once people choose their films, direct contact at the local Regional Office or Branch is not with a person in charge of the film library who has a working knowledge of the films themselves, but with a booking clerk.

My first step in the project was to revisit the Halifax Regional Office. Halifax was important because of the pilot project Booking/Control System. Just being implemented at that time, the system has subsequently undergone evaluation and is now working extremely well. There are plans for its introduction in other Regional Offices and ultimately across Canada. Briefly this is a computerized system containing three modules: booking, reporting, and file control. Communication with the system is on-line through terminals located at each Branch, with the Regional Office as co-ordinator. The system includes a film file (information about each film, including how many prints are available in each Branch), a client file (alphabetical and by client number), a shipping file, a refusal file (which indicates when and where more prints are needed), and a notice file. Advance bookings are confirmed and recorded instantly, with machine-generated instructions for shipping and, if necessary, the mailing of notices. Intra-location loans are possible through the on-line scanning of bookings in each Branch, with all transactions confirmed through the Regional Office.[3]

It soon became obvious that any linkage between the Booking/Control System and an information indexing and retrieval system would have to occur through the booking system's film file. The film file at the present time is fully adaptable, with each film record containing several empty data elements reserved for specific cataloging and classification information.

After detailed investigation of the Atlantic Regional Office in Halifax, I visited the Regional Offices in Toronto, Ottawa, and Montreal. It was necessary to observe first-hand the situation in these regions, each with its own quite different user constraints. In each Office I asked the same questions, both of the booking staff and of typical users such as a Toronto high school English teacher. What I needed to know was: what information, not now available, do Canadian film users need in order to obtain the most suitable NFB-distributed films?

I was expecting the answers to my questions to vary in these three different situations, but instead they were remarkably similar. The most frequently mentioned need was for better subject access to the films. "What do you have on such-and-such a subject?" is an ever recurring question.

Even though it is true that users very often request specific films by title, it soon became clear that these users spend many hours poring over the catalogs before requesting that title. And if the particular film is not available, the inevitable question is, "What else do you have on that subject?" At this point, the booking clerk usually has no ready answer.

The need was for specific subject information. For every film request on recreation there are many for such things as canoeing in Canada's National Parks. A teacher doesn't usually ask, "What do you have on psychology?" but, "Do you have a film on the problems of adolescent boys? I'm especially interested in the feelings kids in urban slums have, and how it affects their behavior." There is at least one NFB film on this particular subject, entitled *Paper Boy*. It's the 37th entry in the English *Film Catalogue* under the general heading of "Sociology". The annotation is excellent, but it takes a fairly long time to find.

It is important to note that the primary need was for an alphabetical subject approach, not a numerical classification system. It seems clear that the films in the NFB film libraries will continue to be assigned a fixed location on the racks which is determined, in part, by the size of the container. Each film already has its unique number, assigned to the film upon release, and used in the booking process. An additional number would be both unnecessary and confusing. However, a numerical classification system might prove useful in arranging the catalogs by subject. It would definitely be a useful service for multi-media libraries which buy NFB films and intend to assign to them either Dewey Decimal or Library of Congress classification numbers, if these numbers could be provided. The provision of a Universal Decimal Classification number would be desirable as a link with the Canadian Film Institute, the *British National Film Catalogue*,[4] and the catalogs of the British Universities Film Council.[5,6] But as far as direct user and staff access to the subject content of films is concerned, retrieval with words would be far less confusing than retrieval with numbers which stand for the words.

However, users still felt the need for *some* sort of generic or classified approach. I therefore began to concentrate upon the possibility of finding a system which would provide for alphabetical subject access while at the same time, achieving a truly classified arrangement of the film content through the capability to generate tightly constructed thesaural relationships.

An additional requirement for the alphabetical approach was based on Canadian Federal law: the subject headings must be in both English and French.

And, of course, there was the expressed need for all information to be as up-to-date as possible.

While on my Toronto-Ottawa-Montreal trip, I also visited the University of Toronto Media Centre, the College Bibliocentre, the Metropolitan Toronto Library Board, the National Library of Canada, the Canadian Film Institute, and the National Film Archives. I conferred with the Senior Film Officer under the Secretary of State. I sought out information concerning the University of Toronto Library Automated System (UT/LAS), and the Ontario Universities Library Co-operative System (OULCS)—now UNICAT/TELECAT.[7] The University of Toronto Library Automated System, with one of the largest data bases in the world, includes the files of the Media Centre, the College Bibliocentre, the Metropolitan Toronto Library Board, and the UNICAT/TELECAT system. I corresponded with La Centrale des bibliothèques in Montreal, which had plans for automating by joining what is now UNICAT/TELECAT. Internationally, I concerned myself with developments in the United States and in Great Britain.[8-13] I found myself enmeshed in a labyrinth of systems and schemes and plans, all of which in some way contributed to the proposal of a system for the National Film Board of Canada.

A complete description of the information indexing and retrieval system proposed can be found in my report.[14] For the purposes of this paper, I would like to concentrate on the recommendation for meeting the need for alphabetical subject access.

Basically, of course, other than highly specialized or local schemes, four types of system providing an alphabetical subject approach are in existence today:

(1) computerized title key-word systems such as KWIC or KWOC;
(2) chain indexing;
(3) subject headings from authority lists such as *Library of Congress Subject Headings*[15] and *Sears*;[16]
(4) the set of working procedures for the creation of computerized subject entries known as PRECIS.[17]

A keyword index based on titles would have been easy and quick—except for the fact that NFB film titles are not an indicator of subject content. *Paper Boy* doesn't begin to cover the concept of the socio-psychological impact of an inner city environment upon the behavior of an adolescent boy, yet this is what the film is actually about. Nor does the film title *At Long Last* give a single clue that the film is really about the National Library of Canada. Other titles which immediately spring to mind are *Nell and Fred* (about the pros and cons of entering an old people's home), *One Hand Clapping* (about noise pollution), *The Medium is the Massage, You Know, The Colours of Pride, Do Not Fold, Staple, Spindle or Mutilate, Wow,* and *The Heat Wave Lasted Four Days* (described in the NFB annotation as a "fast-moving murder mystery"). Even an enriched KWIC for these and hundreds of similar titles would have to be all enriched and no KWIC. The intellectual effort of determining each film's "aboutness" would still have to be made.

Chain indexing, not practiced to any extent in North America, is normally used to provide an alphabetical index for a classified catalogue. Since NFB has no need for a numerical classification scheme, the idea of a chain index was not pursued.

Which brings us to subject headings. Even though the file is now small, *Sears* headings were not considered specific enough for film content. But the use of *Library of Congress Subject Headings (LCSH)* had to be given very serious consideration. Certainly the use of *LCSH* would have put NFB squarely in line with current North American library practice. I have worked directly with *LCSH* for more than ten years—as a cataloger, as a user services librarian, and as an instructor in cataloging and classification. I have also made it my business to begin to understand somewhat the medium of film. Precisely because of this knowledge and experience, I could not recommend the use of *LCSH* to the NFB.

First of all, Library of Congress subject headings are built upon the way Charles Cutter, one century ago, viewed the problems of subject access to information. At that time, recorded knowledge was available principally through the medium of print, more specifically the monograph. These monographs were usually not about multi-faceted subjects, rarely were they interdisciplinary as we understand that term, nor were they produced at a mind-boggling pace. It is well to bear in mind that a general theme in the United States' centennial year—1876— as expressed at the lavish Centennial Exposition in Philadelphia, was that the world—or certainly the United States—had reached its peak of knowledge and understanding; henceforth there would be little new under the sun to know or to write about. It was a time before Einstein and his theory which revolutionized epistemology as well as all of science, before a technology based on electricity, before television, before atomic power, before the full emergence of sociology as a discipline, before air travel or space travel, before computers.

In the second place, the medium of film, more than any other medium, facilitates communication on the intuitive as well as on the rational level. Except for some forms of animation, film presents direct images of reality rather than reality as encoded in the straight-jacket of language or other abstract systems of symbols. Moreover, new subjects are very frequently captured on film before they are written about. It is a question whether *any* indexing system using words can provide adequate access to a subject conveyed through the medium of film. Certainly any word system used must be as exact as possible, as context-enriched as possible, and as flexible and current as possible.

My third reason was this: it is a known fact to those in the business of systems design and systems analysis that there is a limit to the tinkering that can be done to a given system. No amount of tinkering or redrafting or computerizing of *LCSH* can make beautifully faceted, tightly constructed, hierarchically sound thesaurical relationships out of the present system of references. A computerized subject authority file of *LCSH* will still produce relationships between terms and phrases which are inexact, convoluted, and which in some cases turn back upon themselves—all the computer can give to these is the element of incredible speed. They will appear as before, only faster.

Fourthly, the National Film Board is beginning with a small file. The work to be done retrospectively is minimal. The factors of economy and expediency which must at least be considered when a very large file is involved are not relevant in this case.

And finally, *LCSH* is an unilingual list. Laval headings,[18] similar to *LCSH*, have been used in Canada for French language materials, but to my knowledge the National Library's efforts toward the creation of a computerized authority file of both the French and the English headings does not include a plan for the

intermarrying of these headings into a single thesaurus capable of access in
French or English or both by means of a switching capacity.

Having decided, after due consideration, against the first three types of alphabetical subject approach, I turned to the fourth possibility. Permit me to quote
for you the first section of the chapter in my report entitled: "The Proposed
System":

"Out of the maze of developments in the bibliographical control of film information and subject access to it, it is now necessary to chart a course for the
Film Board. The system proposed is intended to consolidate the best of what
presently exists, together with what is moving in with the changing currents. It is
designed to be efficient, to satisfy user needs effectively, to be sophisticated in
its utilization of computer technology, and at the same time to be as simple and
straightforward as possible.

    (1)   *IT IS PROPOSED THAT*, because

- NFB users have specified that their primary need is for improved
  subject access to film content
- film content is both specific and complex and requires a subject
  indexing system which is competent to provide satisfactory access
- subject access must be kept up-to-date with the release of new
  films
- a computer-generated subject indexing system can be used most
  effectively in conjunction with NFB's pilot project on-line automated booking/control system
- a system is required in which subject access to NFB films will be
  available in both English and French
- a system of subject access is required in which terms can easily be
  clustered into hierarchical groups of concepts, so that a subject
  area can be approached generically and not only by specific
  terms in alphabetical order
- subject access to NFB films must be compatible with most probable future practice

and because

- the Preserved Context Indexing System (PRECIS) is the only existing and available subject indexing system which satisfies all of
  the above requirements
- it is estimated that 40-45% of NFB films have already been indexed by PRECIS at the College Bibliocentre, Toronto, and the
  required computer software is operational there
- the College Bibliocentre, its records compatible with the other
  users of UT/LAS whose data base it shares, has expressed willing-
  ness to co-operate with NFB

*PRECIS be the subject approach adopted by NFB for its information
system.* "[19]

Nothing happened overnight, although I have been told by those more
knowledgeable of the workings of Federal governments than I am, that things
are indeed proceeding at a fast pace. To begin with, there was the matter of tim-
ing and coincidence. It just so happened that the day the final report was received in Montreal, in mid-October 1975, a meeting of representatives of all film

agencies in Canada was being held in Ottawa to discuss the very idea of a Canadian information system for film. A copy of my report was rushed to the meeting, where excerpts were read. As can be imagined, no other input at the meeting was of comparable relevance. So immediately, instead of much later, the recommendation was put into the much wider context of a national system, i.e., the terms of reference of the long-term objectives. Further action was that the NFB, which incidentally is under the same Federal branch as the National Library, was given the mandate to proceed with an information system for film. The development of an information system, along with the development of a distribution system, was given top priority in NFB's budget for the current fiscal year. Furthermore, in this year of large Federal cutbacks, the budget was not cut.

In midsummer 1976 I was again approached by the Atlantic Regional Director. He feared that while plans for a national system were being considered in all their ramifications, *rigor mortis* might conceivably set in and in the end nothing concrete would happen. He suggested the local publication of a *Film Catalogue* supplement, complete with a PRECIS index manually produced. Very quickly I found myself taking a week of my vacation in which I wrote the PRECIS strings, taught a person at the NFB Atlantic Regional Office how to produce the entries, and determined the necessary references. Compatibility with future efforts was ensured by means of several phone calls to the University of Toronto Media Centre and by the use of the Authority files of the College Bibliocentre and the *British National Bibliography*.

The *Film Catalogue* supplement, currently at the printers, is scheduled to appear shortly. It will be circulated to the Regional Offices across Canada. Users will be encouraged to express their reactions. Although no feedback can be reported at this stage from the Canadian public, NFB staff members who are thoroughly familiar with the films indexed and who have seen the draft are enthusiastic. Two small examples will show why.

No annotation was available for the film *Still in One Piece, Anyway*, so the film was screened. With PRECIS it was possible to provide entries giving an exact indication of what the film is about, and covering all reasonable approaches:

> **Chedabucto Bay.** Nova Scotia
>> Middle East oil. Transport by super-tankers. Environmental aspects
>
> **Environmental aspects.** Transport of Middle East oil by super-tankers.
>> Chedabucto Bay. Nova Scotia
>
> **Nova Scotia**
>> Chedabucto Bay. Middle East oil. Transport by super-tankers. Environmental aspects
>
> **Oil.** Chedabucto Bay. Nova Scotia
>> Middle East oil. Transport by super-tankers. Environmental aspects
>
> **Super-tankers.** Chedabucto Bay. Nova Scotia
>> Transport of Middle East oil. Environmental aspects
>
> **Transport.** Middle East oil. Chedabucto Bay. Nova Scotia
>> By super-tankers. Environmental aspects

This same film was indexed with Library of Congress subject headings for the UT/LAS data base as follows:

> 1. Ships

A second example is the film *Bill Loosely's Heat Pump.* The NFB annotation for this film reads:

"A short film to be used as a companion piece to 'Bate's Car. . .' and as one of a series of short films on alternative energy sources. For more than 20 years, William Loosely has heated his Burlington, Ontario home with the heat collected from the ground around his home, by using a heat pump."

The following entries were produced with PRECIS:

Alternative energy sources. Heating systems. Houses
    Heat pumps

Energy sources. Heating systems. Houses
    Alternative energy sources: Heat pumps

Heat pumps. Alternative energy sources. Heating systems. Houses

Heating systems. Houses
    Alternative energy sources: Heat pumps

Houses
    Heating systems. Alternative energy sources: Heat pumps

Once again it is interesting to compare these entries with the Library of Congress subject headings this film was given:

    (1)   Mechanical engineering
    (2)   Physics
    (3)   Dynamics
    (4)   Dwellings—Heating and ventilation
    (5)   Heating

Will an automated on-line information/booking/control system for film in Canada be fully operational in the near future—a complete delivery service, enabling Canadian film users to choose suitable films by means of scanning a PRECIS index, book these films and receive them by mail, all by means of a single computer transaction? My horoscope keeps giving hints which could be construed as encouraging. My crystal ball, reliable every once in a while, keeps showing a faint image of what I believe is a penguin from the Canadian north.

A Federal Task Force is now being formed, subject to Treasury Board approval, to consider the proposed system. (A Task Force is necessary in Canada before anything can be implemented at the national level.) I hope that this will ultimately lead to the adoption of my proposal, and the large-scale use of PRECIS for the indexing of films in Canada.

[The views expressed in this paper are those of the author and not necessarily those of the National Film Board.]

NOTES

1. Forsyth Hardy, ed., *Grierson on Documentary* (London: Collins, 1946), p. 151.
2. National Film Board of Canada, *Between Friends/Entre Amis* (Ottawa: The Board, 1976).

3. Dymaxion Research Ltd., *Film Booking/Control System: An Outline* (Halifax, Canada: The Company, 1975).

4. *British National Film Catalogue* (London: British Film Institute, 1963-   ).

5. *Audio-Visual Materials for Higher Education* (London: British Universities Film Council, 1973-   ).

6. *Higher Education Learning Programmes Information Service (HELPIS) Catalogue* (London: British Universities Film Council, 1976-   ). (Previously issued by the National Council for Educational Technology.)

7. Ralph E. Stierwalt, "UNICAT/TELECAT: A Report on the Development of a Union Catalogue in Ontario," *Ontario Library Review* (September 1976), pp. 180-85.

8. *Index to 16mm Educational Films*, 4th ed. (Los Angeles: National Information Center for Educational Media, 1973).

9. *NICEM Newsletter* (Spring 1975).

10. Leslie A. Gilbert, "A British Documentation System for Non-Book Materials," *Educational Media International*, no. 3 (1973), pp. 13-21.

11. Leslie A. Gilbert and Jan W. Wright, *Non-Book Materials: Their Bibliographic Control*, Working paper no. 6 (London: National Council for Educational Technology, 1971).

12. British Library, Systems Development Branch, *MERLIN (Machine Readable Library Information System): An Introduction for British Library Staff.* (London: The Library, 1975).

13. Christie Quinn, "Running a National Filmography" (Report on the *British National Film Catalogue* for the International Film and Television Council).

14. Mary Dykstra, *An Information Indexing and Retrieval System for the National Film Board of Canada: A Proposal and a Plan for Its Implementation.* (Montreal: National Film Board of Canada, 1976). (Internal document. To be published by the School of Library Service, Dalhousie University, under joint contract with the National Film Board in the Schools' *Occasional Papers* series.)

15. United States, Library of Congress, Subject Cataloging Division, *Library of Congress Subject Headings*, 8th ed. (Washington, DC: The Library of Congress, 1975).

16. B. M. Westby, ed., *Sears List of Subject Headings*, 10th ed. (New York: Wilson, 1972).

17. Derek Austin, *PRECIS: A Manual of Concept Analysis and Subject Indexing* (London: Council of the British National Bibliography, 1974).

18. Université Laval, Bibliothèque, Service de catalogage, *Répertoire de vedettes-matière*, 7th ed. (Québec: La Bibliothèque, 1972).

19. Mary Dykstra, op. cit., pp. 19-20.

ADDITIONAL REFERENCES

1. Bonnefoi, Claude, "The Audio-Visual Media: Problems of Document Processing," *Educational Media International*, no. 3 (1973), pp. 6-13.

2. Robinson, C. D., "Indexing the Film Catalogue: With Comparisons Between LCSH and PRECIS Entries," *College Bibliocentre Newsletter*, v. 8 (June 1973), pp. 7-13.

3. Sinkankas, George M., *A Study in the Syndetic Structure of the Library of Congress List of Subject Headings* (Pittsburgh: University of Pittsburgh Graduate School of Library and Information Sciences, 1972).

4. Wellisch, Hans (Hanan), "Subject Retrieval in the Seventies — Methods, Problems, Prospects," *Subject Retrieval in the Seventies: New Directions*, ed. Hans (Hanan) Wellisch and Thomas D. Wilson (Westport, Connecticut: Greenwood Publishing Company, 1972).

5. Wright, G. H., "Catalogue Subject Headings: An Indication of the Problem," *College Bibliocentre Newsletter*, v. 14 (December 1974), pp. 5-10.

The Practical Possibilities of PRECIS in North America

C. Donald Cook
Faculty of Library Science, University of Toronto

To begin, I should like to set some parameters to qualify my subsequent remarks. First of all, the organizers of this Workshop have chosen as a commentator on "practical possibilities" someone who is unencumbered by practical experience in PRECIS, and who, therefore, may be freer to speculate on its possibilities than might be those who are familiar with its problems under operating conditions. Second, my comments will pertain to "North America," not because I reside and work in Canada, but because of the exceedingly close relationships of the United States and Canada in most matters of bibliographic control. Finally, I shall limit myself to the potential cataloging uses of PRECIS; certain comments may also be relevant to periodical indexing, abstracting and other related activities, but these are not being examined specifically.

In assessing the practical possibilities for PRECIS, I propose to look at the system in terms of certain selected criteria for the evaluation of information retrieval systems (borrowing heavily from Kent[1], Vickery[2,3] and Taube[4,5]); interspersed with these comments and at the conclusion are certain speculations on what we might consider seriously for PRECIS now and in the near future.

Initially, there is the problem of familiarity: what is familiar is comfortable. PRECIS is new and unfamiliar to a very large number of librarians in North America and those who are familiar with it know it mostly in an abstract sense or through use of the *British National Bibliography* (*BNB*) Subject Index. I would hazard the guess that the use by librarians of this Index is largely unevaluative; a subject index is present, and that, by and large, suffices. Virtually all of our library users, however, have no knowledge of PRECIS. If the Index locates what a user is seeking, he is usually unaware of the system by which this is accomplished — if PRECIS in *BNB* does not locate, both librarian and user simply turn to some other means. (It is possible that the unobtrusiveness of a system of subject analysis is a valid criterion of its value, but this is another topic.)

However, familiarity with a system of subject analysis is quite another matter for the librarian using a system to catalog materials for a library. While certainly there have been numerous other methods used in North America, the Library of Congress system of subject headings has predominated for three-quarters of a century to such an extent that serious consideration of any general use of another system may be viewed as a genuine example of bibliothecal "future shock."

There are, of course, quite real as well as psychological problems. Most North American libraries are so dependent on the bibliographic products of the Library of Congress that consideration of another method of subject analysis approaches the unrealistic unless the Library of Congress is willing to do so as well. For this reason, many of my comments relate directly to the Library of Congress and its system of subject headings.

However, for the present, let us optimistically assume that we can cross the very real psychological barrier of unfamiliarity, and turn to other aspects.

The crucial criteria of precision and recall are ones which I shall pass over quickly. This is not to diminish their importance in any way, but simply because the evaluation of PRECIS in these terms can come intelligently only from the results of studies such as that of Ann H. Schabas, already described in her paper. It is my intuitive feeling that PRECIS ranks relatively high in retrieval efficiency and that it is relatively easy for a user to ascertain the relevance of entries. However, both of these assumptions require further examination.

PRECIS pre-coordinates in a rather elegant way a sophisticated combination of natural language and controlled vocabulary, and through its reliance on the syntax of language provides a logic not hitherto found in a general system of subject analysis. It will accommodate a variety of semantic forms, permitting a wider representation of relationships among the various aspects of subject matter and their inherent meanings than is present in many systems. A high degree of specificity is possible (dependent in part on the skill of the indexer), and the open-endedness of PRECIS permits the (theoretically infinite) addition of new concepts and subject matter. The RINfile permits a high degree of control of the use of terms, and facilitates the introduction of new terminology to minimize the rate of obsolescence.

This rapid and subjective evaluation of PRECIS in terms of these frequently-used criteria may be supplemented by more specific data. The provision of more access points and of more information per entry often are considered advantages for a retrieval system. An examination of almost 20,000 recent *BNB* records[6] indicates an average of 4.84 significant words per actual title (duplications and unuseful "stop" words having been eliminated). Conventional KWIC or KWOC permutations of these titles would probably result in a slightly higher number of access points per title (since duplication would not usually be excluded), with the words presented as used in their natural language context, and with the advantages and disadvantages well-known to this audience.

Moving from access through the natural language of titles to the controlled vocabulary of the *LCSH*, the average number of distinctive words assigned in subject headings for the same records was 4.09, some fifteen per cent fewer than in the titles of the items themselves. Not all of these words, of course, are access points in the *LCSH*, and they might or might not lend themselves to useful permutation. In a sub-set of some 7,200 records among the 20,000, it was found that, on the average, there were 1.40 LC subject headings per record, representing a reduction of 71 per cent in the number of access points when compared with title access. In these access points from *LCSH*, there might or might not be an organized context which would be comparable to the natural language context of KWIC or KWOC.

Finally, using PRECIS, an average of 5.52 distinctive words occurred per title. Like the *LCSH*, these terms *per se* might or might not serve as useful access points. The increase in the number of words, however, suggests an enrichment over title. So far as access points are concerned, an examination of the current printed *BNB* Subject Index indicates an average of 4.22 "leads" per record. This number compares favorably with the number of access points available from permuted natural language, and has the important advantage that the terms are both controlled and presented in a logical context. This access through PRECIS is almost precisely three times that available through the *LCSH*.

A further criterion which may be considered is that of "suggestiveness" — the reference structure present in verbal analysis or the hierarchical relationships in a classification. There is a highly sophisticated and controlled reference structure in PRECIS, as well as numerous classificatory aspects, the latter not dissimilar in their verbal expression to those of the *LCSH*. There is, however, in the combination of UK MARC and PRECIS an ingenious use of the 082 and 083 fields to provide verbal expression of a classification number (in *BNB*, Dewey), and the provision of a classification number with each index entry.

This quick review of some of the characteristics of PRECIS (thus far, in its favor), now leads to what I shall loosely call "input." The techniques of preparing and inputting PRECIS have been a major concern of this Workshop, and need no further review by me. It is clearly evident that, whatever the merits or disadvantages or practical possibilities of PRECIS may be, specific training for input is necessary; while this is true of any system, it seems probable that training for the skilled input of PRECIS may be more demanding than that for a "standard" system such as the *LCSH*. Here, we return in part to the question of "familiarity" mentioned earlier, and it may be harder to "unlearn" *LCSH* than it is to learn PRECIS. Whatever the case, any practical application of PRECIS in North America will involve substantial training programs. Practicing catalogers would need not only the workshops and seminars of the type Mr. Austin has been conducting, but in-house training in libraries and network offices in order to introduce and use the system. A substantial program of retraining seems inevitable.

Although there is some training in PRECIS available in library schools in England,[7,8,9] schools in North America largely limit a discussion of PRECIS to an abstract consideration of "another" system, if they mention it at all. To my knowledge, there is currently little effort to develop skilled practitioners, as there is for the use of the *LCSH*. This is something of the "chicken and the egg" problem: without the knowledge needed to apply PRECIS, its potential use is limited; without a market for students knowing PRECIS, library schools can scarcely devote much time to it in curricula even now often spread too thin.

To go on to consider the product or products of PRECIS apart from their intellectual or substantive content, it is the "output"—the length of the PRECIS string—that is probably of greatest concern. In the same *BNB* records mentioned earlier, it was found that, without its manipulation codes, the average PRECIS string is some 25 per cent longer than the *LCSH* heading or headings used for the same record. This, of course, has important implications for the appearance of PRECIS entries in hard copy in whatever form, as well as for CRT display. *With* manipulation codes, the difference is substantially greater, PRECIS being 81 per cent longer than the *LCSH*. This affects computer storage directly, and has implications for response time.

The larger number of PRECIS "leads," or entries per title, referred to earlier, may be considered an intellectual advantage, but, practically, this of course means an increased number of entries for a printed or microform catalog and an increased number of cards if used in a card catalog.

On-line search facilities for using PRECIS are, to my knowledge, in their infancy. While it is true that on-line search through headings from the *LCSH* seems not to have been developed satisfactorily as yet, substantial work remains to be done for PRECIS before the "competitiveness" of the two systems can adequately be evaluated.

The last criterion I shall consider is that of cost. I would like to be able to say that PRECIS or the assignment of LC subject headings or the use of another system costs "x" dollars in defined situations, and to compare relative economic efficiencies. I simply do not have this information. The staffs of the British Library, the Library of Congress, and the National Library of Canada may already have or should be able to determine such costs for their institutions, and I would urge them to share this information for comparative purposes.

Even without hard figures, there are, nevertheless, several comments which may be useful. At the time PRECIS was introduced by the *BNB*, Library of Congress subject headings were obviously among the alternatives among which a *BNB* system of subject analysis could be chosen. The fact that PRECIS was used instead of the *LCSH* suggests that PRECIS was felt to be intellectually superior and not prohibitively more costly. The developmental costs for PRECIS, a substantial investment, are now largely over and have been absorbed by the British Library. Certainly I am in no position to speak for it, but one might hope that, should North American libraries (either national or individual) wish to introduce PRECIS, reasonable arrangements might be made for the use here of work already done in England and possibly elsewhere. There would, of course, be the costs which are always associated with transferring a system from one environment to another, but surely the potential availability of principles, methodology and human expertise and experience should be an advantage, even if entirely new computer programming might be required.

Furthermore, it is well to remember that potential costs in North America must be considered in relation to the total span of products possible through PRECIS, a matter I shall come to in a moment.

All of the criteria we have been considering and by which one must judge the practicality of PRECIS are, of course, greatly influenced by the specific environment in which it might be used and by the specific products which may be possible from it. There are relative rather than absolute values which must be attached to each, and informed pragmatic judgements which must finally be made. As the most obvious example, the least expensive system is not necessarily the most desirable. As another illustration, PRECIS can provide the expanded geographic access to materials now being sought by the Library of Congress and others, although the *BNB* chooses not to use this capability to its fullest for both intellectual and economic reasons. Such a list could be extended almost indefinitely.

By now, it is evident that, in my innocence of practical experience with PRECIS, I feel it has distinct advantages, both theoretically and practically, over the *LCSH*. It has been suggested that PRECIS' chief "competitor" instead of the *LCSH*, is post-coordinate indexing. However, to my knowledge, no system of this type has been attempted for the control of the enormous amount of bibliographic data involved in national and general libraries. I have serious doubts, given the present state of the art, that post-coordination can enter into serious consideration. I even suspect that a satisfactory solution of the syntactical problems which accompany post-coordinate systems of retrieval might gradually lead to a system not unlike that of PRECIS.

Earlier in my comments, I mentioned the quasi-monopolistic effect on the North American library community of its dependence on the bibliographic output of the Library of Congress. I should like to return to this now, and to add to the Library of Congress the National Library of Canada which, with some exceptions, tends to extend the practices of LC into Canadian methods of bibliographic control.

Currently, it is quite clear that dependence on the bibliographic data produced by national agencies is increasing rapidly, because the advantages apparently outweigh any disadvantages. Contributed data will be channeled through the appropriate national agency and edited to conform to standards and then be redistributed. At the same time, even though agreement on some international standards seems to be growing, we do not appear to be at the point of unanimity, and so far as subject access is concerned, we are scarcely at the beginning.

I should like to suggest, therefore, that it is probable that we are soon approaching the time when national agencies may find themselves responsible for at least two types of products: one for general distribution, and another, probably a sub-set, for use with their own collections. Already, there is a growing distinction between national and internal functions. The Library of Congress provides Dewey Classification numbers for a substantial part of its output, but does not use these internally; the National Library of Canada does not use the LC classification, but supplies it through *Canadiana*; the *BNB* does not use LC subject headings, but these are available through UK MARC.

It requires no vivid imagination, then, to suggest that subject access through PRECIS might be supplied by the national libraries of both the United States and Canada, whether or not these libraries elect to use PRECIS internally for direct subject access to their own collections. Let us assume that this can be done in North America and, in addition, that the linkage of classification and its verbal expression (the 082 and 083 UK MARC fields mentioned earlier) can be introduced. (All of this does not seem unreasonable, since the *BNB* presently is able to do so.) The prospects for changes in bibliographic control in North America become enormous.

For instance, there have been good reasons until now for the format of the *National Union Catalog* (*NUC*) and the *LC Subject Catalog*, using reproductions of LC cards, but this format need not continue indefinitely into the future. Whenever the proportion of machine-readable data is sufficient (whether from LC itself or from contributed copy), the techniques of computer-activated printing and computer-output-microform would readily permit a *National Union Catalog plus* subject access in a format not unlike that of the *BNB*. *Canadiana* already is appearing in substantially this way. An *NUC* in the format of *BNB* or *Canadiana* would permit considerably enlarged access by title and other entries, as well. It is even possible that such a format might assist in solving the question of the present viability of the *LC Subject Catalog*. One might hope that it could improve currency, since *BNB*, for example, finds it possible to issue its cataloging weekly, and to cumulate more rapidly than we are accustomed to in North America.

Furthermore, there would be no apparent reason why similar patterns of publication could not be introduced for the *Cumulative Book Index* and other major bibliographic tools on this continent. The Wilson periodical indexes would be obvious candidates for examination.

These suggested changes would not, of course, depend solely on the provision of PRECIS by LC and the National Library of Canada. What the introduction of PRECIS *would* provide, however, in addition to improved access to individual collections, is the potential for a bibliographic tool which has hitherto been impractical — namely, the integration of data from the three agencies into an international subject catalog with access through either classification or verbal entries, or both. The apparent adaptability of PRECIS to languages other than English leads one promptly to speculate on whether a multi-lingual international subject catalog in classified order might be possible, which would, of course, be of considerable interest to Canada.

Should LC and the National Library of Canada find it impractical to make PRECIS available on their own, it is possible that a new program of shared cataloging might be begun. We have watched the Shared Cataloging Project at the Library of Congress incorporate bibliographic data from a number of other countries, and adapt these data to LC practices. In the process, LC, in effect, already has PRECIS data available for all those titles in Shared Cataloging which it has derived from the *BNB*. Perhaps the British Library might take the full responsibility for providing PRECIS strings to the Library of Congress and to Canada. Should the National Library of Canada feel "left out" in this expansion of shared cataloging, it might well assume responsibility for access in French, based on the present ability of CAN/MARC to operate bilingually.

Beyond these speculations on the national and international levels, what about networks and individual libraries? Two considerations, I believe, are paramount. First, despite the apparent success of a manual project such as Audrey Taylor's, it seems to me unlikely that PRECIS can be adopted widely where there is no access to computer facilities. PRECIS relies heavily on the computer, and certainly in situations involving substantial amounts of bibliographic data, this is an overriding consideration.

Second, subject access retrospectively through PRECIS is unrealistic in most situations. One can conceive of PRECIS being provided for titles already in the LC and Canadian MARCs (particularly since some of this is already available from *BNB*), but it is highly unlikely that any other substantial retrospective conversion could be undertaken. Therefore, the use of PRECIS is most likely in situations where it is possible to stop and to begin again. This is the case with the *National Union Catalog* and *Canadiana*, already mentioned. Also there is a substantial number of libraries in North America which are considering a variety of "close-and-resume" alternatives for their catalogs. These institutions are in the enviable position of being able to select more effective means of subject access than previously have been available. I need hardly add that the Library of Congress itself is one of these libraries.

In considering networks specifically, I am, quite frankly, somewhat puzzled. Impressive amounts of bibliographic data are now accumulating at a number of locations on the continent, and I know of no one who would seriously entertain the conversion to PRECIS of the data bases at, say, OCLC or the University of Toronto. Yet, if any great number of the libraries which are members of these and other networks are indeed to close and resume, one of the next major problems for networks may be the means by which they, too, can close and resume. It is not a prospect to warm the hearts of network boards and staffs.

My assignment has been to consider the "practical possibilities" of PRECIS, and some of you may feel that I have strayed far from the practical. Certainly, a number of my suggestions require more study before they can be demonstrated to be either practical or impractical. These studies can and should be done. But major changes are imminent in the Library of Congress and in many libraries in North America, and it is incumbent on us to make as many improvements in bibliographic control as are possible in the process. PRECIS is not perfect; it is probable that no system of subject control is perfect. However, PRECIS has been adopted and is proving satisfactory in one of the major bibliographic agencies of the world. It cannot be ignored in North America.

NOTES

1. Allen Kent, "Minimum Criteria for a Coordinated Information System," *American Documentation*, v. 11 (1960), pp. 84-87.
2. B. C. Vickery, *On Retrieval System Theory*, 2d ed. (London: Butterworths, 1965), pp. 154-77.
3. B. C. Vickery, *Techniques of Information Retrieval* (Hamden, Connecticut: Archon Books, 1970), pp. 209-34.
4. Mortimer Taube, "Evaluation of Information Systems," *Studies in Coordinate Indexing* (Washington, DC: Documentation Incorporated, 1953), pp. 101-5.
5. Mortimer Taube, Seminar presentation at Columbia University School of Library Service, paraphrased in: Oliver L. Lilley, "Evaluation of the Subject Catalog," *American Documentation*, v. 5 (1954), p. 46.
6. Acknowledgement is made to Professor Ann H. Schabas for making available the statistical data on which these and other figures in this paper have been based.
7. Ken Bakewell and Eric Hunter, "Teaching PRECIS at Liverpool," *Catalogue & Index*, no. 36 (1975), pp. 3-6.
8. Aldyth Scott, "PRECIS," *Library Association Record*, v. 77 (1975), p. 289.
9. L. S. Simpson, "PRECIS," *Library Association Record*, v. 77 (1975), p. 289.

SUMMARY

The Workshop was evaluated by a panel composed of six participants representing various sectors of the library and information science community. Their comments, paraphrased below, were made in a purely personal capacity, and do not reflect the policy or opinion of the institutions or organizations with which they are affiliated.

Mr. *George F. Heise* (Indexing Services, H. W. Wilson Company). Our present systems of indexing are somewhat like being in a large warehouse of clothes, picking from the rack what the indexer feels best fits the author's work. PRECIS now allows us to select from the author's own wardrobe, which represents the ideas the author wishes to get across in his own words.

The difficult thing in indexing has always been to make the right decisions on subject headings; while anyone can be logical and consistent for about 30 seconds, this generally can not be kept up consistently from 9 o'clock in the morning to 9 o'clock at night. PRECIS, however, provides a mental structure or framework that is extremely useful in decision making. PRECIS can be useful as an indexing system for a newly formed library, especially one dealing with government documents, pamphlets, and reports. For a commercial indexing enterprise, a switch from one indexing system to another becomes immediately a question of dollars and cents, and would have to be considered very carefully before making a decision. Such a switch to PRECIS can be compared with an auto model change at General Motors: the initial cost of retooling in 1976 would be recovered from buyers of autos by GM during the next few years, but the cost of "retooling" for commercial indexing might have to be recovered over a much longer period.

Mrs. *Rochelle R. Reed* (Wake County Public Libraries, Raleigh, NC), considered the economic aspects of introducing PRECIS into a medium-sized to large public library. Wake County is working with a manual system but expects to switch to an automated system sometime in the future. There has long been a feeling that, with the aid of computers, something better than LC subject headings could be produced. The PRECIS system seems to be more adequate for the retrieval of specific information, which is wanted in public libraries as much by the "general" user as by the subject specialist in an academic library. Also, information on subjects presented in many different material forms—book and nonbook, monograph and audio-visual—would be better presented by PRECIS headings.

I now have some valid points in trying to convince people that a system should not be automated based on methods that were not created for that purpose but only for manual use. Computer systems should be utilized in a way that their inherent possibilities are fully realized. The use of PRECIS would allow such optimal use of computers in a public library.

Ms *Olivia O. Kredel* (National League of Cities/U.S. Conference of Mayors Library), speaking as a special librarian, emphasized that her library is somewhat unusual for U.S. conditions, since it has a classified subject catalog. A chain index used as a key to the system has been found not very helpful, especially since its terminology is largely out of date. PRECIS seems to be a very good system to achieve precise subject indications with an up-to-date terminology. This library does not have access to a computer, so that a manual application of PRECIS might have to be considered. The capability of PRECIS to aid and maintain indexer consistency is impressive. Another possible area of application could be a weekly abstracting service on urban affairs now produced by this library; in this case, the techniques discussed in Mary Dykstra's paper on the National Film Board of Canada would be useful. If and when this organization converts to computerized methods in the library, PRECIS might be exactly the thing needed.

Mrs. *Patricia G. Oyler* (School of Library Science, Simmons College), considered PRECIS in the framework of a library school. There are two groups of users, and two ways of handling the issue. The two groups are the library school students and the people in the field who attend continuing education programs. Students ought to be taught a system which is now coming into its own and could soon become an international system. Although I could present PRECIS in my classes, I do not know enough about the system to be able to answer questions on problems that might arise. Therefore, there is an urgent need for more training in PRECIS for library educators in the United States.

Library school students also need more training in order to evaluate the system for their own use. In the Boston area, which has a large number of special libraries, former students are constantly asking their teachers for advice on how to handle certain problems. For special libraries, dependence on Library of Congress subject headings is not as crucial as for public and university libraries. PRECIS might be the right system for this type of library, where much individual subject indexing is now going on. The use of PRECIS instead of homemade subject heading lists could greatly improve access to subjects. Library schools should also play a role in making former students familiar with the system, these students being the grass-roots people who will in time move up to higher levels and be tomorrow's decision makers. For this to be effective, there would have to be an existing model of PRECIS indexing in the United States before one could think of continuing education programs.

Mrs. *Lenore A. Stein* (United States Information Agency). USIA libraries and cultural centers have become a part of a large audio-visual information network, particularly in Western Europe. They are looking for ways and means in which information can be disseminated more accurately and quickly by establishing an information data bank in Western Europe. The first phase of the data bank will be a foreign affairs information system, to go into effect in August 1977, to be followed by an American studies data bank. PRECIS will provide many different access points for this kind of information and the type of questions expected. However, more training facilities for American PRECIS indexers will be needed. In conclusion, PRECIS will be a prime candidate for consideration as an indexing system for the USIA data banks.

Mr. *Edward J. Blume* (Subject Cataloging Division, Library of Congress). The presentation of PRECIS and the enthusiasm of its practitioners are impressive. Technology has made a heavy impact on the means for provision of information, and the Library of Congress is very much aware of the limitations imposed on it by tools that have been developed in a different age, and for manual applications. The LC system has been developed for cataloging monographs that are not dealing with very specific subjects, and for a card catalog. In the past it worked well because it was economical to run. It does not work well now, because monographs have become much more specific; there are more interdisciplinary works. Due to these problems, the card catalogs of LC are about to be closed down. A reexamination of methods is therefore needed at this point. The question is when to make the shift.

The LC system is one that also considers context, but it does so only for titles, relying on a very elaborate reference structure. This structure is very often not found in other libraries using the LC subject headings. In addition, titles have become less indicative of the contents of a work, especially in the social sciences. It must be emphasized that the LC subject heading system is not a closed system as far as the Library of Congress itself is concerned (although it *is* one for other libraries). Subject headings can be created as needed, but often catalogers choose not to do so. Many of the bad examples of LC subject indexing cited by various speakers are not examples of the limitations of the system as such, but rather examples of extremely bad cataloging.

Catalogers at LC should have an opportunity to study PRECIS indexing, if for no other reason than to learn how to approach the description of the contents of a work, even if they would not produce PRECIS strings. They would learn that the whole work is to be considered and they would have to look at what aspects there are and how to index them. Such a procedure could perhaps be initiated gradually as advocated by C. Donald Cook. Whether or not to adopt PRECIS as the method of indexing in America is not so much a question of providing more points of access, it is rather an administrative problem.

LIST OF PARTICIPANTS

Frank Adamovich
University of New Hampshire
Durham, New Hampshire

Derek Austin
British Library
London, England

Francis A. Ball
University of Maryland
College Park, Maryland

C. David Batty
University of Maryland
College Park, Maryland

Ann H. Bein
University of California
Los Angeles, California

Carolynn E. Bett
Saskmedia Corporation
Regina, Saskatchewan, Canada

Kendra A. Biddick
University of Maryland
College Park, Maryland

Edward J. Blume
Library of Congress
Washington, D.C.

Lucille M. Boone
Wollongong University
Wollongong, New South Wales, Australia

Barbara A. Booth
University of California
Los Angeles, California

Valentina de Bruin
University of Toronto
Toronto, Ontario, Canada

Ronald L. Buchan
University of Maryland Eastern Shore
Wallops Island, Virginia

Sister Claudia Carlen
Plymouth, Michigan

Elizabeth Chambers
Northern Illinois University
DeKalb, Illinois

Frances W. Chin
University of Rhode Island
Kingston, Rhode Island

Bogomir Chokel
World Bank
Washington, DC

Doris Clack
Tallahassee, Florida

Kenneth B. Clansky
University of Maryland
College Park, Maryland

Ilze Cockburn
Ontario Educational Research
Information Systems
Toronto, Ontario, Canada

Allen Cohen
Pennsylvania State University
University Park, Pennsylvania

C. Donald Cook
University of Toronto
Toronto, Ontario, Canada

John C. Cosgriff
Virginia Polytechnic Institute & State
University
Blacksburg, Virginia

Rebecca W. Davidson
National Library of Medicine
Bethesda, Maryland

Sue Dodd
University of North Carolina
Chapel Hill, North Carolina

Deborah F. Donaghue
Control Data
Minneapolis, Minnesota

Shauna B. Dorskind
University of Toronto
Toronto, Ontario, Canada

Arlene T. Dowell
North Carolina Central University
Durham, North Carolina

Mary Dykstra
Dalhousie University
Halifax, Nova Scotia, Canada

Elizabeth C. Fake
University of Maryland
College Park, Maryland

Violet Forgach
Case Western Reserve University
Cleveland, Ohio

Eugene T. Frosio
Library of Congress
Washington, DC

Judy Gardhouse
University of Toronto
Toronto, Ontario, Canada

Sally L. Godshall
Wake County Public Libraries
Raleigh, North Carolina

Alan R. Greengrass
The Information Bank
Parsippany, New Jersey

Peter E. Greig
National Library of Canada
Ottawa, Ontario, Canada

Shirley F. Harper
Cornell University
Ithaca, New York

George F. Heise
H. W. Wilson Company
Bronx, New York

Elizabeth S. Herman
University of California at Los Angeles
Los Angeles, California

Joyce D. Herndon
Ferguson Library
Stamford, Connecticut

Frances Hinton
Free Library of Philadelphia
Philadelphia, Pennsylvania

Judith Hopkins
University of Michigan
Ann Arbor, Michigan

Alexis J. Jamieson
University of Maryland
College Park, Maryland

Robert W. Karrow
The Newberry Library
Chicago, Illinois

Paul F. G. Keller
University of Maryland
College Park, Maryland

Rosemary King
Pennsylvania State University
University Park, Pennsylvania

Olivia O. Kredel
National League of Cities
Washington, DC

Signe E. Larson
U.S. Department of Interior
Washington, DC

Mary S. Lewin
Library of Congress
Washington, DC

Peter W. Lisbon
Harvard University
Cambridge, Massachusetts

Irene McCordick
York County Board of Education
Aurora, Ontario, Canada

Judy C. McDermott
Library of Congress
Washington, DC

Gordon W. MacLean
Ontario Educational Communications
   Authority
Toronto, Ontario, Canada

Martha L. Manheimer
University of Pittsburgh
Pittsburgh, Pennsylvania

June R. Morroni
Pennsylvania State University
University Park, Pennsylvania

Andre Nitecki
University of Alberta
Edmonton, Alberta, Canada

Beila S. Organic
Rockville, Maryland

Harriet Ostroff
Library of Congress
Washington, DC

Patricia G. Oyler
Simmons College
Boston, Massachusetts

Tavor T. Paldi-Fleischer
Engineering Index, Inc.
New York, New York

David A. Peele
Staten Island Community College
Staten Island, New York

Maryann G. Phillips
Fairfax, Virginia

Sydney J. Pierce
Emory University
Atlanta, Georgia

Mary D. Pietris
Northwestern University
Evanston, Illinois

Elizabeth T. Pope
Illinois State University
Normal, Illinois

Barbara M. Preschel
Queens College
Flushing, New York

Rochelle R. Reed
Wake County Public Libraries
Raleigh, North Carolina

Gerald E. Reid, Jr.
Library of Congress
Washington, DC

Michael Reynolds
University of Maryland
College Park, Maryland

Phyllis A. Richmond
Case Western Reserve University
Cleveland, Ohio

Leo R. Rift
Ithaca College
Ithaca, New York

Michael Rissinger
Hospital of the University of
    Pennsylvania
Philadelphia, Pennsylvania

C. Derek Robinson
College Bibliocentre
Don Mills, Ontario, Canada

Eris E. Roth
Social Security Administration
Baltimore, Maryland

Theodore Samore
University of Wisconsin
Milwaukee, Wisconsin

Ann H. Schabas
University of Toronto
Toronto, Ontario, Canada

Peri L. Schuyler
National Library of Medicine
Bethesda, Maryland

Elizabeth Sharer
University of Maryland
College Park, Maryland

Gladys E. Siegel
H. Lundeberg School of Seamanship
Piney Point, Maryland

Judy K. Sindel
Anaheim, California

Arlene Farber Sirkin
University of Maryland
College Park, Maryland

Rochelle R. Skalsky
Wake County Public Libraries
Raleigh, North Carolina

Jutta Sørensen
Bibliotekscentralen, Copenhagen,
Denmark

Lenore A. Stein
United States Information Agency
Washington, DC

Jennifer A. Stephenson
Northwestern University
Evanston, Illinois

Patricia Ann Stevens
University of Maryland
College Park, Maryland

Maydelle B. Stewart
National Agricultural Library
Beltsville, Maryland

Yvonne Stroup
University of Utah
Salt Lake City, Utah

Kris Subramanyam
Drexel University
Philadelphia, Pennsylvania

Thomas E. Sullivan
H. W. Wilson Company
Bronx, New York

Audrey Taylor
Aurora High School
Aurora, Ontario, Canada

Joe K. Taylor
Virginia Polytechnic Institute & State
   University
Blacksburg, Virginia

Gladys Todd
Simcoe Composite School
Simcoe, Ontario, Canada

Irene Travis
University of Maryland
College Park, Maryland

Garnet G. Trivett
Simcoe Composite School
Simcoe, Ontario, Canada

Theresa S. Varnedoe
Florida State University
Tallahassee, Florida

Harriet S. Velázquez
University of Toronto
Toronto, Ontario, Canada

Hans H. Wellisch
University of Maryland
College Park, Maryland

Marilyn D. White
University of Maryland
College Park, Maryland

Harry Winton
United Nations Institute for Training
   and Research
New York, New York

Maria Z. Woroniak
National Agricultural Library
Beltsville, Maryland

Cheryl A. Zimmerman
University of Toronto
Toronto, Ontario, Canada

INDEX

Entries are filed word by word. Abbreviations are filed as words. Numerals are filed before the alphabet. Page numbers followed by the letter *r* indicate a bibliographical reference. Page numbers followed by an asterisk indicate an illustration.